UNEQUAL UNDER SOCIALISM

Race, Women, and Transnationalism in Bulgaria

Unequal under Socialism examines the formation of racial, gender, and national identities and relations in the socialist state. With a specific focus on Bulgaria, a former socialist country in the Balkans, Miglena S. Todorova traces the intertwined local and global forces driving racialization, socialist state policies, and Eurocentric Marxist and Leninist ideologies, all of which led to valued and devalued categories of women. Roma women, Muslim women, ethnic Bulgarian women, sex workers, and female factory and office workers were among those marked by socialist authorities for prosperity, accommodation, violent reformation, or erasure.

Covering the period from the 1930s to the present and drawing upon original archival sources as well as a constellation of critical theories, *Unequal under Socialism* focuses on the lives of different women to articulate deep doubt about the capacity of socialism to sustain societies where all women prosper. Such doubt, the book suggests, is an underrecognized but important force shaping how women in former socialist countries have related to one another and to other women in the global North and South.

MIGLENA S. TODOROVA is an associate professor in the Department of Social Justice Education and Director of the Centre for Media, Culture, and Education at the Ontario Institute for Studies in Education, University of Toronto.

Unequal under Socialism

Race, Women, and Transnationalism in Bulgaria

MIGLENA S. TODOROVA

UNIVERSITY OF TORONTO PRESS
Toronto Buffalo London

© University of Toronto Press 2021
Toronto Buffalo London
utppublishing.com

ISBN 978-1-4875-2840-9 (cloth)   ISBN 978-1-4875-2843-0 (EPUB)
ISBN 978-1-4875-2841-6 (paper)   ISBN 978-1-4875-2842-3 (PDF)

Library and Archives Canada Cataloguing in Publication

Title: Unequal under socialism : race, women, and transnationalism in
   Bulgaria / Miglena S. Todorova.
Names: Todorova, Miglena S., author.
Description: Includes bibliographical references and index.
Identifiers: Canadiana (print) 2021022570X | Canadiana (ebook)
   20210225785 | ISBN 9781487528416 (softcover) | ISBN 9781487528409
   (hardcover) | ISBN 9781487528430 (EPUB) | ISBN 9781487528423 (PDF)
Subjects: LCSH: Women – Bulgaria – Social conditions – 20th century. |
   LCSH: Women – Bulgaria – Social conditions – 21st century. | LCSH:
   Minority women – Bulgaria – Social conditions – 20th century. | LCSH:
   Minority women – Bulgaria – Social conditions – 21st century. | LCSH:
   Women and socialism – Bulgaria. | LCSH: Feminism – Bulgaria.
Classification: LCC HQ1712 .T63 2021 | DDC 305.409499–dc23

This book has been published with the help of a grant from the Federation for the Humanities and Social Sciences, through the Awards to Scholarly Publications Program, using funds provided by the Social Sciences and Humanities Research Council of Canada.

University of Toronto Press acknowledges the financial assistance to its publishing program of the Canada Council for the Arts and the Ontario Arts Council, an agency of the Government of Ontario.

Contents

List of Illustrations   vii

Acknowledgments   ix

Introduction: Epistemology of Doubt   3

Chapter One: Race, Women, and Nation-Building in the 1930s and 1940s   26

Chapter Two: Socialist Racialism: Desired and Undesired Genres of Women, and the Paradoxes of Socialism   56

Chapter Three: Women's Work: Gendered and Racialized Socialist State Governmentality   75

Chapter Four: Second and Third World Women: Socialist State Feminisms and Internationalisms   102

Chapter Five: Challenging the Modern/Postmodern Duality: Race, Socialist Masculinity, and Global American Culture   128

Conclusion: Postsocialism, Anti-Racism, and Transnational Feminisms   149

Notes   173

Bibliography   187

Index   205

Illustrations

1. Roma neighbourhood at the outskirts of Sofia, 1932   31
2. A Bulgarian ethnic couple displaying material prosperity, 1924   31
3. Fashionable urban Bulgarian ethnic women, 1928   32
4. A Roma boy with a bear, Varna, 1925   33
5. Middle-class travellers at the Bozhuriste Airport near Sofia, 1928   33
6. An elderly Roma woman smoking a pipe, 1928   34
7. A Muslim Roma man in rural Bulgaria, ca. 1930   35
8. A Bulgarian female teacher and her Muslim students, 1936   85
9. Female workers in a tobacco factory, ca. 1970   96
10. Indira Gandhi and Lyudmila Zhivkova in India, 1976   115
11. Roma Bulgarian music artist Azis in *Erotic*, 2014   165

Acknowledgments

This book has been long in the making. My graduate training in American Studies at the University of Minnesota and the work of inspirational mentors in the early 2000s motivated the questions, the archival research approach, and the interdisciplinary frames that anchor the book. Historians, sociologists, and cultural and social theorists David Nobel, Elaine Tylor May, Lary May, Jennifer Pierce, and Roderick Ferguson created a nurturing environment where budding scholars like myself could imagine and pursue postnationalist American Studies that displaced the United States as the centre of the world and history and asked questions about broader formations that connected peoples and realities. My research and teaching in the areas of transnational feminisms, postsocialism, globalization, and anti-oppression began in these conversations about links, relations, and political solidarities I first encountered in Minnesota. I am especially grateful to Roderick Ferguson for his mentorship, friendship, and support over the years. His work, relational thinking, and kindness have inspired me continuously.

I am also grateful for the support of Ralitza Dimitrova, whose skills in locating and retrieving archival materials in Bulgaria enabled me to collect important primary data upon which this book rests. The insightful feedback provided by four anonymous reviewers of the book manuscript blew wind under my wings and guided my revisions of the text. The professional editorial advice of Stephen Shapiro and the copyediting skills of Charles Anthony Stuart at the University of Toronto Press helped me tremendously in making decisions about formatting, presenting, and revising various aspects of the manuscript. Support and passionate conversations about a better future with colleagues and students in Social Justice Education at the University of Toronto where I teach have further inspired my desire for scholarship that crosses cultural, racial, and national borders.

I could not have written this book without the support of my family. My parents' life stories and nourishment anchor me as a person and intellectual so that I never forget where I come from and what truly matters in life. The unconditional love of my partner in life, Plamen Todorov, has sustained me throughout personal losses and professional struggles but also achievements and joys that further inspire this book. I offer them the most profound expression of gratitude.

UNEQUAL UNDER SOCIALISM

Introduction: Epistemology of Doubt

This book is about the making and remaking of differently racialized, ethnicized, sexed, and classed groups of women in the Balkans focusing on the case of Bulgaria before, during, and after state socialism, covering the period from the 1930s to the present. It is about intertwined local and global processes of racialization, gendered state valorizations, bourgeois, socialist, Marxist, Leninist, and neo-liberal ideological patriarchal formations creating different and unequal genres of Roma (also known as Gypsy) women, Muslim women, and ethnic Bulgarian women marked for prosperity, accommodation, violent reforming, or erasure. These historical constructions of gendered difference and inequalities amid Bulgarian state capitalism and socialism, the book suggests, put into a stark relief the ontological deficiencies and inability of both state socialism and liberal capitalist democracy to create social life where all women prosper. It is important to emphasize and reiterate the limitations of these dominant modern social and political forms in order to transcend them. Envisioning, attempting, and eventually realizing novel, alternative, and more equitable ways of social and economic being depends especially on continuous and critical evaluation of the emancipatory capacities of the theoretical and utopian modes of Marxism and socialism anchoring critiques of capitalism and visions of better societies yet to come.

The postsocialist feminist analytic driving this book engages with Marxism and socialism as lived lives and social and material practice from the viewpoints of race and women's experiences. By analytic, I mean a conceptual and methodological approach examining past experiences in order to identify patterns in events, forces, social behaviours, and effects and to use these patterns to anticipate what could come. The purpose of the analytic is to help expand the conceptual horizons of Women Studies, specifically the area of transnational feminisms, by contributing new and expanding existing knowledge about gender and race in liberal, socialist, and postsocialist states and economies. This conversation is especially important in transnational feminisms concerned with social difference and inequalities that inhibit the emergence of more and stronger feminist political collectives advancing women's issues and politics locally and globally. Speaking about feminist gaps and bridges from within Bulgaria could shine light especially on the role of Marxist, socialist and postsocialist ontologies responsible for women's political aligning or distancing in a region of the world that has been underappreciated as a location of feminist knowledge production pertaining to race, culture, power, social formation, and women's identities and relations.

Generations of women and men in Bulgaria, and the Balkan region more generally, have lived through distinct and contrasting forms of social and political organization within a single century: early twentieth-century nation-building and modernization under a constitutional monarchy followed five centuries of Ottoman domination; state socialism and a collectivist planned economy replaced the monarchy in the mid-1940s, followed by the collapse of the socialist state in 1989 and the emergence of crude capitalism and radical privatization and redistribution of wealth. Within the same century, Bulgarians and other peoples in the region were also imagined and narrated as "semi-Orientals" and backward others to the West and Europe; a few more decades down the road, they are living throughout their own "re-Europeanization" as members of the European Union and NATO. Along the way, British, French, Hapsburg, and Soviet Empires and hegemony as well as Cold War armament and divisions also shaped their lives.

This history is personal. My grandparents, born in the early 1900s, bowed to a tsar and paid taxes to a kingdom. My parents, who were born in the 1930s, participated in a dramatic redistribution of wealth and lived in a vastly different state led by a communist party. I belong to a generation raised under state socialism in the 1960s and 1970s but maturing amid its collapse and transformations under the pressures of global capitalism and neo-liberalism. My mother worked the fields near the small village where she was born and wore sole-less pigskin shoes until the age of fifteen. She tasted chocolate for the first time when the German Army invaded Bulgaria in 1941; an army mobile kitchen was stationed in her village so the cook gave the local children scraps of food. My father came from a working-class family that kept a small house on the outskirts of the capital, Sofia. He started working in the local factory at the age of fourteen. My parents donated countless hours of free labour to help build roads, bridges, and buildings and harvest the agricultural fields so that the new socialist society could prosper. My father died before socialism crumbled. My mother lived to see and experience the ensuing postsocialist transformation and privatization, leaving her in old age with a miserable pension after life of hard socialist work. She refused to participate in any kind of political elections, democratic or not.

I followed my parents to the factory floor, where I worked for seven years; socialist education predestined me for that route in the 1970s and 1980s. And I followed the masses of proletarians marching the streets of my hometown of Sofia in celebrating socialism and the worker. But on 1 May 1986, International Workers' Day, we breathed the poisoned air released a couple of days earlier by the nuclear plant accident in Chernobyl, Ukraine. We also ate food exposed to radiation in the weeks immediately after the accident because the state did not warn the people of the risk. Rumours about thousands of women in Bulgaria terminating their pregnancies because of exposure to higher levels of radiation and worries about a generation of children suffering from developmental issues went undocumented in the history books because the Soviet Union bullied its satellite states into preventing the collection of such information. I carry Chernobyl on my neck. A scar marks the irradiated thyroid gland removed from my body. After state socialism collapsed, I joined a generation of young Bulgarians embracing life in diaspora in a search for answers and new paths. In the early 1990s, my path led to the United States and Canada, where postsecondary education and social, political, and professional experiences amid neocolonial capitalist patriarchies and racisms formed further the multiple selves from within which this book is written.

These travels, ruptures, turns, contrasts, and transformations, which I share with others who grew up under socialism, have produced postsocialist subjectivities, modes of consciousness, and personal and group relations marked by *doubt*: emotional and cognitive awareness that the political, social, and economic formations through which one has lived lack elemental truthfulness; hence they have to be continuously critiqued, examined, distrusted, and replaced. The kind of doubt illuminated by this book is a ceaseless evaluation of core values to which state and society are committed, leading to unease with Marxism, socialism, capitalism, and liberalism and seeking novel ways of being in the world that transcend these modern Eurocentric ideologies that have arrested our imaginations and politics. Postsocialist feminist doubt is also a continuous refusal to join Marxist and socialist projects constructed by feminists in the global North and South unless we fully interrogate and understand how state socialism in the twentieth century enfolded race, patriarchy, heteronormativity, and violence.[1] Marxist and socialist utopias also inform social movements, politics, and knowledge production envisioning "democratic socialism" as a platform for gender justice.[2] A recent treatise on the power of socialist ideals and political economy penned by an American anthropologist even suggests that "women have better sex under socialist conditions";[3] that is, unless one is a poor, racialized Indigenous, Roma, or Black woman whose concern is not having satisfying sex but surviving racist patriarchal heteronormative neocolonial societies stretching from the former Soviet Union in the East to the United States and Canada in the West. Marx's and Engels's notions of expanded and changed human consciousness and collectivized economy are common features of utopias and theories moving us closer to "good societies."[4] For a postsocialist subject, however, Marx's theories of human development leading to transformed consciousness and socially useful work in the socialist public economy may not be liberation but the site of state governmentality and violence. And for a postsocialist subject, Marxism and socialism constitute not the future but the past and lived lives posing important but unresolved questions: How and why did state socialism produce differently racialized, sexed, and gendered subjects? How could understanding and documenting root causes and driving forces of racialization, patriarchy, and violence under socialism support anti-racism and social justice in former socialist countries in the Balkans and globally?

These questions guide and organize the contents of this book, using race and women's lives as entry points to examine the kinds of social and political formations produced in the socialist state. The book advances analyses of these formations seeking *useful knowledge*: widely disseminated epistemology that moves "beyond critique to help in producing new political programmes and movements."[5] Such move beyond critique requires consideration of who is served by our writing and what kinds of political actions could be induced or supported by our work. The purpose of this book is to provide deeper understanding of race, women's lives, ideology, and inequality before, during, and after state socialism, thus serving anti-racism and gender equality programs and politics. The other objective of the book is to bridge gaps between ethnic minority and majority women, and Muslim and Christian women in Bulgaria and the Balkans, and between postsocialist women in the region and women in the global North and South. The book attempts such bridgework by engaging concepts and issues that are important to women racialized as non-white: race, nation-building, work in the family and the formal economy, globalization of culture and capital, power, hegemony and colonialism, state and epistemological violence, patriarchy, and heteronormativity, all of which organize the histories, ontologies, and polemics presented in this book. Yet this book alone does not purport to constitute such useful knowledge; its chapters seek purposeful historical data, observations, and connections to other bodies of knowledge that place social difference at the centre of analyses of temporal, political, cultural, and social experiences of groups of women under socialism. Scholarly and discursive practices centred on social difference, like this book, could support contemporary anti-racist, anti-homophobic, and feminist mobilizing and efforts in Bulgaria and other Balkan postsocialist countries by constructing difference (based on race, ethnicity, sexuality, class, religion, or citizenship) not as the occasion for a competition over resources or comparisons producing hierarchies of women-victims but as a site from which to observe how local, national, and international powers and hegemony have actually produced these differences between women across socialism, Marxism, Leninism, liberalism, capitalism, and neo-liberalism, inhibiting in turn relational thinking and politics of togetherness and mutuality that are so needed in postsocialist Bulgaria and the world today.

Why Race and Women in Bulgaria? Second and Third World Women Transnational Feminisms

Race, gender, sexuality, and class are neither distinct and separate nor bonded, but these signifiers of social difference "are coming into existence *in and through* relation to each other – if in contradictory and conflictual ways."[6] Therefore, race changes studies of women under state socialism by making questions about difference, inequality, and power central to the inquiry. Such critical postsocialist race feminisms are lacking in Bulgaria and the Balkans. Postsocialist race-based feminism is also scarce in women and gender studies and transnational feminisms research and teaching programs enacted in Western academies.

Only recently have transnational feminist studies that are focused on women in the so-called Second World consisting of former socialist states begun to explore the absence of postsocialist women in feminist theories and research pertaining to postcolonialism, women's politics and relations, and the globality of capital.[7] These inquires have linked the silence of postsocialist women in the theorizing of these phenomena to the historical domination of white Western feminists, whose needs and politics have shaped women's studies globally.[8] The limited presence of the postsocialist Second World in transnational feminist theories and research has been further attributed to the political and epistemological genealogies of area studies, postcolonial studies, and gender and sexuality studies, especially in the United States revolving around histories and relations between white and non-white women across the First and Third World.[9]

Importantly, the absence of postsocialist women and locales in women's studies practised in the West, and the social sciences in general, is noted and interrogated predominantly by women from former socialist states in Central and Eastern Europe, the Balkans, and the former Soviet Union. Third World women and feminists – identified in the literature as women racialized as non-white in countries in the global North and South – have not responded or taken up the issue to the same extend. This dynamic, I believe, relates to the historical political and cultural proximity of former socialist societies to European and Euro-American modernities. From the perspective of the transnational feminist theories that emerged in the United States in the 1990s as a critique of the domination of white feminism, European colonialisms, and racism, socialist countries and societies in the Balkans could appear as cultural and political extensions of "Europe" and racial whiteness. The current membership of former socialist countries in the European Union, NATO, and other international alliances dominated by Western countries exacerbates such views. These perceptions, however, misunderstand the distinct and very different geopolitical and cultural locations of postsocialist societies in the Balkans, which are often enfolded under homogenizing banners such as "Eastern Europe" or "the Second World." Latvia, Poland, Bulgaria, and Albania, for example, have all been included into Cold War categories such as "Eastern Europe" because they were all socialist and because they played the role of peripheral others against whom Western Europe emerged historically. These countries and peoples are in reality vastly different linguistically, culturally, and geopolitically. Unlike, for instance, Latvia in north-eastern Europe, which traces its history to Christianity and Viking, German, Polish, Swedish, and Russian conquests, Bulgaria and Albania in the Balkans have been spheres of influence and domination of Ottoman, Russian, and Hapsburg Empires and both Christian and Islamic conquests and influence. And unlike Western writing and constructions of "European Latvia," countries in the Balkans have only recently been associated with "Europe." Transnational feminists in academies, especially in the United States and Canada, have not made these distinctions, thus failing to grasp the distinct historical geopolitical and epistemological location of the Balkans under and between colonial and economic powers that have impacted women in the global South as well, albeit differently.

Transnational feminist writing and politics enacted in the United States as well as Canada and Western Europe have also relied on Marxist epistemologies extensively to critique and grasp the intertwined local, national, and global aspects of capitalism and its effects on women, especially women of colour.[10] This epistemological practice has not been questioned from the perspective of that important feminist realization that one woman's empowering and liberating epistemology could be another woman's site of violence, oppression, inequality, and deep doubt. Marxist thought, in its various iterations, has emancipated myriad feminist voices and epistemologies amid capitalism and colonialism; it has produced, however, violence, assimilation, erasure, and silencing of as many women under state socialism. Therefore, Marxism – as a critique, philosophy, ideology, or aspiration – is dividing women within former socialist states as well as groups of women in former socialist states and self-identified Marxist and socialist white and non-white women and feminists in the United States and other countries.

That division is extended by academic discourses and everyday conversations where postsocialist feminist doubt is dismissed as speaking from a place that was not "truly socialist" and "really Marxist."[11] My own academic career, and that of others originating in the socialist Balkans but living and working in the West, has been shaped by such continuous epistemological discharges suggesting that socialism and Marxism did not succeed in Eastern Europe and the Balkans because it was twisted and corrupted by peoples and cultures not fit for it, or because communists in these locales used Marxist ideas to rationalize a society Marx did not intend or envision. More advanced and civilized peoples and intellectuals in the European and Euro-American West, however, can and would foster real socialism(s), or "democratic socialism," free of racism, sexism, and other inequalities, these dismissive gestures further suggest.[12] Postsocialist feminist assertions highlighting the Eurocentrism of Marxism and violence inflicted on women in the name of socialism seem uncomfortable to some women and feminists in Western academies, especially in the United States, whose theoretical repertoires revolve overwhelmingly around Marxist thought in order to imagine something that is deeply desired (utopia), to deconstruct capitalism and its oppressive effects (critique), to test a cluster of concepts (theory), or to use these concepts exclusively to interpret the world (ideology). Distinctions notwithstanding, at their core, Marx-inspired epistemologies and praxes gain efficiency and meaning in relationship and contrast to concepts and practices of capitalism. Marxism and subsequently socialism thus depend on a duality that impedes connections, better mutual understanding, and collaborations between women and feminists who are conditioned by the starkly different and opposing economic, cultural, and philosophical principles of Marxism, socialism, liberalism, and capitalism. Back in 1974 amid burgeoning women's movements in Canada, the United States, and other Western countries, Charnie Guettel defined feminism as an extension of Marxism:

> Women of the Left, are looking to Marxism to discover the basic causes of our oppression, and to give us the scientific understanding of our society that will enable us to develop a strategy to organize for liberation ... The main contradiction is not between men and women, but between the forces of production, people's labour power, machines, materials, etc., and the property relations of production, the ownership of almost everything by a few capitalists who produce only for profit. Capitalism tries to use reproduction, sexuality, masculine-feminine socialization of children in such away as to make us more exploitable ... Herein lies the special oppression of women as women, as well as of women as workers.[13]

Yet the concept of "capitalism," organizing Guettel's and similar definitions of women and their oppression, is actually "the Soviet gift to the United States" because "capitalism," as a concept, did not have meaning and salience in American political and scientific discourse before the Soviet revolution of 1917.[14] "Capitalist" and "capital" were used to refer to the economy but "capitalism" emerged as a concept against the articulations of "Marxism," "socialism," and "communism" advanced by the revolutionary forces and changes in the Soviet Union in the early twentieth century. The temporal and dialectal relationships between theories and concepts of socialism and capitalism in the Western social sciences, therefore, call into question what we really know about capitalism. It also calls into question what and how we have come to know about socialism. "As a result," Steven Marks writes, "American conceptions of capitalism have been, and still are, imbued with economic and cultural science fiction of the right, as well as of the left and center."[15]

Transnational feminists in Western academies claiming a Marxist viewpoint have not considered how the Marxist-capitalist epistemological duality impacts women's relations in and outside academia, presuming instead that both Marxist theory and socialist practice are equally and universally embraced by all women who are critical of capitalism.[16] *Unequal under Socialism* conveys postsocialist feminist doubt and seeks feminist standpoints from where to produce a deep critique of both capitalism and socialism in order to encourage thinking beyond binary epistemologies: these present a failure of imagination and signal our inability to see that which may lay beyond and above Marxism, socialism, and capitalism. We have generated a vast body of knowledge critical of capitalism but we lack such a rigorous and extensive critique of socialism. Critical theories linking socialism and communism to "totalitarianism" launch such a critique,[17] yet these theories lack gender and sexuality analysis. They are also reductive in the context of the Balkans, where the idea of total subservience to the socialist state and "streamlined modernity"[18] does not and cannot capture the depth, heterogeneity, and complexity of socialist nation-building and the subjectivities it supported. Equating state socialism in the region with totalitarianism further dovetails notions of passive Balkan citizenry lacking agentic capacitates and transformative consciousness in the face of power – a dehumanizing notion as well.

While self-described Marxist and transnational feminists in the global North and South "do not see" postsocialist women, postsocialist feminists in the Balkans "do not see" race. Postsocialist feminist intellectuals have spent much attention and energy describing how empires and colonial regimes of power have impacted women in Eastern and Central Europe and the Balkans but have *not* interrogated the role of race in their foundational views of the world. Instead, postsocialist feminists have presumed that the domination of Western and white middle-class feminisms over Second and Third World women affords enough shared experiences to sustain feminist alliances, mutually beneficial projects, and collaborations between postsocialist women and non-white women in the rest of the world.[19] In their extensive critiques of the erasure, muting, and absence of socialist and postsocialist women in feminist theory and women's studies practised in the West, yet absence of thinking about race, postsocialist writers have also missed entirely the history of Black international women from the United States, the Caribbean, and Canada who have been deeply engaged with socialism. In the earlier parts of the twentieth century, Black international women studied extensively the experiences of women and men in socialist states to think through if and how socialism and communism could liberate Black people globally. Black women in the American political Left including Louise Thompson Patterson, Claudia Jones, Audre Lorde, Angela Davis, and others, travelled to the Soviet Union and countries in Eastern and Central Europe and the Balkans personally and recorded their observations of socialist nation-building and interrelated issues of class, gender, and race. Some of these Black feminists like Claudia Jones and Angela Davis admired Soviet progress;[20] others like Audre Lorde observed social relations at the flanges of the Soviet Empire and concluded that the thing holding different races together in the Soviet society was a strong and forceful state.[21] Race and the status of women were central concerns of this mode of Black feminist internationalism located in the political Left. Postsocialist feminists in the Balkans seeking inclusion and consideration in transnational feminist studies and theories have not engaged with the role of race in their own societies and socialism despite the fact that such engagement could lay the foundation of an important political bridge connecting postsocialist women to Black women and feminisms.

This book attempts such bridging by making the question of race central to the inquiry about women under state socialism. It centres on race in order to take responsibility for the oppression and marginalization of women racialized as non-white in Bulgaria, the Balkans, and globally. It is inspired and guided by critical knowledges related to gender, race, culture, coloniality, class, sexuality, women's relations, agency, political economy, and feminist solidarities developed by transnational postsocialist feminist intellectuals originating in Bulgaria, the former Soviet Union, Macedonia, and the United States: Madina Tlostanova, Suzana Milevska, Nurie Muratova, Kristen Ghodsee, and Jennifer Suchland; indigenous transnational, postcolonial, and border-theory feminist thinkers with roots in North and South America, Europe, Africa, Asia, and the Caribbean: Chandra Talpade Mohanty, Chela Sandoval, Audre Lorde, Angela Davis, Gloria Anzaldua, Patricia Hill-Collins, Ethel Brooks, Caren Kaplan, and Njoki Wane; and social and cultural theorists Roderick A. Ferguson, Homi Bhabha, Stuart Hall, David Theo Goldberg, and Paul Gilroy, among other whose work has been instrumental in developing my own thinking about racialization, feminist solidarities, and socialism. *Unequal under Socialism* also takes responsibility for my own implication in regimes of power and violence as an ethnic Bulgarian, Christian, "new European," and mobile woman educated in the United States, currently working and living in Canada, and enjoying privileges not given to others. I am also a former socialist subject and factory worker from the Balkans whose own racialized identities defy binary white/non-white designations.[22] I speak about race and women in the Balkans from that location as well.

Challenging "Whiteness" and "Racial Formation" in the Balkans

While postsocialist transnational feminists are yet to take up race as an important issue in women's relations and activism, a handful of Western social scientists contributing to critical race theory, globalization studies, and area studies have begun to tackle the role of race in nation-building, culture, and politics in former socialist states.[23] Although these authors have opened important debates about racial ethnonationalisms and racist cultural productions in former socialist countries, their writing has painted peoples, territories, and itineraries of race in the Balkans in broad strokes, advancing generalizations that obscure the gendered, sexed, and classed aspects of the issue as well as its various local manifestations and effects. These studies also utilize concepts stemming from critical race theory, whiteness studies, and racial formation theory developed within the contexts of European colonialism and United States race relations to describe issues in the Balkans – a transposition presuming that race must have played a significant and similar role in the region's history as it has done in Western Europe, the United States, and world regions subjected to their colonial and political conquests. This presumption is evident in the prevailing methodological approaches used in these studies focused exclusively on those events, people, artefacts, and archival documents showing the presence and impact of race in the region but ignoring all those other forces, agents, or factors that undermined the salience of race in making Balkan peoples and societies. Studies of race and racism in former socialist states also form a body of intellectual work performed in Western Europe and the United States; hence these studies speak to race and racism in the Balkans from the location of historical geopolitical, racial, and epistemological power. These studies and their overwhelmingly white Western authors are thus doing the work of the colonizing gaze. My own early work on race in the region struggled not to extend a Western social scientific gaze to the Balkans. I attempted to guard against it by rooting the work I produced in the early 2000s in ideas and arguments developed by the Black British historian of Guyanese heritage Paul Gilroy, whose theorizing of a "Black Atlantic" countering European modernity inspired my ideas of a "white Atlantic" and Balkan immigrants in the United States who approximated American racial formation but were not its originators or natives.[24]

This book wishes to undermine that Western gaze and the knowledges it produces further by addressing processes of racialization in the Balkans as well as forces countering these processes. In so doing, the book challenges theories of "racial whiteness" in Balkan societies presented at recent conference panels and workshops dedicated to the subject.[25] Racial whiteness is a theoretical paradigm originating in the fields of US labour history, American studies, American sociology, anthropology, and other related fields positing that White people are made and not born, and that membership in the White race has determined the distribution of material wealth, political and cultural privileges, and wages in the United States. State socialism in Bulgaria, and to the best of my knowledge in other socialist countries, collectivized the material tools of production and reorganized class structures profoundly, giving material and political power to workers regardless of their ethnoracial background. Such material privileging of the worker was apparent in the distribution of wages favouring labourers in plants, factories, mines, and heavy industries versus cultural and intellectual workers, whose wages in Bulgaria were substantially lower than those of the industrial workers. Socialist state authorities in Bulgaria also extended material and social privileges and wages to racialized groups such as the Roma. State policies also enacted assimilationist programs against the Roma, forcing them into public employment and modern housing, and sponsoring mixed marriages between Bulgarian and Roma persons in order to showcase how socialist work fostered human progress and social and material equality. These realities may evoke some of the features of "the wages of whiteness"[26] in the United States, but they hardly fall into the rubrics of foundational whiteness studies and theories developed by American scholars such as Theodore W. Allen, David Roediger, George Lipsitz, Michael Omi, Howard Winant, and others.[27]

Understating the salience of race in identity formations and social relations in Bulgaria and other socialist states is actually undermined by insisting on "racial whiteness" as a viable explanatory category in the Balkan region. As John Hartigan Jr. warns us, notions of racial whiteness solidify and make real what are in actuality cultural and social racial constructs.[28] Whiteness theorizing also lumps different people into a single mass obliterating the possibility of a much more nuanced understanding of the instability and constantly shifting nature of racial, ethnic, or gender identifications in the Balkans. Instead of focusing on "whiteness" as emerging against the "Blackness" of the Other, Hartigan invites us to shift our attention to the study of the pliability, temporality, locality, and liquidity of racial imaginations. Besides, it is in this kind of inquiry into the shifting of racial meanings that we are more likely to find both examples of racialization and racism as well as instances of anti-racism and anti-whiteness. Finding such examples and anti-racism inspirations is a major objective of this book about race and women in socialist Bulgaria.

Unequal under Socialism further challenges prevailing theorizing of "racial formation" in Balkan societies. It is very tempting to address racial thinking and imaginations in the Balkans using various iterations of racial formation theory. Concepts such as "racial projects," "racial order," "racial myths," "racial change," or "racial innocence" provide potent explanatory paradigms tracing the ways in which ideas about racial origins and racial difference organize structures and relations in a given society, provide rationale for material production and distribution of wealth and privileges among the members of that society, explain claims to colour blindness, challenge racist practices, spread racial thinking globally, and anchor individual and group identifications.[29] At the heart of racial formation theorizing is the question about the role and salience of race in processes of ascribing meaning to human beings, and social and material realities, and using these valorizations to grant political rights and social, economic, and cultural privileges.

Racial formation theory also consists of multiple epistemological aspects and processes resulting in social stratification; yet the presence of some or all elements of the theory is not required to perceive a historical, cultural, social, discursive, or political phenomenon as racial formation locally or globally. The intellectual pliability of racial formation theory is evident in its continually expanding historical and geographic scope, as scholars in countries worldwide have utilized elements of the theory to speak about the role of race in defining societies in Latin America, Europe, Asia, and more recently Central and Eastern Europe and the Balkans.[30] "Racial palestinization," "racial southafricanization," "racial latinamericanization," and "racial europeanization" are recently coined signifiers capturing the subtle yet powerful historical ways in which scientific, artistic, cultural, political, and legal scripts have worked together to normalize racialized views and hierarchies globally.[31] Likewise, notions such as "red racism," referring to racial views under state socialism, or "racial ethno-nationalism," presenting eugenics and racial hygiene as ingredients in Balkan nation-building, showcase the power of racial ideas and racial sciences in the making of Balkan countries and societies.[32]

This book challenges theories of racial formation in the Balkans by exploring the issue from the perspective of multiple and contradictory events and experiences. Focusing on race and nation-building in post-Ottoman Bulgaria before, during, and after state socialism, the book reveals how processes of racialization in that country are linked directly to the global order of power, rendering people in the Balkans recipients and subjects of British, German, French, Russian, and American racial sciences and modern ideologies. Yet the book shines light on purposeful and accidental local events, social forms, and knowledges that curbed the trajectories and impact of racial epistemes. My entry points to such a reading of race and racialization in Bulgaria include public scientific discourses about the origins of Bulgarian and Roma races, state demographic data collection practices, popular views related to human difference in and outside the young Bulgarian nation state, Bulgarian women's politics and activism, oral histories of Roma and Muslim women, transgender cultural productions, autoethnographic events, and other experiences that illuminate the unstable itineraries of race thinking in Bulgaria. Together, these archives reveal ambiguity, uneasiness, and stumbling paths and directions of race-based ideas and imaginations in Bulgarian nation-building before, during, and after socialism. Indeed, Western European expansion and power caused conceptual seepage of racial rationalizations that extended local Balkan ethnic, class, and gender hierarchies; however, race did not become a "foundational code" of nation-building in Bulgaria, which is the premise of racial formation.[33]

The book offers the notion of "socialist racialism" as a useful way to distinguish between racial formation conceived within Euro-American experiences and the specific ways in which racial sciences and imaginations operated within the socialist states. It argues that unlike race and racism, which served to divide and separate human groups under colonial and capitalist conditions, socialist racialism sought to include human groups deemed racially different and culturally backward into a political and economic project seeking equity through redistribution of rights and privileges. Both capitalist racism and socialist racialism produced tremendous violence, the former to sustain power and privilege and the latter to create equality. The book chapters observe the violence in the name of inclusion under socialism, calling for novel paradigms that could capture the relationship between socialism, racialized and gendered thinking, and forced inclusion in-depth. Racial formation and whiteness theories originating in the experiences of the United States do not and cannot do that analytical work fully and competently in the context of Bulgarian and Balkan socialisms.

Race, Unequal Power, and Standpoint Analytics in the Balkans

Reconstructing race's uneasy itineraries in marginal and subordinated societies such as Bulgaria in the Balkans further shifts attention to the local as the ground for theory and knowledge production, thus guarding against homogenizing generalizations stemming from a Western intellectual, theoretical, and racial gaze enfolding the Balkans into global racial formations without taking care of the complex geopolitical power relations and European, Russian/Soviet, and Euro-American hegemony under which Balkan assertions of self-whiteness have taken shape. Race-thinking in Bulgaria, this book suggests, supports assertions of self-agency and claims to self-governance in the face of external hegemonic powers that have determined who is "European," "civilized," and "developed," and therefore entitled to a political voice and independence. Indeed, as Dale Peterson reminds us, "the insidious Western conception of the inherent inferiority of the Negro and the

Slavic races, initiated that harmful conflation of race and ethnicity, of biology with culture, that led to the victims of such genetic and climatological theories to adapt similarly racialist and essentialist thinking in their own defense."[34] Mary Neuberger's work extends Peterson's observations from Russia to Muslim-Christian relations in socialist Bulgaria by arguing that external Western orientalizing discourses about the inferiority of Christian Bulgarians fomented not only deep-seated Bulgarian animosity to Muslims but also Bulgarian claim to self-Europeanness.[35] Neuberger further attributes "all Balkan nationalism" to the latter phenomenon; yet her important observations fail to note the role of racialization in organizing social relations under state socialism, thus erasing the experiences of the Roma minority in the country. Neuberger's theorizing of "self-orientalizing" in Bulgaria further omits the role of globally disseminated popular culture seated in the United States and Western Europe in the identity formations the author describes. That omission and the erasure of Roma might be attributed to the lack of critical examination of the geopolitical and epistemological self-location from which this author speaks to and of Bulgarians and Muslims, missing an opportunity to reflect on how a contemporary Euro-American gaze may be shaping who and what primes Euro-American authors who study identities and social relations in the Balkans.

A recent article commenting on the findings of a study of racial biases among "white Europeans" manifests that external gaze further. The author noted that anti-Black views were common in Western Europe but increased in volume and intensity in Eastern and Southern Europe: "The Balkans," he wrote, "look like an exception to surrounding countries."[36] The author speculated that the deviation of data from the Balkans had to be because people in these countries had heard about the racial biases study beforehand, hence their responses did not reflect how they truly felt. The author proceeded to insist on intense and universally shared Balkan racial biases by suggesting that the data deviation could also be due to Balkan people's racial prejudices "not oriented along white-black axis" targeted by the study.

What is defined as "Balkans" and "white" in these conclusive utterings actually consists of heterogeneous and complex locales, where race provided grounds for imagining self and others, but these imaginings were not universally shared by men, women, working-class people, economic elites, ethnic and religious majorities and minorities, and parties aligned with political ideologies to the Left and Right. Racial and racialized milieus in Bulgaria, and likely in the rest of the Balkans, are fractured, uneven, unstable, and constantly negotiated, calling for standpoint methodological and theoretical approaches placing difference (gender, sexual, ethnic, religious, class) at the centre of analyses of race before, under, and after state socialism.

This book attempts such an analytic anchored in temporal, social, and ideological standpoints from which the chapters perceive how state and society negotiate racial meanings constructed in modern science, culture, nation, family, womanhood, ideology, and work before, during, and after state socialism, and how different groups of women both shaped and were shaped by these negotiations and the unstable, contested, and even paradoxical social forms they produced. Feminist standpoint theory originates in critical feminist epistemologies challenging perceptions of "women" as a class of people whose oppression or liberation is tied to common biological characteristics. Feminist standpoint analytics insist on recognizing how and why groups of women are differently positioned vis-à-vis power and the experiences that positioning entails.[37] Therefore, a standpoint approach like that grounding this book asserts that experience produces knowledge and divorcing knowledge from one's historical experience and social location is oppressive and hegemonic.[38] *Unequal under Socialism* delineates yet relates the standpoints of Roma women, Turkish- and Bulgarian-speaking Muslim women, Bulgarian ethnic and Christian women, sex workers, women office and factory workers, urban and rural women, and state feminists in the socialist state who presented forms of difference that cannot be lumped and analysed together as a mass of female socialist subjects.

Chapter 1 begins to map these standpoints by following the loud public debate about the relationship between a people's biology and capacity for culture among leading Bulgarian scientists in the late 1930s. The chapter positions this moment of influential racial discourses in the young post-Ottoman Bulgarian state in relation to the women's movements and activism at the time, Muslim and Roma local life and relations, political mobilization surrounding the treatment of Jewish communities in the country during the Second World War, and other events that curbed the power of race in permeating the foundations of post-Ottoman nation-building and identifications in the country. Racial formation theory developed within the historical context of the United States, the chapter argues, *does not* capture the complexity of race's itineraries in Bulgaria, and probably in other Balkan countries.

Chapter 2 develops a conceptual paradigm where European and Western hegemony over the Balkans and the Eurocentricity of Marxism and Bulgarian socialism resulted in an ideology I dub "socialist racialism" focused on the erasure and forceful inclusion of "belated peoples" into the socialist project. State narratives rationalized the inclusion by actively reproducing cultural logics that mimicked the comparativism and hierarchies produced by the racial sciences that justified European and Russian colonial conquests. In the 1950s and 1960s, the Bulgarian socialist state thus promoted racial equality in public education, the state constitution, and mass culture; however, this book suggests, the embedded Eurocentrism of Marxism and socialism still engendered culturally perceived racialized socialist subjects and subjectivities marked for prosperity or social and cultural death. Racialized Roma and Muslim women, sex workers, unmarried or childless women, and those not engaged in socially useful labour were devalued genres of womanhood and biologized cultural aberrations threatening the socialist project and the scientific claims of Marxism and Leninism. Moral, modern Bulgarian and Christian ethnic wives, mothers, and workers supporting socialist men and raising proper socialist citizens claiming membership among the "European races" were tasked by the state with the reformation and assimilation of the undesired female kinds. This history, the chapter suggests, both enables and inhibits local women's relations conducive to feminist solidarity and political aligning.

Chapter 3 explores how places of work and work-related activities performed by women in the socialist state became a major site of state violence against women. Racially and ethnically privileged Bulgarian women involved in state instrumentalities for managing social deviation carried socialist assimilationist and eradicating agendas targeting undesired female types; but the archives also show that as many women resisted the roles assigned to them by the state, expressed doubt in the emancipatory properties of both socialism and capitalism, and formed strong bonds with women subjected to state violence. These archives anchor a theory of gendered socialist mode of governmentality centred on women's work that contributes new knowledge about the relationship between gender, socialist political economy, and state violence in women's studies and transnational feminisms.

Reforming and power-based relationality between groups of women in the socialist state extended internationally through travel and discursive productions by racially and socially privileged female intellectuals and writers attached to the state and/or men in positions of power. Chapter 4 analyses how these women contributing to the influential state-supported journal *Zhenata Dnes* (Woman today) constructed raceless yet deeply Eurocentric depictions of white and non-white women in Africa, South and North America, the Soviet Union, Asia, and capitalist Europe in the 1960s and 1970s. The chapter relates these depictions to state socialist internationalism that brought to Bulgaria thousands of students and migrant workers from Vietnam, Nigeria, Kenya,

South Africa, and other colonial locations, but which guests faced perceptions and treatment illuminating socialist racialization in the form of state patronage over non-white peoples struggling against racism and exploitation in the global North and South. One highly influential socialist woman, however, formed different kinds of relations and promoted a mode of socialist internationalism that helped change the course of Bulgarian history.

In the late 1970s and early 1980s, Lyudmila Zhivkova, who was the Minister of Culture and daughter of Todor Zhivkov, the chair of the Bulgarian Communist Party, fostered a strong personal friendship with India's prime minister, Indira Gandhi. Driven by doubts about the course of Marxism and state socialism, Zhivkova reached out to Eastern and Indigenous philosophies and practices as soulful and spiritual human expressions that could revitalize a failing socialist project. Focused on socialist workers' declining productivity yet increasing political alienation, Zhivkova embraced ideas about the foundational role of culture in organizing social life advanced by intellectuals in the emerging international New Left committed to democratic and humanistic socialism. Zhivkova's work changed the Bulgarian socialist cultural landscape profoundly, opening it to increased Western and Eastern cultural influences simultaneously. These examples of socialist feminist internationalism, the chapter argues, left an important albeit mixed legacy of Second and Third World women's relations that provides an important political compass for contemporary postsocialist feminists building their own transnational women's networks.

Chapter 5 expands understanding of this legacy by engaging with the domestic cultural policies that opened socialist Bulgaria to a powerful influx of racist masculine globalized popular culture originating in the United States, especially American action movies, which became popular among socialist male youth audiences. This cinematic stream energized male desires for political freedom and resistance to an overbearing and controlling socialist state; yet US-based cultural streams presented an influential visual and sensory epistemology of race, gender, and capitalist materiality conducive to postsocialist transformations marked by the rise of racist and ultranationalist politics targeting Roma, Black people, queer individuals, women, Muslims, refugees, and others living on, or merely crossing, the Bulgarian land.

Simultaneously, a Roma transgender artist named Azis became the most innovative, beloved, and popular figure of Bulgarian postsocialist mass culture in the 2000s and 2010s further calling into question the racial formation paradigms used to describe contemporary postsocialist Bulgaria and the Balkans. The book's conclusion reviews recent programs dedicated to the integration of Roma communities and preventing violence against Roma women in Bulgaria and other former socialist countries implemented by the European Union, individual donor states, and local and international NGOs. The analysis evaluates these programs in light of the historical forces causing race-thinking, racism, and anti-Gypsysm in Bulgaria mapped in the book's chapters. It illustrates the short-sighted logics of these anti-racism initiatives and gestures to Azis's music and art as a postsocialist cultural "third space" embodying hybridity, cosmopolitanism, and open-ended gender, sexual and racial forms that imbue postsocialism with tremendous optimism, anti-racism, and social energies of a new kind. Through their art and politics, this Roma artist openly challenges socialist and capitalist racist, sexist, and heteronormative scripts and locates freedom, democracy, and notions of "future" in non-white bodies and feminist and queer political alliances transcending both socialism and capitalism. The chapter links these politics of a third postsocialist cultural space to the history of resistance against oppression and violence staged by Roma, Bulgarian, Turkish, Muslim, and Christian women in Bulgaria. It further links these modes of defiance to transnational anti-racist feminisms embodied by Gloria Anzaldua, Chandra Talpade Mohanty, Audre Lorde, and other women of colour whose work and struggles against racism and patriarchy provide further insights to how anti-racism in Bulgaria and the world could be staged. The book ends by calling for more and extended critical conversations, memory work, formal and informal education, and cultural productions inspired by that history shared by women in Bulgaria and transnational feminists of colour so that together we can dream up and realize societies where all citizens prosper.

Clarifying Key Terms (and What This Book Is Not)

This book is not a proper history of race or women and gender in Bulgaria, or the Balkans, despite the fact that it is rooted in primary archival documents. Rather, it is a social and interdisciplinary critical reading of events and documents in order to promote a viewpoint and enter into a debate with existing literature and interpretations. The book also falls under the category of "locational feminism":[39] in this case, locational postsocialist feminist texts and analytics positioning differently raced, sexed, and classed women's experiences in the Balkans as the basis of globally used and debated theories, interpretive frames, and issues falling under the umbrella of women's studies. Locational feminism is further related to "transnationalism." *Unequal under Socialism* rests upon a methodological analytical approach that is vertical in the sense that my interpretations of events, social forms, women's relations, and power connect local, national, and global forces that together impact and shape the lives of women.[40] This approach embodies the feminist concept of "transnationalism," which, in feminist theory and practice, rejects horizontal and centre-margin analytical paradigms because they confine our understanding of race, patriarchy, and women's identities within colonial power relations or nation states thus being "helpless to recognize the complex and nuanced manifestations of transnational circulations of people, goods and information."[41]

Throughout the book, I use other terms and signifiers that are unstable and contested. I refer to the case of Bulgaria but also leap to speak of the Balkans. These leaps are not meant to suggest that somehow Bulgaria represents the whole of the Balkans; rather, it is one distinct location and a case among multiple cases that must be studied and analysed in order to map shared experiences and distinctions all of which constitute the Balkans as a geopolitical, social, and cultural region. Hegemonic external power, multiple empires, an alliance of all socialist countries in a single political block under Soviet control, and globalization of European and Euro-American ideas and cultures impacting countries and regions of the world simultaneously allow for assertions of what is specific to Bulgaria while gesturing to what Bulgaria likely shares with other peoples in the region.

The term "postsocialism" refers to a cognitive and emotional state of being shaped by doubt. It also refers to time and place: life in countries that used to be organized by Marxist and socialist/communist political and economic principles in the past but are now transformed and operating under neo-liberal political global regimes.[42] In the Balkans, these transformations are related to the end of the Cold War; hence postsocialism also refers to a world defined by globalization of culture and markets where all countries partake in an emerging geopolitical order propelled by the collapse of socialist states and its leader and hegemonic power, the Soviet Union.

The notion of "racialization" used extensively in this book evokes processes where state and social agents and powers create racial meanings and assign these meanings to human groups and material life within their own society and globally. These racial meanings further unfold and spread alongside gendered, sexual, religious, and classed hierarchies that organize socialist and capitalist societies alike. My usage of "racialization" draws from the work of sociologists who do not think "race" is a useful concept because the term has taken so many and diverging meanings rendering the notion useless in the social sciences. "Racialization" displaces focus on what "race" means to what racial ideas do; racialization thus refers to processes of categorizing, defining, and representing others using or alluding to presumed biological characteristics associated with them.[43] Put differently, racialization signifies the ways in which people, structures, and ideas are given racial interpretations at the level of culture, highlighting the unstable and fluctuating meanings of race and its usage in the construction of gender, sexual, religious, cultural, and economic hierarchies and divisions.[44] This book focuses on how processes of racialization under state socialism impacted different groups of women and their relations to other women locally and internationally.

Like "racialization," the terms "orientalizing," "semi-Orientals," and "the Orient" in this book refer to historical processes of constructing the Balkans and Western signifiers depicting the region as an extension of and a door to lands called "the Orient." I am aware that these terms are outcomes of colonial projects and have been used to dehumanize peoples and diminish their cultures. My usage of these terms in the book is not meant to extend these offensive meanings but to name and deconstruct the power dynamic underlining these constructs.

I continue to refer to First, Second, and Third World women and locales throughout the book although these terms have been rejected by some women because their origins in European and American colonial conquests for power connote a hierarchy of developed and undeveloped societies, cultures, and races. I use the terms because they are meaningful to postsocialist women and ontologies where the "East" and "West" of Europe and the world viewed from within the Balkans continue to denote historical sociocultural and geopolitical locations and inequal relations of power that play a central role in how contemporary women encounter and relate (or not) to other women locally and globally.[45] These categories have also been claimed by scholars and activists within the field of transitional feminisms, where I locale my scholarship and this book.[46] In addition, I use "global North" and "global South" to refer to economic exploitation and political and cultural appropriation of women south of the equator. This signification marks the material prosperity of societies in the global North versus the continuous impoverishment and exploitation of women in countries located in the global South.[47] A "Third World woman" thus stands for women racialized as non-white in both Western countries where they are the descendants of slaves, migrants, refugees, and colonized peoples and non-white women residing in countries in the global South who cope with histories of external colonization and exploitation.

"Second World" in the book refers to former socialist countries in Eastern and Central Europe, the Balkans, and the former Soviet Union. During the Cold War, socialist states were commonly described as more economically advanced than countries in the so-called Third World, yet politically and culturally inferior to the First World: hence the term "Second World." But in this book, "Second World women" also connotes social differences between groups of women in order to recognize the various and distinct ways in which these women have been marginalized or privileged. By "Bulgarian women," therefore, I do not mean all women in the country called Bulgaria but a class of women enjoying racialized ethnic, religious, cultural, and material advantages not afforded to Roma women or Turkish and Bulgarian-speaking Muslim women in the same country.

"Women" in this book is not a biological but a *political category* describing citizens whose productive and reproductive qualities have been targeted for control by both socialist and capitalist/neo-liberal states. "Socialist state patriarchy" is a related notion describing a society committed to socialist and communist ideals of social justice that sustain and extend deep inequalities between men and women, and between heterosexual and queer and transgender citizens and subjects. These concepts inform another important term I use throughout the book: "postsocialist women" refers to women born and coming of age under state socialism who are now looking back at these experiences critically, generating new knowledge enriching and expanding conversations about socialism, communism, Marxism, and capitalism. Yet "postsocialist women" should not be used lightly because those of us who came of age and worked and lived under socialist conditions differ significantly from younger women born in socialist states in the 1980s and thereafter who barely remember socialist life. These younger women, brought up in the transition from socialism to capitalism, many educated in American and Western European universities, and acculturated under the Europeanizing influences of the European Union, theorize and think of socialism differently. These younger women are the daughters of those of us who grew up on the factory floors, worked the fields in the socialist agricultural collectives, studied in vocational schools to support the socialist economy, and never travelled abroad. That privilege to travel or study in a university was reserved for another category of elite postsocialist women from the affluent political classes who controlled the Communist Party and the state and who benefited from socialism in ways other women never did. These classes of women experienced socialism but not as equals or equally. "Postsocialist women" in this book highlights the differences.

Unequal under Socialism examines how Russian/Soviet, European, and American racial and racist sciences and imaginations intertwined with local and national forces to produce these differences and inequalities between women in socialist Bulgaria. It also shines light on countering and connecting forces and feminist socialist and postsocialist imaginations that bridged the divides produced by race, unleashing relational and non-violent identifications that also mark Bulgaria. Along the way, the chapters and arguments invite feminists, political activists, and intellectuals to reconsider the capacity of socialist and collectivist modes of material and non-material production in fostering social equality – a dialectic deeply ingrained in Marxist theories and praxes dominating Western academies. It serves as an occasion for reflection and reassessment of the increasing body of academic and popular work, especially in the United States, born out of the crises of neo-liberalism. Many authors have proposed changes within industry and culture as ways to transform unjust capitalist and racist neo-liberal societies by creating socialist structures and forms: a large public economic sector; more Marxist, materialist, and class analyses within academic research and education; new cooperatives; and fostering teamwork, crowd outsourcing, and collectivism. This book serves as a cautionary tale amid presuppositions that socialist and collectivist economic and cultural production will necessarily foster social relations conducive to racial and gender equality, expanded democracy, and the "good society" – racializing, valuing, and devaluing different groups of women in socialist Bulgaria testifies to that.

Chapter One

Race, Women, and Nation-building in the 1930s and 1940s

In the spring of 1939, Germany invaded the former Czechoslovakia, sending shockwaves throughout Europe and the world. In the Balkans, peoples recovering from the horrors of the First World War worriedly awaited the consequences of the German conquest unravelling. In Bulgaria, anxious publics followed closely the political manoeuvring of Tsar Boris III and his government in response to the invasion. Upcoming general elections, the growing popularity of the Bulgarian Communist Party, and the women's vote also preoccupied the government's agenda. A few blocks away from the National Assembly buzzing with political activity, a curious crowd of students, academics, and citizens gathered in Auditorium 15 at Sofia University to hear prominent speakers, among them Professor Dimiter Mihalchev, who delivered critical lectures on the links between "race," "culture," and "nation."[1] Mihalchev's talks responded to widely debated studies of the origins of the Bulgarian race by anthropologist Methody Popov published in 1938. The polemic further included leading biologist and eugenicist Stefan Konsulov and distinguished sociologist Ivan Kinkel, whose descriptions of biological and cultural difference between the Bulgarian, Roma, and Jewish races had captured public attention centered on independence, nation-building, and modernization after five centuries of Ottoman presence, domination, and exploitation that ended in 1878.

Yet, as this chapter will show, the racial debates raging in Bulgaria in the 1930s involved ideas about biological and cultural difference that were still novel in the Bulgarian context. The archives suggest that the issue of race and the question of the Bulgarian racial type engaged urban male scientific and political elites educated in European universities who commanded positions of power. Women belonging to the Bulgarian ethnic majority evidently did not find the issue as important, judging from their political actions that focused on the women's vote and access to education and the professions. Ethnographic accounts of life among Roma and Muslim minorities in the country also show that women in these communities actually practised fluid identities and relationships revolving around the hardships of poverty and rural life. Fluidity and regional cosmopolitanism of identifications in the young Bulgarian nation were further suggested by revolutionary imaginations dominating the previous century.

For example, throughout the nineteenth century, Bulgarian writers, intellectuals, and revolutionaries struggling against Ottoman imperial rule imagined a post-Ottoman multicultural federation of Balkan peoples organized by principles resembling those governing the United States. The press in the Bulgarian domain of the Ottoman Empire published hundreds of stories, journalistic reports, and editorials throughout the period, constructing the United States as an example of egalitarian democratic society where all kinds of people lived together.[2] Bulgarian intellectuals and supporters of an uprising against the Ottomans further shared the belief that the United States was a potent force unfriendly to both the Ottomans and the British who collaborated with them. The American revolutionary war against Great Britain, abolition of slavery, constitutionality, and multiplicity of races, languages, and cultures made the United States an attractive political example that could instruct the establishing of a "Balkan Union," which Bulgarian progressives and revolutionaries imagined as a federation of Christian peoples and Balkan territories that recognized each other's distinct cultural and linguistic features yet lived in political solidarity extending to collective protection from external domination and conquest.

In 1878, it was not the United States but a coalition led by Russia and the Russo-Turkish War that liberated Bulgaria and other Balkan territories. The ensuing Bulgarian post-Ottoman nation-building took a very different turn and away from the federalist and egalitarian Balkan-centred thinking marking the nineteenth century. The reasons were multiple and related to a new political configuration positioning Bulgaria and the Balkans for political subjugation and cultural and economic domination by European, Euro-American, and Soviet colonial powers whose intertwined racial sciences, racialized liberal, Marxist, Leninist, and fascist ideologies, and shared cultural constructions of human difference would help shape Bulgarian views and discourses on self, other, and the nation not just in the 1930s but throughout the twentieth century. This chapter begins to map women's politics, epistemologies, and relations that are equally important but understudied forces and ways of knowing routing, curbing, resisting, and redirecting these itineraries of race during the period.

Catching up with Racial Modernity

In the decades after gaining independence in 1878, Bulgarian society experienced great political, economic, and cultural transformations under the banner of modernization. Two generations of Bulgarian bourgeoisie educated in the capitals of Europe conceived and carried out economic, cultural, social, and political projects envisioned as catching up with modern Europe.[3] Notions of Bulgarian membership in Europe coupled with cultural, political, and economic deprivation from participation in European modern history caused by Ottoman and Muslim domination served as a powerful impetus for the reforms. Members of the Bulgarian ruling classes understood the task of uplifting the masses as their duty to the nation. Sharing a sense of urgency, the elites designed state and public institutions copying European social and political forms.

In 1879, an assembly of "educated, well-known, contributors to their mother land ... intelligentsia of educators, doctors, lawyers, publicists and writers ... among the urban classes" drafted a Bulgarian constitution fashioned after the Belgium constitution.[4] The assembly established post-Ottoman Bulgaria as a constitutional monarchy resembling "advanced Europe." But there was no royalty in Bulgaria to lead the new monarchy. Therefore, the assembly elected a tsar. He was Alexander Battenberg, the nephew of the Russian emperor Alexander II, who was also a member of the British extended royal family, a German officer, and an Austrian general. The Bulgarian choice of a monarch permanently connected the new state to the hegemonic powers of the day. Balkan peoples were not invited to the Berlin Congress (June–July 1878), where Germany, Russia, England, and France determined their fate and territories following the era of Ottoman domination by dividing and redesigning the geographical and human boundaries of the region. The Bulgarian constitutional assembly elected a tsar whose connections to European centres of power would provide Bulgaria with political leverage and the ability to determine its own faith. The newly elected monarch arrived in Bulgaria in 1879. He immediately appointed a government that quickly set about organizing the state institutions. Bulgaria's National Assembly embedded in these institutions the principles of European bourgeois democracy and the visions of the first Bulgarian political parties: conservatives advocating slow democratization and modernization of post-Ottoman Bulgaria following the "natural evolution" of Western Europe, and liberals standing by the most liberal traditions of the West.[5]

Bulgarian elites further initiated and carried out sweeping reforms in banking, taxation, trade, agriculture, land distribution, law and order, and transportation. Between 1903 and 1906, a major educational reform also took place. In the words of the minister of education at the time: "Only through expansion of education ... state support of the cultural institutions and state stimulation of arts and sciences ... would turn Bulgaria into a modern country ... following the examples in education of the advanced European countries."[6] Enacting modernization through mass education, the Bulgarian state sponsored more than 250 promising intellectuals to study in Western Europe. The state also funded academics' attendance at professional conferences abroad, so that Bulgarian scholars would be acquainted with the latest achievements in the arts and sciences. The Bulgarian Ministry of Education also provided scholarships so that teachers could travel to European capitals to study or perfect their proficiency in the German, French, Italian, or English language.[7] State support for individuals obtaining education in European universities and acquiring language skills privileged members of the middle and upper classes and the Bulgarian ethnic majority perceived as bearers of European culture. Members of these mostly male elites brought back to modernizing Bulgaria racialized thinking and racial identifications of different kinds and intensity. The following account of the "Gypsy town" in Sofia from 1931 illustrates local male liberal bourgeoise racial perceptions vividly.

Racializing the Roma: Loving All Races but Despising Some Cultures

In the autumn of 1931, an article published in a magazine called *Az Znam Vsichko* (I know everything) explored the "Gypsy town" on the outskirts of Sofia. Penned by the magazine's editor, Hristo Brazitsov, the short urban travelogue provided rich descriptions laced with dormant racial qualifications of Roma life at the margins of society:

> I like the people from all races, with the exception of the bad people even if they are Bulgarians. And I respect more a hard-working and good-natured Gypsy who masterfully carves a trough than a Minister in the so-called great France ... I am saying this so that you are not bewildered about why I am interested in Gypsies and so that you do not hold your noses, oh, you wonderful readers of non-Gypsy origin. I will tell you some other time when you really have to make this gesture.[8]

Brazitsov's narrative articulated common notions of separate and distinct Bulgarian and Romani races. The editor further invoked a widely shared belief that Roma embodied a non-white race originating outside of Europe – a notion related to historical texts tracing Roma in Bulgaria to Egypt. Brazitsov described a Roma man he encountered as "a real heir of the pharaons: black, curly hair with playful eyes." Yet the editor blurred the corporeal markers that distinguished Bulgarians from Roma by describing "the head of the Gypsy neighbourhood" as a man dressed like Brazitsov, "even a bit white with good pronunciation of the Bulgarian words." The man was surrounded by "blond polished physiognomies ... If I met them in the centre of Sofia," Brazitsov wrote, "I would not believe they were Gypsies."[9]

Brazitsov explained further that according to "the head of the Gypsies," more than four thousand people, or seven hundred families, lived in the neighbourhood, most of them from the Muslim faith, making living as basket makers, musicians, tinsmiths, and porters. Brazitsov defined the Gypsy imam as a "fanatic" who wanted Turkish schools for the Gypsies. "Better," proclaimed Brazitsov, "Gypsy children [should] learn the language of the country in which they live ... It is better that Gypsies rear amongst them a youngster who will finish a university to take on to defend the rights of the Gypsy tribe in Bulgaria!"[10] Brazitsov linked the lack of education and leadership among members of the Roma community to cultural inferiority signified by the "filth" of Roma houses and neighbourhoods, the "fanaticism" of their faith, and "disorderly and careless" behaviours signified by group dances on the street that the Bulgarian journalist observed and described but did not join.

An archive of photographs from the 1910s, 1920s, and 1930s entitled "The Lost Bulgaria" provided visual representations of Brazitsov's discursive constructs.[11] The images assembled by the curator in a folder titled "Gypsies" reflected the inner world of a privileged social, cultural, and political Bulgarian gaze embodied by intellectuals like Brazitsov who "loved all races" but despised inferior and non-European cultures. Photography in the early twentieth century was the hobby of members of the Bulgarian middle and upper classes, who could afford to buy cameras and dedicate time documenting aspects of their lives. From the standpoint of their privileged gaze, Roma men and women depicted in the pictures conveyed powerful racial and cultural foreignness: Romani subjects appeared as exotic dark-skinned others and pre-modern difference marked by Asiatic attire, unconventional behaviour, such as elder women and young children smoking pipes or cigarettes, and spatial proximity to animals and caravans. In contrast, the fashions, materiality, and urban landscapes surrounding the images of ethnic Bulgarian men, women, and children in the archive gestured to their racial whiteness signified by their European fashion and modern materiality symbolizing political, social, and economic power. Standing by automobiles,

Fig. 1 The Roma neighbourhood on the outskirts of Sofia in 1932. Hristo Brazitzov, the editor of the local magazine *Az Znam Vsichko*, used the notes from his visit to this same neighbourhood in 1931 to pen an article calling on ethnic Bulgarians to "love all races." lostbulgaria.com.

Fig. 2 An ethnic Bulgarian couple displaying their material prosperity and enthusiasm for modern machines and travel in 1924. lostbulgaria.com.

Fig. 3 Fashionable ethnic Bulgarian women in Sofia in 1928. The European fashions and lifestyles of the Bulgarian bourgeoisie is vividly displayed by the posing women. lostbulgaria.com.

Fig. 4 A Roma boy entertaining the guards in front of the royal summer residence in the city of Varna in 1925. Bulgarian love for the new hobby of photography often reproduced racialized perceptions of Roma in a state of nature and Bulgarians who are members of European modernity. lostbulgaria.com.

Fig. 5 An elegant party of middle-class travellers at the Bozhuriste Airport near Sofia, 1928. lostbulgaria.com.

34 Unequal under Socialism

Fig. 6 An elderly Roma woman smoking a pipe while observed by curious non-Roma onlookers in 1928. lostbulgaria.com.

Fig. 7 A Muslim Roma man in rural Bulgaria circa 1930. lostbulgaria.com.

airplanes, and boats departing for lands far away, the folder of photographs depicting Bulgarians also gestured to their worldliness and mobility – qualities attributed to affluent Western European travellers, adventurers, and colonizers.

Interestingly, while popular visual and discursive narratives communicated racialized perceptions of self and others, the post-Ottoman

Bulgarian state did not collect population information based on race. Census data emphasized instead cultural, linguistic, and religious differences. Between 1887 and 1934, state authorities collected demographic data based on three socio-demographic categories: religion or faith, nationality, and mother tongue.[12] The term "nationality," referring to "national belonging" and a member of a nation, tribe, or people was used interchangeably with "ethnicity" because of the latter's origin in the Greek *ethnos*, meaning nation or people. Based on these indicators, religious and ethnic minorities in the country included self-identified Turks, Roma, Jews, Armenians, Romanians, Russians, and Greeks. Together, these minority groups constituted approximately 20 per cent of the country's population throughout the first three decades of the twentieth century. Bulgarians were the dominant majority, comprising 83 per cent of the total population in 1926. Romani people comprised 2.4 per cent of citizens in 1934. Turkish- and Bulgarian-speaking Muslims constituted 14 per cent of the population.[13]

State census practices suggested that cultural, religious, and linguistic characteristics of the population were much more salient in the new Bulgarian state than racial differences. One reason was post-Ottoman Bulgarian aspirations for consolidation of historical territories and concern about Bulgarian minorities left outside the state due to the Treaty of Berlin in 1878. The so-called national question underlined the country's international and domestic affairs focused on uniting groups of ethnic Bulgarians scattered as ethnic minorities in neighbouring states emerging out of the ruins of the Ottoman Empire. Moreover, overarching notions of national unity in the region perceived cultural traditions, language, and religion as foundations of any nation. Such understanding evolved out of Balkan peoples' historical experiences. The Ottoman Empire moved culturally and linguistically distinct populations across its Balkan domains according to its economic or military needs, creating in the process deeply fractured yet manageable, populations out of which emerged independent nation states.

Contemporary scholars in and outside the region defined these processes as a root cause for distinct modes of ethnonationalism that define the Balkans. That view, equating ethnicity with nation and state, according to these experts, organized and governed state policies in Bulgaria, and the Balkans, for over a century, explaining past and contemporary ethnic conflicts in the region. The sweeping observations reducing Balkan identities to "ethnicity" are short-sighted. Bulgarian popular and scientific debates pertaining to race, culture, and nation raging in 1938 and 1939 challenged state demographic practices in Bulgaria, directing attention to the importance of biological and racial difference in fostering national and territorial cohesiveness and strength. Questions pertaining to the role of race in determining a people's capacity for culture were at the centre of a debate involving influential public figures: Dimiter Mihalchev was the chair of the Bulgarian Academy of Science and a former Bulgarian Ambassador to the Soviet Union; Stefan Konsulov was a prominent international scholar teaching biology in German and Bulgarian universities; Methody Popov was the country's leading anthropologist; while Ivan Kinkel chaired the Bulgarian Sociological Association. These distinguished intellectuals filled with globalized scientific and ideological meanings Bulgarian perceptions of social difference.

Racial Origins of Bulgarians: Among the European Races and Peoples

Two scientific studies of the origins of the Bulgarian race by Methody Popov published in the summer of 1938 attracted the full attention of the Bulgarian scholarly community because the works presented "the first non-translations, serious, scientific studies on the subject written in [the Bulgarian] language."[14] The publications were entitled *Nasledstvenost, Rasa i Narod: Rasova Prinadlezhnost na Bulgarite* (1938; Heredity, race, and nation: Racial belonging of Bulgarians) and *Bulgarskiat Narod Mejdu Evropeiskite Rasi i Narodi* (1938; The Bulgarian people among the European races and peoples). According to contemporary observers, Popov's studies responded directly to the "well-known but misleading notion" that Bulgarians were of non-European mongrel racial origin advanced by the Nazis, who ascribed racial impurity and barbarism to Southern Slavs more generally.[15] Historical European constructions of racially ambiguous and "semi-Oriental" Balkan races embodying violence, unpredictability, and cultural backwardness supported Hitler's hatred for the Southern Slavs. Popov defined these views as outcomes of "racial self-overvaluing among known circles in certain countries (North America, England, Germany, and Scandinavian countries)."[16] Responding to these racial valorizations, he set to prove scientifically that Bulgarians belonged to the European races utilizing widely accepted European and American scientific models and racial theories.

Popov opened his arguments with a review of Darwin's theory of natural selection, Lamarck's ideas about the effects of the natural environment on changes in organisms, and Mendel's laws of heredity. Based on these theories, he defined race as "a group of people with a smaller or greater number of common hereditary factors, or genes," further determining "the spiritual make-up and mentality" of that human group.[17] But the original pure races, Popov argued, no longer existed because historical contacts between the world peoples had allowed mixing of "valuable races" producing physically and mentally stronger racial cohorts with even higher reproductive capacities.[18] Popov constructed the Balkans as a zone of such racial mixing based on anthropological studies of blood types and human skull measurements of more than ten thousand individuals from different regions of Bulgaria.[19] He attributed the Nordic blood in the Bulgarian race to the Thracians, who were "tall, slim, blond hair, with blue eyes."[20] The Slavs, who also belonged to the Nordic race, according to Popov, would settle in what would be Bulgaria later, mixing there with an "insignificant number" of proto-Bulgarians who came to the region from Asia and had Mongol blood.[21] Mediterranean racial genes would also inoculate the Bulgarian race through the Romans, who ruled over the Balkans, and via the conquests of Alexander the Great from Macedonia, who was also from the Nordic race.[22] Popov demonstrated his argument by lining up the portraits of twenty distinguished Bulgarian men, among them classicists of Bulgarian literature, prominent educators, and national heroes leading Bulgarian resistance against the Ottomans.[23] Gazing at the portraits, readers could perceive for themselves the "favourable racial mixing" of European racial types in the physiognomies of these men at the forefront of Bulgarian culture and European civilization.

Bulgarian readers could also study the elaborate globalized comparative tables of blood types provided by the author.[24] The tables traced and compared the percentages of blood types A and B between European and Asiatic races. The higher the percentage of blood type A, the more originally European the race in question, argued Popov. While the Bulgarian race's blood type firmly placed Bulgarians among the European races, along with Swedes, British, French, Norwegians, Italians, and Germans, the scientific racial taxonomies crafted by Popov identified Roma, Jews, and Armenians who were also present in the Bulgarian state as members of the group of "Asiatic races" alongside "Indians, Koreans, Chinese and Japanese."[25]

Popov's arguments drew power from a scientific methodology combining external measurement of the Bulgarian body with its internal blood type. The approach endowed Bulgarian Europeanness and genetic heritage with the mantle of legitimacy that only science could provide. Armed with that knowledge, Popov urged Bulgarians "to become proud again, bold in endeavours, and with a sense of self-respect" because "our belonging to the European races … the favourable racial mixing in our people [is an] important biological basis for cultural and spiritual advancement."[26] So talked about and debated were Popov's studies in 1938 that the philosopher Professor Dimiter

Mihalchev felt compelled to enter the polemic embracing the European racial heritage of Bulgarians but disputing Popov's claim that one's race determined one's mentality and capacity for civilization.

Philosophizing the Nation: Enfolding Marxism, Sovietism, and American Racism

Dimiter Mihalchev was an internationally renowned Bulgarian philosopher who had studied in Germany under the mentorship of the famous German thinker and writer Johannes Rehmke. In 1909, Mihalchev published his first book critiquing some of the best minds of European philosophy at the time. His audacious work received positive reviews in British, German, and Bulgarian journals, earning Mihalchev the position of chairman of the Bulgarian Academy of Sciences. The philosopher's brilliant career throughout the 1920s led to his political appointment in 1934 as the Bulgarian ambassador to Soviet Russia. Thereafter, Mihalchev's ideas and writing exhibited uneasy yet deep intellectual involvement with Marxism-Leninism and historical materialism, while refusing to be labelled "Marxist" or "socialist."

In the summer of 1939, Mihalchev published his views on the relationship between race, culture, and nation in the Bulgarian journal *Folosofski Pregled* (Philosophical review), which the professor edited. His article entitled "Rasizmut kato Filosofsko-Istoricheska Teoria" (Racism as a philosophico-historical theory) was a critical narrative on the ideological underpinnings of racial thinking in Bulgaria. According to Mihalchev, "the question about the essence of the races" was popularized by intellectuals and ideologues located at the communist and fascist ends of the Bulgarian political spectrum.[27] These ideological fractions engaged in a "fierce battle for control over Bulgarian history and especially over who are the heirs of the 'ideas and testament' of the Bulgarian Renaissance."[28] At the heart of the struggle, according to Mihalchev, was the question of "Bulgaria-ness" itself, dovetailing definitions of the nation, therefore race and culture as well.

Addressing the ideological Right, Mihalchev identified a Bulgarian "philosophizing racist camp" inspired by the French count Arthur de Gobineau's treatise entitled *The Inequality of Human Races* (1854). The Bulgarian Right also drew inspiration from the works of British and German scientists Huston Stuart Chamberlain and Ludwig Woltmann, who glorified the "German race" as a pure breed of the highest quality and the creator of civilization elsewhere in the world. The Bulgarian philosopher passionately disputed claims of German racial superiority by pointing out that "blond, tall, blue-eyed people" had nothing to do with technological inventions in ancient China and Egypt.[29] Nor had "German blood" created ancient Bulgaria "as a great cultural centre." Such theories of the relationship between race and culture, Mihalchev argued, served as "the ideological mask" covering German aspirations for power in Europe and the world. Mihalchev further qualified as "strange" the conclusions of European and American racial scientists who had argued that persons with darker skin or hair were more likely to engage in delinquent behaviours, or that the French Revolution was a racial conflict between racially inferior Celts fighting racially superior individuals with German blood. For Mihalchev, these arguments implied the static nature of human groups rather than their evolution: "From the writings of some travellers who in earlier times had crossed the Bulgarian lands, we learn that the Bulgarian is religious, hospitable, and fond of his land," wrote Mihalchev, but "the Bulgarian is not a still substance. Everything flows, everything changes."[30]

Race and culture, according to Mihalchev, were distinct phenomena: "Race ... is a group of people, whose peculiarities are acquired through birth, or through physiological heredity." In contrast, Mihalchev argued, "culture is that which a person acquires after birth through education and upbringing and through the influence of environment, no matter what this environment is."[31] Therefore, Mihalchev concluded, racial origins did not determine a people's cultural development, or history. "Look at the Jews," wrote Mihalchev, "the characteristic Jewish nose, which we all know from caricatures, was not found among all Jews in Western Europe, Eastern Europe, and the United States."[32] Moreover, Mihalchev stated, the American anthropologist Franz Boas had proved that the skull, another permanent racial feature, "enlarges among immigrant children in the United States," as they acquire higher Euro-American culture. Therefore, every race was capable of change and capable of acquiring culture under proper conditions, much like Sicilian brains changed, or enlarged, under American civilizing influences.[33]

However, equality of the races did not mean that cultures were equal as well. Rather, Mihalchev constructed a hierarchy of "savage" and "modern" cultures that replicated hierarchies of unequal white and non-white races. He used the example of "American Negroes" to illustrate the point: "It is usually argued that Negroes are incapable of any culture. However, last summer in Paris at the International Philosophical congress I met Negroes who were delegates and took part in the discussions."[34] Mihalchev attributed African-American delegates' capacity for a higher order of thinking to their upbringing in the United States. In a sharp conceptual turn, Mihalchev also narrated American Blacks as still culturally and intellectually inferior: "It is true that

American Negroes have not gone much ahead. They, who began living as humans just a few decades ago, still today behave as a mass of ignorance, despite that they have a university for their elite."[35] The philosopher further established the cultural inequality between "cultured European peoples," "Australian savages," and "African and American Negroes" living in cultural "darkness."[36] Mihalchev would add to this global racialized hierarchy of unequal cultures Roma in Bulgaria, Siam people in Asia, Indians (Native Americans) in the United States, and Kyrgyz and Tunguska peoples in Soviet Russia. In this map, Bulgarian Roma emerged as a cultural difference linked to non-white races in Africa, North America, Russia, and the United States.

A few months after his first publication in the summer of 1938, Professor Dimiter Mihalchev published a second article entitled "Rasizmut pod Zakrilata na Biologiata" ("Racism under the protection of biology"). There, the Bulgarian philosopher advanced the argument that "culturally belated races" and "forgotten peoples" in Bulgaria and Soviet Russia were "capable of civilization under favourable conditions" and through assimilation into culturally superior societies.[37] Mihalchev argued that "Bulgarian Gypsies" had not produced scientists, statesmen, and artists but only street musicians not because of biological or racial inferiority but because of the social, more specifically labour, conditions under which Roma specialized in earning a living by playing music and singing.[38] "Everybody knows that Gypsies everywhere lead a nomadic life: not just here but everywhere in the world!" Mihalchev added. "They rarely go to school and no educational law catches them. They have no contact with this cultural environment, which influences and changes a person. And you want from such a population to show its gifts! ... How can you seek statesmen and leaders among a people who are isolated, or have isolated themselves from normal social and civic life?"[39]

According to Mihalchev, a Roma person could become a scientist if he "is under the direct and intensive influence of the Bulgarian cultural environment."[40] In Bulgarian villages, where Roma had settled permanently and mixed with Bulgarians, Mihalchev saw further proof of how Roma absorption of Bulgarian culture uplifted them. The philosopher pointed out distinguished intellectuals who were of Romani origin, yet one was "an excellent judge," while the other was "a wonderful linguist."[41] Not just Bulgarian Roma but "African savages" could also learn culture, Mihalchev argued. His example for such cultural emancipation included African peoples under French colonial rule: "The French, who created some conditions for the cultural development of the Negroes in some of their colonies, soon realized that Negroes were taking fast steps forward ... Some Senegalese are even members of the French parliament." However, Mihalchev cautioned, "No one is arguing that if you take an African savage and put him under the same university conditions under which our [Bulgarian] children study, the savage will catch up right away ..."[42] "But in a longer historical period, of let's say one hundred to three hundred years, a favourable social environment would affect the brain of even the least developed human race."[43] Yet it was the responsibility of Bulgarians to make sure that the educational laws "catch the Gypsy" and force them to attend schools. Mihalchev had in mind a schooling system delivered in the Bulgarian language and rooted exclusively in European and Euro-American modern sciences and arts. The matter was not of time but principle, Mihalchev concluded again, while effectively displacing onto Bulgarian Roma racial and cultural traits attributed by European colonial science to Black people in Africa and North America.

Mihalchev's ideas were inspired by personal observations of Soviet modernizing policies targeting Roma people and Indigenous societies in the Russian North: "Soviet Russia decided to put an end to their roaming and with a hard hand put the Gypsies into collective agricultural units. Thus, Soviet Russia created conditions for cultural life among the Russian Gypsies. In 1926, the Gypsies even received an alphabet."[44] Moreover, Mihalchev added, "The October Revolution gave to all peoples inhabiting the Soviet territory the right to have full and well-rounded national development.[45] The Bulgarian philosopher marvelled at Lenin's policies of cultural uplifting of Kyrgyz and Tunguska peoples, as Lenin had ordered the Soviet Academy of Sciences to invent alphabets for those peoples who did not have a written language and "to modernize" the alphabets of those who had some. "Today, twenty years later," Mihalchev boasted, "these insignificant until then peoples woke up to their cultural life."[46] Dimiter Mihalchev articulated further a notion of race relations as relations between cultures at different stages of development; hence, his writing mixed racial and ethnic designations as the philosopher referred to "Negroes," "Gypsies," "French," and "Bulgarians" as examples of both races and cultures. Simultaneously, his theorizing of the difference between these human groups signified uneven stages of cultural development that could be remedied by political conditions conducive to belated peoples "mixing into" and "mingling with" culturally advanced nations associated with racial whiteness and European civilization.

Mihalchev's views enfolding and collapsing race and culture onto each other weaved Marxist historical materialism as well. He believed that history and social relations depended not on "race" or biology but on "the labour process ... in which all people take part ... and which envelops social relations that grow on the soil of this overarching process; people's customs and morals, their judicial and moral relations, national ideals, class struggle, sciences, arts, wars, everything in which we are 'entangled' as far as we are participants of this historical reality."[47] Marxist historical materialism thus better explained for Mihalchev social reality than did race. The philosopher further envisioned Marxist and Leninist modes of socialism as the more just social order that would soon replace exploitive and imperialist capitalism. In Marxist internationalism and solidarity, and in the spreading around the world of socialist ideals and revolutions, Mihalchev saw "the culture" with truly homogenizing influences; one that could best and justly assimilate within itself culturally inferior peoples. His examples of how the Soviet state firmly absorbed and thus "awakened" Roma and Indigenous peoples for cultural life embodied Mihalchev's vision of Marxism and socialism as international culturally and racially emancipating forces.

In 1939, Mihalchev gave a series of public lectures entitled "The Nation as a Historical Reality." There, he defined "nation" as social bonding based not on biology or genetics but history, common experience, and culture.[48] He exemplified his argument by pointing to what he described as a "Bulgarianized" Jew: "By blood and race he is a Jerusalemian Semite. But he is no 'Jew.' Growing up in our culture, living with the sorrows and happiness of our people, participating in our social and cultural life ... he is in no way a worse Bulgarian than any other Bulgarian."[49] A Bulgarianized, educated, and therefore uplifted Roma, according to Mihalchev, was also a member of the Bulgarian nation because his cultural traits were replaced by Bulgarian culture and spirituality. Other scientists vehemently disagreed.

Eugenics and Racial Hygiene in Making the Nation

Stefan Konsulov was a distinguished Bulgarian biologist who had studied in Germany. He was thus among the privileged intellectuals who gained higher education abroad and participated in the advancement of the state project of modernization after the period of Ottoman colonization. Konsulov was also the chair of the Union of Bulgarian Teachers – a professional but also a political position that assured public attention for his articles and public lectures on race and nation. In February and May of 1939, Konsulov published two articles in the monthly journal published by the Teachers Union entitled "Shto e Natsia?" ("What is a nation?") and "Edin Filosof, Competenten po Vsichko" ("A philosopher, competent in everything"). Konsulov felt urged to respond to Dimiter Mihalchev because in his view, his Marxist propaganda among Bulgarian educators around the country spread misinformation regarding the races. Additionally, he had received letters where "teachers expressed their surprise and concern with the lectures of Prof. Mihalchev."[50] Konsulov took an especially strong position against environmental arguments framing human types as outcomes of nurturing and social forces rather than biology. Biological or racial heredity worked along with environment, Konsulov argued, but racial heredity and racial temperament overrode the influences of any environment. Therefore, Konsulov wrote, the races were biologically unequal and the cultural achievements of a particular race depended on its biological mental capacities. Mihalchev was also using "racism" as a derogatory term, Konsulov complained, while in fact, correctly used, "real racism" was the same as "racial hygiene or eugenics," which he contended was a scientific field.[51]

If the races were biologically equal and were equally capable of culture, Konsulov asked, how would anti-racists explain that the Roma in Bulgaria, "as the example of a race, which has some valuable qualities … has not given anything significant … They have given nice music but not scientists … Where are their [Gypsy] people of science, where are their statesmen and social builders?"[52] Scattered around Europe, the Roma had lived under the same cultural and material conditions for centuries alongside superior races, including Bulgarians, French, Germans and British. While the latter groups "had proven their racial talents," Konsulov stated, Roma produced nothing but "nice music." "But what about the Jews?" he asked further. "They too had lived scattered among other peoples. With their racial qualities, however, they managed to take a position among the other peoples, so that these peoples felt threatened and economically enslaved by the Jews … And by the way, this caused the anti-Jewish movement: the struggle for independence of a people against a racially strong opponent in the economic field."[53]

While distinguishing between a weak "Gypsy race" and too strong "Jewish race," Konsulov suggested that both races could not belong to the Bulgarian nation, which he compared to a beehive: "Biology teaches us that humans belong to that category of living beings which, like the bees, have social instincts … No matter what the external conditions, the bees, always sticking with their hive, would not start living like spiders … These biologically inherited social instincts are connected to something else, to the feeling of what is 'mine.' The social instincts of the bee were directed to 'its' hive, and not to all hives or bees on earth."[54] Similarly, people's social instincts were directed to their nation only and not to all peoples around the world. And, like the bees, according to Konsulov, those social instincts and solidarity were strongest among the members of the same race because shared racial genes and qualities represented natural closeness upon which depended national consciousness.[55] Eugenics, in Konsulov's framework, was the practice of racial hygiene that secured and preserved nations; hence, he considered the preservation of the Bulgarian nation through racial hygiene to be a social obligation: "It is our public duty to ensure improvement of the social conditions so that the good qualities of the [Bulgarian] people manifest themselves ... But it is our duty to also think about the protection and improvement of the people's racial gifts because without such care, racial retardation is inevitable. Then, no improvement of the social and labour conditions will help us. This is the objective scientific truth of the matter."[56] Another prominent intellectual, Professor Ivan Kinkel, would soon confirm that "truth."

Sociological Constructions of Bulgarian Race and Nation

Professor Ivan Kinkel was the chair of the Association of Bulgarian Sociologists. Fluent in German and English after studying abroad, he had published his work in Bulgarian and foreign journals. In 1940, Kinkel intervened in the debate because he felt that the question about the relationship between "nature and society" was too important to ignore. Therefore, like his colleagues, Kinkel delivered public lectures around the country under the title "Sociology and Biology." At these gatherings, he was asked by "student delegations, by many persons among our intellectual circles and even some of my university colleagues, to speak as a sociologist on the question that has so highly engaged our intelligentsia."[57] Addressing that intellectual reader, Kinkel argued that both Auguste Comte's sociology emphasizing "the mental development of human society" and Marxist sociology, based on "the development of the means of production," understood that society was governed, along with sociological beginnings, by "various influences of natural powers, especially biological laws."[58] The biological laws of heredity, Kinkel explained, determined the spiritual and mental qualities of individuals who make a society, shaping further said society's cultural production and social behaviours.[59] Referring to what European and American scientists of race called "racial temperament," Kinkel explained further that hereditary processes presented "the constitutive racial qualities" determining "national psychology" or the "national character" of a people.[60]

Kinkel described "national psychology" and "national character" as the sum of the racial qualities of those who were present in the national space. A Bulgarian nation that included inferior Roma might be on its way to decline, he suggested.[61] Natural selection securing the survival of the fittest, the strongest, the smartest, and the most advanced meant that "weak" and "unfit" Roma could not belong to the Bulgarian nation. Kinkel evidenced his assertions with "the study of the psychology of Slavs by the famous Russian psychologist and psychiatrist Sikorsky and many studies on national and racial psychology, published in the last decades in the German, French and Anglo-American literature" proving the existence of biologically based national consciousness.[62]

The Bulgarian sociologist appealed further to a myriad of racial epistemologies to envision the nation. He referred to a synthesis of natural and social principles developed by Auguste Comte and Herbert Spencer, Lamarckian and Darwinian laws of evolution and adaptation, and Mendel's laws of heredity to explain the formation and survival of biological racial qualities from generation to generation. The ideas of British historian and theorist of "civilization" Henry Thomas Buckle informed Kinkel's point on the influence of natural laws on the organization of society and on the character of its members. The writings of French sociologist Gabriel Tarde lent support to Kinkel's claim that biological laws governed human communication. Kinkel discussed the theory of historical materialism authored by Karl Marx and Fredric Engels at length to explain how nature affected people but they, through labour, changed and mastered nature. But we did not need look as far back as these nineteenth-century thinkers, Kinkel wrote. The contemporary "very modern" sociological studies of well-known, prominent, and "solid" American, European, and Russian eugenicists and sociobiologists best demonstrated for Kinkel the explanatory and scientific power of "biological sociology."[63] Kinkel admired the work of the prominent American geneticist Raymond Pearl, who supported the eugenics movement in the United States. Kinkel also highlighted the shared theories of American and Soviet eugenics to prove biology's great significance in studies of society. He referred to two Soviet eugenics journals available in Bulgaria to make the point: *The Soviet Eugenics Journal*, published since 1925, and *News Bureau on Eugenics and Genetics*, available since 1922. Kinkel emphasized that both journals were published by the Soviet state in order to support the engineering of a socialist society. Yet he conveyed a sense of Bulgarian epistemological inferiority by complaining about scholarly dilettantism in the country: "We see how every intellectual, though having only secondary education, having read two or three brochures on social matters, considers himself competent 'to solve' various sociological problems that are highly complicated, while first-year students in the social sciences are writing articles for newspapers and journals on most complicated contemporary sociological questions."[64] Kinkel urged Bulgarian scientific dilettantes "to specialize" by reading the European, American, and Soviet literature on race, biology, and nation.

The racial epistemologies grounding Kinkel's notions of racial self and national character in the earlier part of the twentieth century were thus not native to Bulgaria. Rather, they were transnational and hegemonic racial scientific knowledges originating in the conquests, needs, and racial projects of the Russian, European, and American Empires. Kinkel and other prominent Bulgarian men of science translated these racial knowledges from the Balkan margins of a Eurocentric geopolitical order where Bulgarian racial self-valorizations presented acts of seeking dignity and independence in the face of power. Still, these masculine and privileged scientific postures did not represent the otherwise heterogeneous ontologies and identifications present across the Bulgarian social landscape. Ethnic middle-class Bulgarian women belonging to the social majority, for instance, campaigned for access to higher education and the right to vote. Racial debates concerned them only where biologized notions were used to explain women's difference and social and political status. Roma and Muslim women's narratives from this time period did not express racial self-identifications either; rather, these women practised inter-group social solidarities constituting a longitudinal historical thread also warping the fabric of the young nation.

Women, Race, and Making the Nation

The scientific debate about the role of race and culture in determining national character reflected deeply gendered and patriarchal structures supporting Bulgarian scientific identifications with racial whiteness and European civilization. When the distinguished biologist Methody Popov lined up the portraits of Bulgarian national male heroes to illustrate the European racial origins of Bulgarians, his assertions hinged upon widely shared perceptions of these patriarchal political and cultural figures as "fathers" of the nation. Professor Stefan Konsulov extended gendered national imaginations further by arguing that Bulgarian women had special responsibility for preserving the race from which emerged the nation: "Talented women represent the genetic treasure of the nation, but instead of bearing many children they often prefer to work in science and to stay childless. They squander their valuable genes; the number of intellectually gifted will decline in the long run."[65] Konsulov's remarks spoke directly to women across the country active in the Bulgarian Women's Union and similar organizations seeking political and educational rights for women.

In fact, the public scientific debates about the relationships between race, culture, and nation took place during a time period marking the beginning of women's suffrage in Bulgaria. A special decree from 1937 finally allowed women in the country to vote, but the right was not extended to women without children or women who were university students. Later in the same year, these voters were included but then excluded again from the electoral list in 1939. Women also struggled for equal access to higher education and the professions. In the academic year 1938–9, quotas and other prohibitive systems established against the admission of female candidates in the universities was challenged by female students, intellectuals, and activists.[66] Both liberal and conservative governments in the 1930s also passed legislation banning educated women from practising law. Educated women dominated only the teaching profession, which was considered a natural vocation for a middle-class ethnic Bulgarian woman. Yet a special survey about the marital status of female teachers in the country conducted in 1930 attracted commentaries from both civil servants and other citizens. The survey showed that 50 per cent of teachers in the country were women; of them, half were not married.[67] The percentage of unmarried women was highest among female teachers with postsecondary education. Male leaders of professional and state institutions called the trend "abnormal" and a threat to public, state, and social interests. Public figures like Professor Stefan Konsulov chastised unmarried and childless female teachers for being too picky in choosing marriage partners, bringing their nervousness and pretensions to their work, and staying unmarried, thus not meeting their racial obligations to the nation as well. Similar ideas about women's biology and natural roles as childbearers and nurturers underlined state and public discourses on women's suffrage and professionalization.[68] Political pundits doubted publicly women's ability to make appropriate decisions as voters and expected women to vote following the choices of their husbands.[69] Women's professional performance as teachers or lawyers was similarly viewed as the outcome of women's marital status and emotional and cognitive biology.

Environmental and sociological views of the so-called woman question inspired by Marxist theory and socialist ideologies were equally prominent at the time. In fact, socialist and Marxist ideologies, including leaders in the women's movements in the country, perceived material structures rather than biology as the engine of women's emancipation and equality with men. Socialist women shared Marxist and Leninist formulations of the so-called woman question as a question of class and material inequalities. Women's emancipation, they believed, depended on industrialization and modernization because industries drew women out of domesticity into the public economy, providing them with income and therefore independence. Rooted in this ideology, the Socialist Women's Union, established in 1914, positioned itself against the Bulgarian Women's Union, claiming the latter's bourgeois aspirations did not and could not represent the interests of women workers. According to the leader of the Socialist Women's Union, "A conscientious woman would not vote for bourgeois political representatives regardless if they wear trousers or a dress. It would mean to multiply her enemies. We stress the conflict between feminism and socialism so that women comrades would not be seduced by the sweet talk of the feminists who want to use women workers for their purposes but then turn their backs on them."[70]

Women's politics to the ideological Left and Right represented overwhelmingly the interests, needs, and ideals of urban middle- and upper-class women and also members of the Bulgarian ethnic majority. For example, the Bulgarian Women's Union focused exclusively on the limited access of women to higher education and the professions, paying special attention to Bulgarian female teachers, who constituted the core membership of the union. An archive of private correspondence and albums reveals that young Bulgarian female students aspiring to the teaching profession in the 1920s were highly aware of the Union's political agenda and shared its political goals. The letters articulated the young women's commitment to serving the modernization of the nation in the role of teachers spreading light among the masses. The young women also addressed each other using the title "Citizen, Maria" instead of the conventional gendered title "Miss Maria," thus claiming political and citizenship rights as independent persons rather than in relation to men.[71]

In one letter, a seventeen-year-old female student travelling across Europe wrote to her girlfriend: "I am wishing you Europe, not the village."[72] That wish for Europe rather than the Bulgarian village reflected a prevailing state social and political approach charging Bulgarian women with the modernization, civilizing, and enlightening of both themselves and the masses of rural and working-class people, transforming them into European citizens worthy of national independence. Young Bulgarian women's professionalization as teachers often dispatched them to practise in small towns and villages where they served ethnically diverse communities of Roma, Turks, and Bulgarian-speaking Muslims described in popular and scientific texts as racialized difference, and culturally belated races in need of education, modernization, and uplifting. However, some young women preferred life in Europe and a suitable husband over service in the Bulgarian village. That desire and longing for "Europe" suggested self-distancing and alienation both from state projects of modernization and local politics of women's emancipation positioning young women as teachers yet, in the words of the young female student, also committing them to isolation, loneliness, and spinsterhood.[73]

Well known in urban elite circles, the writer and translator Fani Popova-Mutafova enacted a brand of women's activism that supported female desire for domesticity and personal happiness versus professionalization and public work. Inspired by biological arguments associated with racial science and citing examples of women-related policies in Germany, Italy, France, the Soviet Russia, and the United States, Popova-Mutafova argued passionately that Bulgarian ethnic women bore the responsibility to rear fit, educated, moral, and patriotic children who would in turn support a mighty modern nation state.[74] She identified declining fertility rates in 1930s Bulgaria as a serious threat to the nation and urged the state to invest not only in armaments but also in the physical and mental well-being of mothers and wives. Popova-Mutafova celebrated the genetic inheritance and beauty of ethnic Bulgarian women and mothers. In fact, Roma, Muslim, Black, and other racialized women in and outside the country presented the backdrop against which Popova-Mutafova's passionate assertions of women as protectors of the Bulgarian genetic stock crystalized and took shape.

Neither were racialized Roma, Turkish Muslim, Armenian, or Jewish women on the radar of the influential Socialist Women's Union in Bulgaria. In speeches, essays, and personal letters, leaders of the socialist women's movement subsumed those racialized as non-white and non-European groups of women into the class of "proletarian women" whose ontologies preoccupied socialist feminist agendas at the time. Lamenting the lack of new cohorts of women workers joining the socialist movement, its leader Vella Blagoeva argued that the socialist women's organizations did not provide much-needed political enlightening to cultivate women's class consciousness and attraction to labour and socialist causes. "The liberation of proletarian women," she added, "should be the act of women from all social classes. This objective can be achieved only through the common struggle of all working-class people regardless of gender."[75] Agrarian and peasant women were of special interest to male and female socialist and communist writers in the early twentieth century as well as generations of young girls from small towns and villages who migrated to the larger cities seeking and gaining employment as domestics, babysitters, and low-wage industrial workers. Some of these young girls came from Roma and Muslim families but their lives and struggles as racialized, culturally devalued, and marginalized subjects were silenced by socialist womanism and activism targeting women from the lower social classes for political education.

Likewise, documents drafted by members of the Bulgarian Women's Union rarely addressed peasant, working-class, and Roma and Muslim women in the country; when they did, liberal and bourgeois feminist discourses penned by women belonging to the privileged middle class constructed lower-class women as subjects ripe for indoctrination in order to elevate their consciousness as oppressed subjects and position them for much-needed membership to support the women's unions and their agendas. For example, in a memo to local branches from 1931, Dimitrina Ivanova, the chair of the Bulgarian Women's Union, outlined a plan of activities to strengthen the position of the Union. Highlighting the lack of women's organizations in small towns and villages, as well as the decline of existing women's organizations in rural areas in general, the memo called on the branches to intensify work and reach out to rural and peasant women "to elevate the village ... and wherever possible, establish women's committees."[76]

Divisive racial ideologies did not serve these political purposes of growth in numbers and shared women's consciousness. That may be one reason why literature produced by the women's unions lacked explicit engagement with popular and scientific conversations about racial and cultural difference prominent at the time. Instead, women's organizations ignored and subsumed these differences into homogenizing signifiers such as "women" and "working-class women," emphasizing either shared biology or class under the patriarchal economic mode of production. In either case, early twentieth-century middle-class women's activism took the interests of ethnic Bulgarian women as representing those of all women in the young state.

The archives do not allow for deeper understanding of how Roma and Muslim women experienced these realities. The reason is that their marginality and otherness in Bulgarian feminist, scientific, and national narratives erased and silenced these women's histories. A recent ethnography seeking to fill the gap revealed some of the material and social aspects of Roma and Muslim women's lives through personal stories like that of Kudrie, who was born in 1938 in a small village in Southeastern Bulgaria: "There was not enough bread or clothes for me," remembered Kudrie, the youngest of nine children in a Turkish Muslim household, whose mother worked day and night ploughing and gardening other people's land for a piece of bread and pennies. Recalling hard times, Kudrie shared further the following episode conveyed to her by her older siblings:

> [My mother] has given birth ... as the baby comes out of her womb, she wraps it up in a shirt, cuts the umbilical cord with a sickle and ties it with a string of her own hair ... My older brother comes and says: "Mom, the horse is in some people's cornfield ..." Mother instantly got up and went to the yard, the placenta hanging from her, bleeding ... "Where are you going?" a neighbour asked her. "To get the horse because they will fine me for the corn it ate and I have no money to pay ... Children, I may be dying but don't be scared. Take care of the baby," replied Kudrie's mother.[77]

The presence of surveying and punitive state apparatuses loomed large in Kudrie's story, as the threat of a fine and punishment caused a bleeding woman to rise out of bed and face death. The distant and intense public scientific debates about the racial and cultural origins of those like Kudrie, her mother, and their community moved and shaped these apparatuses supporting racialized ethnic, gender, and class structures in the young post-Ottoman Bulgarian nation. The life story of Sevda, a Roma woman born in 1924, illuminated yet defied those social edifices gesturing to harmonious social relations between Roma and Bulgarians that also marked the early twentieth-century, newly independent nation:

> My father worked in the mill; mother in the local industrial plant. When they went to work, I took care of my [five] younger siblings. I got up very early to feed and clad them. Then I prepared lunch for my parents ... took it to their workplace. We lived next to a Bulgarian family and got along very well ... My childhood was short. Based on our traditions, my father gave me in marriage at age eighteen. My husband was older and already had five children. But he was a skilled blacksmith ... I worked with him in the smithy, did the domestic work and took care of the children, ours and his. We lived in a large house at the centre of the town. Our neighbours were Bulgarians with whom we had good relations, helping each other a lot.[78]

Sevda's memories of Bulgarian and Roma living in social harmony, solidarity, and mutuality, despite perceived racial and cultural difference, stood in stark contrast to the urban travelogue penned by Hristo Brazitsov depicting Bulgarians holding their breath and noses encountering members of the "Gypsy race" in Sofia in 1931. Memories of peaceful coexistence of Roma, Bulgarians, Turks, Muslims, and Christians preserved in the archives demonstrates the fluidity of identities and social relations especially in rural Bulgaria at the time. Such fluidity and mutuality could be attributed to Roma and Bulgarian ontologies rooted in shared Ottoman subjugation, religious beliefs, and historical memories originating in a pattern of population settlements created by the Ottoman Empire. Roma communities in Bulgaria and across the Balkans consisted of distinct ethnoreligious subgroups whose customs, cultural traditions, and world views responded to local economic, social, and political circumstances further supporting pliable, flexible, and fluid Roma identifications conducive to peaceful coexistence with other groups. Dynamic Roma identifications also drew from distinct historical myths of Roma origins in early India and Egypt and stemming diasporas reaching the Balkans, which diverged significantly from the racial and racist mythologies of genetic heredity and difference created by European conquests and modern science.

Bulgarian views of Roma, Turkish, and other minorities present in the newly independent nation were also fluid and responsive to their changing broader contexts. A few years after scientific racial and racist constructions of Bulgarian Roma charged the public sphere in 1938 and 1939, Bulgaria ended up fighting during the Second World War on the side of Germany. In 1940, rightist and pro-German factions in the Bulgarian National Assembly proposed and passed with the help of centre-left political counterparts the so-called Zakon za Zashtita na Natsiata, or Nation's Defence Law. In many respects, the law copied the anti-Jewish laws in Germany, as it denied Jews Bulgarian citizenship, forbade the election or hiring of Jews in government and public positions, imposed devastating taxes on Jewish property, restricted Jewish access to educational institutions, prohibited legal marriage between Jews and Bulgarians, and prohibited Jews to employ Bulgarians as servants. The same law applied to the Roma, who were also prohibited from marrying Bulgarians. Roma were further subjected to acts of violence by nationalistic groups, discriminated against in the war distribution of rationed foodstuffs, and limited in their freedom of movement. The growing power of pro-German and pro-fascist factions in Bulgaria further prepared the stage for the deportation of Bulgarian Jews and Roma to the Nazi concentration camps. The anti-Jewish campaign was spearheaded by Tsar Boris III, whose German and Austrian origins tied his politics and interests to these countries closely. In March 1941, under the influences of the tsar and his pro-Nazi prime minister, Bulgaria joined the so-called Tripartite (Axis) Act, which cemented the wartime alliance between fascist Germany, Italy, and Japan. In 1943, pro-fascist government officials and the monarch collaborated with the

Nazis in the deportation of nearly eleven thousand Jews from newly added territories of Macedonia, Aegean Thrace, and Pirot, which were conquered and added to the Bulgarian state as a result of the war and the tsar's collaboration with Germany. In fact, the recuperation of territorial losses dividing Bulgaria after the Russo-Ottoman War played a major part in the tsar's and government's decisions to assist the Nazis, who in turn would give back Bulgaria these territories. The deportations of Jews from the annexed territories, however, sparked public outrage and resistance in Bulgaria.

Letters and petitions to the tsar and the government by professional associations, literary circles, the national leadership of the Bulgarian Orthodox Church, former cabinet ministers, and public intellectuals protested vigorously against the treatment of Jews and condemned the new laws targeting their rights and freedoms.[79] As much support and courage came from ordinary ethnic Bulgarian and non-Bulgarian citizens whose compassion, honour, and sense of responsibility for others who were different saved Bulgarian Jews and Roma from the Nazi concentration camps. In his insightful interpretations of the events, the Bulgarian-French historian and philosopher Tzvetan Todorov concluded that the saving of reportedly forty-five thousand Bulgarian Roma and Jews from the Nazi camps happened because of a chain of random events as well as the actions of moral and courageous individuals, which Todorov used to theorize "the fragility" of human goodness.[80] Other observers point to the Jewish and Roma lives that were nevertheless lost in this tragic historical moment as evidence for Bulgarian responsibility and participation in the genocide. Bulgaria, they argue, is both a rescuer and perpetrator who refuses to take responsibility for the death of some Jews and Roma but uses the saving of as many to claim its own humanity, morality, and capacity for goodness.[81]

These judgments on Bulgarian "goodness" or "evilness" could and have supported theories constructing Bulgaria as a racial formation and a people who committed racial "terror and viciousness" against Roma and Jews.[82] But the events and people depicted in this chapter, I suggest, paint a complex picture resisting qualifications gesturing to racial formation. Race, in the final analysis, did not really become the foundation of the political, institutional, social, and economic structures that established the independent modern Bulgarian nation state in the early twentieth century. Yet racialized imaginations and identifications existed, suggesting that the 1930s and 1940s was a dangerous moment conducive to the emergence of a Bulgarian racial state amid globally diffused and intensified European, Soviet, and Euro-American modern racial sciences presenting themselves as truths about human life and experience. In 1944, an uprising led by the Bulgarian Communist Party put the country on the path to state socialism and communism. Race would take on new meanings, illuminating further the deep ambiguity yet persistence of racialized cultural constructs in the making of a Bulgarian socialist nation.

Chapter Two

Socialist Racialism: Desired and Undesired Genres of Women, and the Paradoxes of Socialism

Bulgarian state socialism was marked by a paradox: ideological commitment to anti-racism and anti-colonialism nationally and internationally, yet enforcement of racialized policies and reforms targeting minority populations like the Roma perceived as "smears" on socialism. For example, the newly drafted state constitution in 1947 proclaimed the right of all citizens to vote regardless of their race, gender, or ethnicity and made every kind of preaching about racial, national, or religious hatred punishable by law. The concept of "race" was muted by ideological and cultural discourses describing socialist subjects as members of "nationalities:" a Leninist definition of social groups who shared culture, religion, and language but were not entitled to independent nationhood. Similarly, educational textbooks in socialist Bulgaria barely engaged the topic of race; where they did, they presented the human races of the world as different but equal. Political and cultural documents further articulated Roma, Jews, Turks and other groups – identified as non-European races prior to the communist revolution – as subjects of a single nation state. Socialist authorities referred to "Bulgarian Turks," "Bulgarian Muslims," and "Bulgarian Gypsies" instead of just "Gypsies" or "Turks," thus emphasizing that these groups were members of the socialist nation state.

Internationally, socialist authorities supported anti-colonial and anti-racist movements in countries in Africa, Asia, and North America, denouncing racism and colonialism as mutually supporting forces responsible for exploitation and oppression, especially that of Black people. In the 1960s and 1970s, Bulgaria, like other socialist countries, hosted hundreds of "freedom fighters" from Angola, Kenya, Mozambique, El Salvador, Guatemala, Cuba, and other countries, training them in the Bulgarian Marxist Academy of Social Sciences and Social Management to stage revolutionary struggles against colonialism, apartheid, and capitalism. A select group of Bulgarian lecturers taught these international activists about tactical and organizing techniques and Marxist-Leninist theories pertaining to social uprising, anti-colonialism, political leadership, and socialist governance. Socialist Bulgaria also supported the civil rights movement in the United States, inviting prominent figures in that movement to visit the country; these included the African-American feminist icon and communist Angela Davis, who visited Bulgaria in 1971.[1]

Simultaneously, socialist discourses and policies pertaining to anti-racism and anti-colonialism presented powerful narratives constructing Roma communities in Bulgaria as backward and intolerably different, demanding their reform or eradication. For example, state documents emphasized Roma origins in Asia and India, and referred to "Gypsy roaming," "Gypsy immoral behaviours," and "Gypsy uncleanness and illiteracy" as major problems in socialist nation-building and threats to the foundational tenets of Marxism.[2] Beginning in the 1950s, the socialist state initiated a number of special policies targeting Roma communities for resettlement, education, and placement in the public economy. These policies also involved changing the personal names of Muslim Roma residing in rural parts of the country with Christian names; Roma women, many of whom were Muslim, were targeted explicitly by policies seeking to change "backward and deviating minorities" one woman at a time. These policies articulated the affinity between racial, colonial, and Marxist ideologies, thereby exposing the ambiguous, tenuous, and gendered relationship between socialist and racialized systems of thought.

Specifically, the relationship between socialist state-building and modern Eurocentric epistemologies involved a discursive comparison, measuring different human groups and their cultures against a "white European man" and "European civilization," considered the epitome of development and social and cultural progress. Eurocentrism and comparativism were built into Marxist and Leninist ideologies and socialist social formations, whereby peoples and cultures deemed vastly different and unlike the modern subjects signified by "Europe" were assigned meaning, value, and location within material and symbolic socialist hierarchies of desired and undesired subjects framed as either advancing or inhibiting the objectives of socialism and communism.

Race, Eurocentrism, and Marxism

"Eurocentrism" is a form of knowledge production and interpretation in which race plays a central role: biologized classifications of social groups in and outside Europe emerged as mutually constitutive signifiers. White and non-white racial categories have been formed in relation to the idea of "Europe."[3] The concept of race organized discourses that naturalized the exceptionality, universality, and whiteness of "Europeanness" by utilizing "blood" and "culture" as open-ended "cognate tropes" that affirmed the superiority of Europe.[4] Modern ideologies – Marxism, Leninism, liberalism, conservatism – further extended Eurocentrism by diffusing and universalizing theoretical and social categories that are actually specific. Nick Hostettler called this phenomenon a "europic complex" that is embedded in modern epistemes: issues and categories that are presumed to be abstract – freedom, liberty, human rights, equality, wealth, capital, and political economy – are theorized, explained away, and resolved from a Eurocentric historical, social, racial, cultural, and political location.[5] The europic complex within modern ideologies requires a second order of analysis to reveal how the Marxist critique of capital and bourgeois life in Europe was "constrained within bourgeois horizons" – as well as how Marxist visions of the "good society," "authentic" human nature, self-correcting and expanding human consciousness, and social history as a continuous "development" and "progress" may work to reproduce Eurocentricity.[6] British cultural theorist Stuart Hall referred to this reproduction in his influential treatise on the emergence of "the West" and the role of non-European societies he called "the Rest." He attributed the discourse on "the West" versus "the Rest" to Eurocentric systems of thought dominating European expansion since 1492, when Columbus crossed the Atlantic. Hall further analysed the representations of "the West" within various discourses including modern disciplines such as sociology.[7] Karl Marx was the founding father of sociology, and his ideas about social history and the economic mode of production relied on orientalist categories and developmental dualities typical of European comparative imaginations pitting the self-defined "progressive" West versus "the Rest" and "civilized" Europe versus "backward" Asia. In the 1850s, Marx developed his theory of an underdeveloped "Asiatic" mode of production and referred to external factors that made countries such as China, India, and "those of Islam" stagnant and lacking potent and revolutionary classes. He also identified the conditions for capitalism that could transform these societies and move them forward.[8]

Marx's writing on the "Jewish question" has furthered the debate about the racialized tone of his writing, although Marx was of Jewish origin himself.[9] For example, Marx was writing about the political emancipation of Jews in Prussia, a region of what would later become modern Germany: he attributed Jewish marginalization and Prussian anti-Semitism to internal factors, which were as essentializing and racializing as his explanation of the Asiatic. Marx suggested that the greed and egoism specific to Judaism had to be expelled from the public realm so that it became a space for abstract citizenship supporting the evolution of social consciousness. Marx wrote that political emancipation "is a reduction of man, on the one hand, to a member of civil society, an independent and egoistic individual, and, on the other hand, to a citizen, to a moral person." Human emancipation will only be complete when the real, individual man has absorbed into himself the abstract citizen."[10] According to Marx, the problem was that Jewish culture – to him, embodying greed and egoism – not only bred anti-Jewishness but had also permeated the whole of German society, thus becoming a social feature. The social emancipation of the Jew required the emancipation of society from Judaism, he wrote. Marx saw the possibilities for such emancipation in social forms, "which would abolish ... make the Jew impossible. His religious consciousness would evaporate like some insipid vapour in the real, life-giving air of society."[11] Contemporary readers of Marx are sceptical about interpretations suggesting anti-Semitism or prejudice in Marxist thought and theory.[12] Such scepticism, albeit important, does not negate Marx's visions of the modern citizen as both abstract and specific, bearing a universally shared human ability to reason, yet also having a specific social consciousness and cultural and moral characteristics, which excluded those Marx attributed to the Jew and his contemporaries attributed to economies and cultures in Asia.

In the twentieth century, Soviet men building a socialist state upon the remnants of the Russian Empire espoused this Marxist paradox of seeking a universalized socialist citizen who is also culturally and morally specific to European modernity and racial whiteness. The manifestations of this paradox were captured powerfully in the writing of African-American feminist, civil rights activist, and poet Audre Lorde, who visited the Soviet Union in 1976. Lorde used vivid adjectives to describe her dreams after the trip, which reflected her sense of doubt and contradiction about the Soviet places and people she had encountered: "cold," "white," "strange," "ill," and "so different."[13] Lorde compared Moscow to New York before Latino and Black people had settled there, while the Uzbek capital Tashkent reminded her of Ghana and West Africa. Overall, she found these socialist spaces "rather disappointing" and concluded that what held the "Russian and Asian people" together in one socialist country was a strong state rather than a "personal element."[14] Lorde also noted that such state-supervised racial "togetherness" presented an incomplete vision of "socialism" that was imposed on these peoples.[15] She felt that Black people were situated outside the rhetoric and proclamations of solidarity she heard in the Soviet Union, and that Soviet socialism involved "double messages" – privileging white Russians and Europeanness on the one hand, and the goals of a collectivist economy, eradication of poverty, love for books, mass education, and material progress on the other. Lorde concluded that with regard to Black struggles for racial equality – in the United States and globally – "There is no help, except ourselves."[16]

Thinking with Audre Lorde about the double messages of socialism, this chapter develops the concept of "socialist racialism" to describe the gendered and sexed content, texture, flow, and impact of socialist narratives on race and difference, capturing their paradoxical properties of commitment to racial and social equality nationally and internationally but also to Eurocentrism, comparativism, and violence against minority groups such as the Roma. Unlike racism, which produces violence through division and exclusion, socialist racialism produces violence by seeking togetherness, emancipation, and social, economic, and political inclusion. The socialist state authorities in Bulgaria targeted Christian and Muslim Roma communities for emancipation through assimilation into socialist modernity. These communities did acquire access to education, employment, housing, and resources, but this inclusion was predicated on the violent erasure of their Roma and Muslim identities and histories. Socialist policies of inclusion through erasure framed these social groups in terms of hygiene (odour, filth, and disease), culture (undesirable customs, traditions, beliefs, morality, and behaviours), and ideologically (how their capacity to engage in socially useful labour could support a socialist political economy). By clarifying the historical role of Eurocentrism in these processes of valorization and devaluing of social groups, this discussion is central to ongoing anti-racism work in postsocialist Bulgaria and other former socialist countries in the region.

Former socialist states in the Balkans have historically been perceived as marginal to or outside of "Europe" proper. They have spent a good part of their modern history trying to catch up to, resemble, and be like "Europe." Current processes of "(re)Europeanization" within these countries tied to their membership in the European Union (Bulgaria, Croatia, Montenegro, Romania) or aspirations for such membership of the candidate countries (Albania, Bosnia-Herzegovina, North Macedonia, Kosovo, and Serbia) have reignited deeply internalized racialized Eurocentric developmental epistemes.[17] In Bulgaria, commitment to Europe involved the cleansing of racial, religious, and other differences, which has persisted through capitalist, socialist, and neo-liberal nation-building where racialized others (such as Roma, Syrian refugees, or

African migrants) are perceived as alien and threats. European Union governing bodies, Western NGOs, and North American scholars and activists have been rushing to save the Roma from the hands of Romanian, Serbian, Hungarian, and Bulgarian "racists" – but in reality, this chapter suggests, anti-Gypsism in the region is also a by-product of Western hegemony and deeply gendered and racialized Eurocentrism that is not native to the Balkans or Bulgaria. Continuous Western European domination over Eastern Europe and the Balkans as well as contemporary forms of Eurocentrism promoted by the European Union, therefore, ought to be the primary focus of anti-racist initiatives in the postsocialist Balkans, and globally. We will return to the important issue of anti-racism work in more detail in the concluding chapter of the book.

Fostering Socialist Subjects: The Politics of Eurocentric Comparativism

During its reign from 1944 to 1989, the Bulgarian Communist Party state relied on the postulates of scientific Marxism and Leninism to nurture cultured, well-rounded, moral, and conscientious socialist builders, whose main strength was their ability to reason. Logic and science were leveraged to ensure socialist subjects would submit their individual needs and interests to the project of material redistribution, social and cultural homogeneity, and collectivism, with the end goal of equality, liberty, and freedom for all members of society. Ideological documents referred to Reason as a universal human quality regardless of race or gender – the socialist personality, therefore, emerged as an abstract prototype defined by Reason, capable of absorbing class, ethnic, and other differences within the socialist state.

However, that ideal socialist subject was also specific, embodying qualities associated with racial whiteness stemming from European influences. For example, the Bulgarian Communist Party ascribed to the ideal socialist subject an inner set of moral virtues, or a "moral code" for the builders of socialism, which excluded behaviours such as selfishness, drunkenness, idleness, or divorce. A directive by the Central Committee of the Bulgarian Communist Party from 1958 titled "For Increased Fight against Alcoholism" described drunkenness as "bourgeois" and "capitalist" vestiges and "occurrences that are foreign to the socialist order."[18] According to the Communist Party, alcohol drinking demoralized and stupefied workers, thus "diverting them from the revolutionary struggle against capitalism."[19] A state report calling for "New Economic Management" published on 26 April 1966 suggested that selfishness was undesirable because it undermined the mutual aid and collectivism needed to sustain the communist project; similarly, the "New Communist Party Program" presented at the Party's 10th Congress in April 1971 declared that "idleness" would not be tolerated by state authorities because it defied Marxist and Leninist notions about work as human activity constituting the meaning of life.[20] Article 73 of the Bulgarian Constitution from 1947 stated that engagement in "socially useful labour" was the duty of every citizen. Todor Zhivkov presented in December 1967 a thesis entitled "Some Basic Problems in Work with Youth and the Komsomol," where he recognized the family unit as the "bastion of socialist society," such that "bad morals, certain ways of life, poor family relations, divorces, and a blunted sense of responsibility related to parenting" were all violations of the socialist principles organizing the nation.[21]

These narratives constructed a socialist subject who was a cultured, well-rounded master of arts and science – a "conscious" pursuer of high ideals and self-perfection whose work was useful and contributing to human evolution. Still, this abstract socialist ideal embodied moral and cognitive qualities that were linked inextricably with European modernity and civilization. State documents and Communist Party discourses interpreting Marxism and socialism framed ethnic Bulgarians as the biological heirs of the Thracian and Slavonic civilizations described as pillars of European culture. In 1967, the Communist Party chair Todor Zhivkov presented a speech where he defined Bulgarian geneologies as follows:

> Before Slav tribes settled here, our parts were inhabited by Thracian bands, creators of one of the great European civilizations of Antiquity. Thracian blood runs in our veins; we are the legitimate heirs of Thracian history and civilization; Thracian monuments dot our lands ... Thracian civilization ... exerted an influence both on the Roman and the Byzantine civilizations ... we, Bulgarians and Slavs, are the heirs of Thracian culture.[22]

Zhivkov called on educators and society at large to cultivate socialist youth who were schooled in the spirit and values of these civilizations upon which Europe emerged.

Socialist science linked the Slavic and Thracian civilizations to the European, or white, races. In public education, secondary school biology textbooks used in 1953, 1966, 1970, 1979, and 1981 introduced students to three basic races: "white (Europeanoid)," whose representatives included the peoples in Europe and "a great number of Americans"; a "yellow (Mongoloid)" race represented by the peoples in Asia;

and a "black (Negroid)" race inhabiting Africa. These racial categories invited ethnic Bulgarian youth to imagine themselves as nothing else but members of a white European race defined against the races in Asia and Africa. The textbooks further asserted that no races were superior or inferior: given the proper material and political conditions, all races could produce and acquire high culture.

These school lessons drew evidence from a special study of the racial origins of Bulgarians published by the state in 1959. Its author concluded that "the anthropological types which made up the contemporary Bulgarian peoples belonged completely to the European race."[23] Based on skin-colour research involving 4,336 individuals in Bulgaria, the study defined 85 per cent of Bulgarians as having "white" skin; 10 per cent had "light swarthy" skin, while only 4 per cent were "swarthy."[24] In contrast, the author classified Roma, Jews, and Turks as members of Asiatic races. Other state documents lent cultural and social support to these racial qualifications by framing Roma as non-Europeans whose backwardness and stagnation defied the very premise and promise of socialism and communism. Roma, therefore, presented a major ideological and political threat that had to be managed, controlled, and eliminated.

A 1968 state document titled *Tsiganskoto Naselenie v NR Bulgaria po Putia na Sotsialisma* (The Gypsy population in the People's Republic of Bulgaria on the road to socialism) illustrates these processes of racialized and cultural evaluating and meaning-making vividly. It states that the Roma originated in "nomadic tribes in Asia," particularly Northern India, and that historical conditions forced them to leave Central Asia and disperse throughout the world. The text adds cultural qualifications to this story of origin: "[Gypsy] public and family life has preserved many remnants from the tribal organization (especially among the nomads), kin (blood relatives) with a leader. Many Gypsies around the world still have patriarchal social relations with power vested in the elder." The document states further that Roma engaged in "begging" and "theft" while roaming and exerting "un-cleanliness and cultural backwardness," which bred hostility among the peoples who hosted Roma on their territories. It concludes that Roma were slow in their development and in assimilating "into the material and spiritual culture of the more elevated nationality" hosting them.

These qualifications relied on extensive comparativism used by the state to define the so-called Gypsy question:

> Through the years of people's rule, deep changes took place in the life of our country. After 9 October 1944, along with the Bulgarian people,

all minorities in the country received full opportunity and freedom for all-sided development. Such freedom was received by the Gypsy population ... [Despite some success] still, a part of the Gypsy population lags behind the collective development, it is not engaged in permanent labour, does not settle in one place, but leads a nomadic life, engages in begging, fortune telling, theft, and other violations of the public order. In many cases, the Gypsy population spreads diseases and appears the bearer of the utmost backwardness.[25]

Developmental and comparative constructs of Roma in socialist Bulgaria were built on Marxist notions of human emancipation as the outcome of material conditions. The state framed Roma as a people and culture defying a normative Marxist notion: socialism and communism created material conditions under which individuals from oppressed classes would become the makers of their own history by applying reason and consciously choosing socialism and its higher social stage – communism – which emancipated them from the chains of capitalism. According to Bulgarian state ideologues, "grabbing" and owning one's history – one's political emancipation – was a rational choice, but unlike the masses of oppressed Bulgarian workers and peasants building socialism, Roma did not or could not make that choice and instead stuck to their old ways. For that reason, state narratives presented Roma as ideological aberrations of modern history that were racialized: their presumed lack of ability to reason and see what was good for them was viewed as the result of a specific Roma corporeal and psychological make-up that defied both the Eurocentric notion of "human" as a rational being and Marxist theorizing positing that changes in the means of material production would lead to changes in human consciousness and social relations. Roma were perceived as defying these foundational ideas of modern epistemologies.

Leninist concepts of "nationalities," steeped in Russian and Soviet coloniality, also played a role in the narrative encoding of Roma difference. The Bulgarian socialist state referred to the different social groups within the state as "nationalities." The Bulgarian liberal state preceding state socialism used this category as a loose reference to what Western social sciences defined as "ethnicities," but under the rule of the Bulgarian Communist Party, the term "nationality" took on Soviet meanings. With Russian tsarism swept by the communist revolution and secessionist sentiments burgeoning, Lenin felt pressured to conceive a strategy for the "national question" that would allow Bolsheviks to retain cohesion within the Russian Empire while maintaining the

Soviet Communist Party's image as a champion of oppressed peoples. To that extent, Lenin drew from the work on nationalism by Marx and Engels.

Marx and Engels attributed nationalism to the structures of capitalism. They further understood the phenomenon as a kind of "ethno" sentiment pressed upon the working classes by the bourgeoises to prevent workers from developing and acting upon their class consciousness. They also asserted that communists should support a nationalist movement only if it was a movement toward socialism and communism. Yet Marx and Engels insisted that communists had to remain above nationalism for two reasons. First, nationalism might split, thus weakening the communist parties and the global communist movement. Second, "immunity" from nationalism would become the communist movement's "single defining characteristic," which would secure its authority and political legitimacy as the leader of oppressed and colonized peoples around the world.[26]

Marx's and Engels's strategic support for nationalist movements leading to socialism and communism became central to Lenin's policies on the "national question" in the Soviet Empire. Lenin knew that his party could not claim to be the champion of the colonized if Soviet communists did not support the right to self-determination expressed by these peoples. However, Lenin could not allow nationalist and secessionist movements within the Soviet Union to undermine the overarching political objective of globalized Marxist and communist movements. Hence, Lenin designed a rhetorical political strategy, where Turkmen, Uzbeks, Kyrgyz, Kazaks, and others – who had been framed as the "Asiatic" racial other in the Russian imperial imagination – would now be considered separate "nationalities" which Lenin defined as "a people in a pre-nation stage of development, that is to say, a people who, for whatever reason, have not yet achieved (and may never achieve) the more august station of nationhood."[27]

Lenin's "nationality" also signified a group distinguished by its members' shared historical past and cultural and linguistic traits. This notion of "nationality" thus related to the idea of shared character constituting the modern "nation." Therefore, in the Soviet Leninist lexicon, "nationality" also referred to "a segment of a nation living outside the state where the major body of the nation resides."[28] However, Lenin's strategic employment of "nationality" precluded the idea that ethnically and racially different former Russian colonial subjects (e.g., Kyrgyz, Turkmen, and Uzbeks) could form politically independent nation states. Although Roma in Soviet Russia were not perceived as a threat to territorial unity, they too were subjects of the same racialized views praising the exotic cultures of non-European minorities but denying these "nationalities" the right to self-determination and self-governance.[29]

Lenin's political deployment of "nationality" was also intended to displace the racial order and practices privileging self-proclaimed white and culturally superior Russians that had organized the Russian Empire before the October Revolution in 1917.[30] Lenin understood that the racism and chauvinism of "the Great Russians" fuelled local nationalism and the struggle for independence of formerly colonized peoples. Moreover, the superior-to-inferior relationship long practised by Russians impeded another of Lenin's goals: the assimilation of non-Russians into one Soviet socialist homogeneous culture, which represented the values and ideals of the advanced and superior Russian socialist culture. In 1929, Lenin's disciple Kalinin noted that the goal of Leninist nationality policies "was to teach the people of the Kyrgyz steppe, the small Uzbek cotton-growers and the Turkmen gardener to accept the ideals of the Leningrad worker."[31]

Kalinin's statement could be interpreted as a standard imperialist utterance closely resembling the idea of the white man's burden. Indeed, Leninist notions of "nationalities" stressing the cultural heterogeneity of the Soviet state did not displace Russian racial imaginations and identities. For example, at its Twelfth Congress in 1923, the Soviet Communist Party addressed the peoples in Soviet Asia as "brothers of other nationalities."[32] However, in 1937, Soviet ideologues and leaders persecuted a Russian historian who had called the Russian colonization of these brothers "an absolute evil."[33] Moreover, in the years after Lenin's death, his "nationality" policies privileged the proletariat over the peasants. In Soviet Asia, the proletariat consisted mostly of Russian and Ukrainian minorities: white, Christian, and culturally Europeanized minorities, who took the governing positions of power controlling Asian and Muslim majorities. One historian argued that such racialized Soviet policies began "a long process toward the rehabilitation of Russia's historical mission as a mentor of backward peoples."[34] This process of socialist imperial revival was disguised under the discourse of "nationalities" that wiped the word "race" from the Soviet lexicon to maintain a raceless and anti-racist image of an "affirmative action empire" dedicated to preserving multicultural and multiracial difference.[35] Indeed, the silence of "race" varied and shifted throughout Soviet state-building;[36] however, Soviet racializing and racist practices were apparent in the development of Soviet eugenics.[37] Inspired by German anthropology and American eugenics in the 1930s, scores of Soviet scientists and ideologues supported blood studies, sterilization and insemination campaigns, and cataloguing the biological traits of Soviet subjects to better understand and govern the socialist evolution and modernization of the population.[38]

Soviet hegemony in the Balkans opened the region to Leninist racialized definitions of "nationalities" that permeated Bulgarian socialist science and state ideology, providing a powerful rationale for forceful assimilation of groups, including the Roma, into Eurocentric Soviet and Bulgarian socialist modernity. State authorities addressed the issue in a special report issued in September 1958 by the commission appointed by the Bulgarian Council of Ministers to seek "Complete Resolution of the Questions Regarding the Gypsy Population in the People's Republic of Bulgaria":

> Until now, little organization is done to manage the Gypsy population, to push it toward the road of the collective development of the Bulgarian people. In the past years, our people has gone a long way in its cultural and economic development, building heavy industry, collectivizing agriculture, and developing culture and science. In many regards, they [the Bulgarian people] reached and already surpassed many advanced capitalist countries. The Gypsy population, however, living within the borders of our country, lags behind … To leave [the Gypsy population] in the same condition in the future would mean *to smear* socialism and to prevent the common development of the country. Without state special measures, this population cannot alone get out of its state of backwardness.

Gendered and Colonial Techniques of Socialist Inclusion

The Bulgarian socialist state nurtured, celebrated, and invested heavily in "proper" heteronormative socialist women and mothers embodied by idealized female figures exemplifying the values of Bulgarian culture and Christian morality. Roma women engaged in begging, pickpocketing, or sex work as well as veiled Romani-, Turkish-, or Bulgarian-speaking Muslim women, divorcées, and pregnant teenagers all represented aberrations of socialist morality and womanhood in need of surveillance, rescue, and reform. State archives – only recently opened – reveal that socialist authorities were especially concerned with the "Turkization" of Roma in regions of the country dominated by Muslim Bulgarian- and Turkish-speaking communities. In 1962, socialist policymakers attributed the growing number of Muslims in Bulgaria to the propensity of Roma to identify with Islam and give their children Arabic and Islamic names.[39] According to socialist scientists, Roma traditions such as early girl marriage, bride pricing and marketing, high divorce rates, and sexual relations out of state-sanctioned marriage were attributable to barbaric Islamic customs, nomadic lifestyles, and persisting tribal social forms – all considered intolerable under socialist law and morality. Panhandling and pickpocketing by Roma women and children were persecuted as especially immoral delinquent acts. Roma women were framed as lazy and uninvolved in meaningful work as well as failing mothers depriving their children of hygienic homes, discipline, and proper education. Deeply rooted state and popular beliefs attributed the roots of Roma sexual promiscuity, prostitution, and the spreading of venereal diseases in Bulgaria to Ottoman domination and Turkish sultans who tolerated and even normalized sexual behaviours that were foreign to the Bulgarian character and culture. In stark contrast, socialist mass culture celebrated Christian and Bulgarian mothers, sisters, and wives as moral and normative gendered subjects who epitomized socialist womanhood. These proper socialist women were tasked with the rearing of good citizens who could build and sustain socialism and its higher form: communism. Cultural, ideological, and institutional narratives further stressed heteronormative socialist ideals of womanhood emphasizing a woman's reproductive role and her capacity for socially useful labour.

Not surprisingly, the Bulgarian socialist state sought to reform Christian and Muslim Roma through laws and political directives explicitly targeting women. In 1958, Roma women were the subject of a special order forbidding vagrancy and begging in the People's Republic of Bulgaria. All persons engaging in vagrancy and begging had to join organized production and engage in socially useful labour. The state ordered local governments to place Roma women and men in plants, factories, and agricultural cooperatives. The Council of Ministers further ordered municipalities and local Communist Party divisions to regulate, urbanize, and improve the hygiene of Gypsy neighbourhoods. The Ministry of Public Health was responsible for organizing a systematic anti-epidemic educational propaganda campaign among Roma women to increase the sanitary culture of that population. The state also charged the People's City Council of Sofia to remove Roma who lived in neighbourhoods near the city centre to more "appropriate areas in greater Sofia." An earlier draft of the order from the same year specified that the resettlement of Roma should not allow their concentration in compact groups. The state also required the Ministry of Culture and Education to implement a campaign bringing all Roma children to schools for compulsory education. To foster a "Gypsy intelligentsia," the state ordered the building of boarding schools in three major cities, where Roma children were expected to acquire the values of civilization away from the negative influences of their mothers, fathers, and communities. This initiative was recommended by the State Commission on the "Gypsy Question," whose members felt that "without the creation of Gypsy intelligentsia and qualified Gypsy cadres in production, this population would not overcome its present state of illiteracy and backwardness."

In 1961, Todor Zhivkov decided to expand this process, and new boarding schools were built in all parts of the country, housing three thousand Roma pupils; by 1968, about nine thousand Roma students were being taught in residential schools.[40] According to state authorities, "Removed from their family and neighbourhood environment, placed in good conditions, in only a few months [Roma and Muslim] children were transformed."[41] The "good conditions" included full control, cultural isolation, and mentoring by Bulgarian "special teachers-trainers."[42] Roma children in residential schools were taught about socialist and modern values, with the hope that they would in turn transmit them back to their families and communities. Meanwhile, state health activists educated Roma women in personal hygiene and good parenting. The propaganda in the form of lectures and meetings included topics such as "What did the people's rule give to the Gypsy population?" "Hygiene in the family," "Family and schools," "The morality of the new person," "Protection of the socialist property," "Harm from alcohol drinking," and "Child delinquency and the fight against it."[43]

The boarding schools housed hundreds of Turkish- and Bulgarian-speaking Muslim Roma and non-Roma girls – many extracted from their homes forcefully and against their parents' will. These young women were channelled into gendered educational programs designed to cultivate professional and work skills as well as aesthetic and cultural tastes appropriate for a modern socialist woman. These girls formed an ideological and political feminized state-led vanguard whose purpose was to reform Roma and Turkish Muslim communities from within. Socialist educators trained Muslim girls and young women as seamstresses, teachers, nurses, dentists, veterinarians, librarians, and social workers, but just as many women and girls were enrolled in vocational programs preparing them for industrial and manual labour in the textile and food industries. State campaigns against the veiling of Muslim women, including Roma, also intensified. A state document from 1960 explicitly linked the unveiling of Muslim women with their liberation – both as citizens and workers – from oppressive and backward Islamic dogmas:

> The religious elements in the clothing deteriorate people's health. The wearing of veils prevents the sunlight from reaching the eyes of the

women. The veil restricts the movement of the woman's body and reduces her ability to work. Wearing a veil in the hot summer days exhausts her organism entirely. Is that what the hard-working women of the Rhodope region deserve?[44]

Framing Roma and non-Roma Muslim women as "deserving" of free physical movement, good personal health, and improved working conditions provided a powerful rationale justifying the use of socialist state force and punitive measures where education, propaganda, and elevated consciousness did not produce the effects desired by the socialist state. Oral histories from the period reveal the pain and vulnerability of parents, especially fathers who refused to send their daughters to boarding schools or educational programs in the large cities. Fathers and mothers were strongly pressured by local representatives of the state, and some were denied public services including health care, access to stores, and basic goods as well as access to public transportation. Some Roma and non-Roma Muslims who had their male children circumcised were even imprisoned. State repression intensified during the implementation of policies seeking the full assimilation of Roma, Bulgarian, and Turkish Muslims by forcing members of these groups to change their personal Muslim names for Christian and Bulgarian names. Muslim men who refused to change their name and the names of their children were arrested and beaten, and some were sent to labour camps.[45] Roma Muslim women resisting these policies were dismissed from their places of work and denied access to professions, such as teaching, nursing, and social work.

Overall, these socialist reforming initiatives evoked the colonial technologies used by European and Russian/Soviet Empires seeking to subdue colonized populations by controlling women. Anne McClintock explored the gendering of European colonialism in maps, pictorials, stories, and literary imaginations authored by European male explorers, travellers and administrators. These European men of science and travel, dispatched by imperial courts to traverse unexplored territories, populated their maps with depictions of naked female bodies, and oversexualized poses representing the "bestial character" of the Indigenous peoples they encountered. Thus, the maps served as gendered, raced, and sexed tropes marking the geographies of unknown lands and peoples with the bodies of local women depicted as a category of nature. The feminized pictorials served to guide and orient waves of European conquerors; they also normalized the subordination of Indigenous peoples and the logic of European imperialisms.[46]

Women – and difference – also provided spatial and cultural orientation for Marxists and socialists. Roma and Muslim women in socialist Bulgaria, and Indigenous and ethnic minority women in Soviet Russia, provided tropes for socialist modernity and progress. Socialist ideologues framed the speed, type, and completeness of socialist nation-building through Eurocentric notions of history: nation-building was considered a form of continuous and linear progress from savagery to civilization and from chaos to organized governmentality and political and moral order. Like their capitalist cousins, socialist ideologues shared the belief that history equals human evolution. Marxists in particular treated history as "a single optimistic chronicle" that some critics have linked to "white mythologies."[47] The framing of groups of women as aberrations of Marxist principles of historical evolution justified violence against them as acts committed in the name of their uplifting, social equality, and well-being. Socialist integration, however, enacted European and Soviet imperial technologies: the boarding schools for Roma and non-Roma Muslim children established in socialist Bulgaria borrowed from the logic of Christian missionaries in the 1800s at the forefront of British colonial conquests. European missionaries considered boarding schools for native and Indigenous infants and children a highly potent tool for inoculating the minds of "heathen peoples" with the values of European civilization and Christianity. In 1814, the Anglican Church Missionary Society clearly stated the colonial intent of these schooling endeavours as using the children of undeveloped peoples to access and control their parents.[48] Anglican missionary schools pursuing similar objective emerged in Canada, New Zealand, and India; they served as inroads for British colonizers, whose migration to and economic domination over colonial vicinities turned Indigenous and seminomadic peoples into "minority cultures" and subjects of colonial governance.

Russian, and later Soviet, colonizers also used special schooling projects targeting the children of "belated peoples" for the purpose of controlling these groups, but these projects built on both colonial and socialist imaginations. In her research among Evenk women in Siberia, Alexia Bloch observed how Soviet residential schools moulded novel gendered subjectivities among Indigenous populations in the Soviet Empire: four generations of Evenk women schooled in Soviet state boarding institutions beginning in the 1920s referred to themselves as historical agents of change and members of a national socialist collective dedicated to emancipation, modernity, and progress. These perceptions echoed Soviet state discourses describing women in the process of modernization as "icons" who showcased the power of socialism and communism in elevating and emancipating girls and women in social groups deemed barbaric, illiterate, and backward. Staffed by Soviet workers and educators, these boarding institutions promoted literacy, European-style hygiene, modern medicine, and industrial work skills among minority and Indigenous women and their children.[49]

Soviet policies targeting minority populations functioned as a form of "socialist multiculturalism" that tolerated modernization of the culturally belated peoples only to the degree where they would not surpass or threaten the hegemony of white Russians.[50] In the Bulgarian version of socialist multiculturalism, some Roma cultural traditions and customs such as dances and music were celebrated in state-supported special cultural events, showcasing the benevolence of socialism. However, these celebrations were accompanied by the attempted genetic erasure of Roma: the socialist state sponsored and encouraged mixed marriages between Roma and Bulgarians; it even provided housing for mixed families and granted special privileges to their children in kindergartens and schools.

Socialist state interventions targeting Bulgarian-speaking Muslim women had a different logic and purpose. Bulgarian-speaking Muslim women and men in rural areas were framed as historical victims of the Ottoman Empire and Islamic domination forced to convert to the Muslim faith. Thus, unlike state and popular discourses constructing Roma as foreign genetic and cultural material associated with Asia, Bulgarian-speaking Muslims were imagined as a domestic population whose evolution was interrupted. And while Muslims in Bulgaria were praised for their industriousness, honesty, and embrace of the emerging socialist order, Roma were constructed as immutably different and historically pathological – unable to reason, and therefore unable to see the emancipatory modern gifts offered to them by Marxism and socialism.

Historic prejudice against the Roma shared by Bulgarians in positions of power and society at large secured the success of socialist assimilationist policies. According to one Roma educator, the mass campaigns for Roma education actually resulted in "homogeneous, segregated schools for Roma children in the ghettos," where Roma children were taught the language, values, and morals of Bulgarians while focusing mainly on practical labour skills appropriate for Roma lifestyles, including sawing and tinsmith – which socialist authorities called "professions." The same author wrote:

> What kind of a society was the one, where the mother Party, through its executive orders, marked the pernicious role of the neighbourhood Roma schools, and even envisioned a policy for mixing of Roma and Bulgarian

children, while, at the same time, the state continued unceremoniously to build such schools without paying attention to the forming of Gypsy ghettos as an ostrich covering its head in the sand?[51]

This was a state calling upon its Bulgarian subjects to help regulate and reform "the worst" and "still unreformed Gypsies ... by creating public attitudes against their bad behaviour, to create around them such an atmosphere of care and control, so as practically to make it impossible for them to influence the rest of the Gypsy population."[52] When it was unable to erase Roma through assimilation, the socialist state literally declared the Roma in Bulgaria to be non-existent.

For example, despite forceful socialist assimilationism, a great number of Roma continued to use their own dialects and practise their cultural traditions and customs, while maintaining tight and homogeneous communities throughout Bulgarian cities and villages. The Bulgarian socialist state and society were aware of this reality, yet state narratives presented to foreign and native observers an image of full Roma assimilation – otherwise, the socialist state and the Marxist-Leninist ideology that guided it would appear weak. Roma resistance to socialist assimilation undermined Marx-inspired claims that socialism, communism, and the people's rule could transform a person. Therefore, to maintain the image of a strong and working socialist state and society that could easily uplift and assimilate culturally and morally backward subjects, the Bulgarian Communist Party state adopted a policy of statistical silence related to the Roma. According to the official public census population data on Roma in Bulgaria from 1956, there were 197,865 Roma in the country; thereafter, all statistical data on the Roma was provided for unofficial use by state authorities, and in the passing years, socialist authorities kept demographic silence where the Roma were concerned.[53] By not collecting or releasing population information on the Roma, the socialist state sought to prove to itself and the world that Roma were rapidly disappearing under the transformative powers of socialist modernity. For example, one unofficial source of 1965 census data listed 148,874 Roma in Bulgaria. In 1975, soon after the last state legislation on "the Gypsy question," unofficial data listed only 18,323 Roma in the country.[54] The purported disappearance of 150,000 Roma during this ten-year period framed socialism as a naturally assimilating force because of its superior and emancipating social, political, and economic character. Socialist ideologues presented Roma assimilation as an organic event predicted by socialist ideology and Marxist theory.

However, unofficial data collected in 1989 by local governments and the people's militia (the police) indicated that 577,000 Roma remained in Bulgaria, which had a total population of about eight million. More recent census data puts the numbers of Roma in Bulgaria at over 750,000 individuals. These figures appear more realistic although observers caution that the actual numbers of Roma in the country likely exceeded any data collected throughout the decades of socialism, because the censuses were based on self-identification. Because Roma were targeted for assimilation and subjected to discrimination, they tended to identify in the censuses as members of groups with higher social standing and as having "Bulgarian nationality." Thus, two simultaneous processes worked to render Roma invisible within the socialist state. Socialist ideology worked to hide the presence of Roma in Bulgaria from the domestic public and the world in the pursuit of social, cultural, and class homogenization and equality. At the same time, socialist racism forced Roma to identify as ethnic Bulgarians to avoid social and state violence. These processes echo racialized assimilationist events in capitalist and liberal states.

For example, American sociologists tackling "the American racial dilemma" in the first half of the twentieth century – especially those in the so-called Chicago school – overwhelmingly conceptualized American race relations and racism against Black Americans as an issue of unequally developed cultures.[55] Chicago sociologists further considered African-American culture as too different, hence the reason for Black social and cultural visibility and prejudice against them. Liberal sociologists linked African-American visibility to cultural traits and social behaviours constructed as the exemplar of social pathologies, evidenced by undocumented marriages, births out of wedlock, non-heteronormative sexual behaviours, non-monogamous relations, and single motherhood. According to white sociologists, these behaviours not only deviated sharply from white and Eurocentric normative cultures considered "American," but African-American cultural and social traits were also framed as creating disorder in an otherwise well-functioning American society. Chicago sociologists concluded that to make African Americans less visible, and thereby address racism against them, Black Americans should be regulated and assimilated into the cultural norms and behaviours of a universal "American citizen" linked to racial whiteness and Euro-American civilization.[56] Thousands of miles away, the Bulgarian socialist state, an American rival in the Cold War, framed Roma as a racialized cultural difference that "smeared" the socialist project. Notions of difference thus connected Marxist, liberal, capitalist, and socialist ideologies during the Cold War, illuminating the intertwined ends of the racialized Eurocentric modern ideologies that set the terms of our imaginations.

Chapter Three

Women's Work: Gendered and Racialized Socialist State Governmentality

Work is a human activity involving physical or mental exertion that has material and symbolic value.[1] The work that women do has been an important site of feminist research inquiring about the relationship between gender and political economy across the disciplines. Feminists have identified women's work in the home (reproduction) and the formal economy (production) as interrelated sites of women's subordination and the backbone of both socialist and capitalist patriarchal formations. Writing in 1977, socialist feminist Zillah Einstein acknowledged that fact. Capitalist production, she explained, created and supported unequal gendered and sexed social classes whose place in the social hierarchy was determined by the kind of work they do – a phenomenon referred to as a gender division of labour.[2] Women's domestic work maintaining a household and raising children is perceived as proper and natural in capitalist societies, resulting in the exclusion of women from the public economy and professions and making these realms the site of male work and privilege. That hierarchy of gendered work anchors capitalist patriarchies and gendered regimes of representation that keep women subordinate and unequal to men. Einstein observed that a socialist mode of production did not abolish patriarchy: "the sexual division of labor exists in the Soviet Union, in Cuba, in China," she wrote. "As we can see, patriarchy is cross-cultural by definition though it is actualized differently in different societies via the institutionalization of sexual hierarchy."[3]

Transnational feminist scholar Chandra Talpade Mohanty extends the notion of gendered division of work to the global. In her highly influential work titled *Feminism without Borders: Decolonizing Theory, Practicing Solidarity* (2003), Mohanty constructs a critical Marxist and feminist paradigm enfolding *gender*, *class*, and *race* from where she observes how the globalization of capital and international production chains entrench the subordination especially of racialized poor and working-class women in countries in the global South.⁴ These women, she argues, perform low-paid, precarious, and, in some cases, dangerous jobs because they are women. Therefore, Mohanty locates unleashed global capitalism at the Third World woman's body; women's work, she argues, constitutes the site where we can comprehend how global capitalism naturalizes racial and class hierarchies and inequality. She further theorizes women's work in the global economy as the site of women's relations that could support political solidarities among working women across geographical, cultural, and linguistic borders. In conceptualizing these solidarities, Mohanty acknowledges that the collapse of socialist states created a new "post-1989 global political and economic landscape," but her vision of women's solidarities based on work and class does not extend to poor or racialized women in former socialist states who too were engulfed into the emerging neo-liberal economies that Mohanty analysed.⁵ Mohanty further roots her theorizing of women and work in a Marxist-feminist anti-capitalist framework whose total eclipse of women's work in socialist societies could be interpreted to suggest that women and their work in socialist economies could not be subjected to similar important inquiries about women, difference, and solidarity in places of work.

In this chapter, I take on the challenge and seek to examine how a socialist economy constructed and positioned women for work and relations to each other. Such an inquiry, I believe, extends transnational feminist theories of women's work while enriching and pushing further understanding of how different women worked and experienced their labour in a socialist political economy. The burgeoning literature on women and work in former socialist countries has not taken up this question of difference presuming that neither racialized thinking nor ethnicity, religion, or language mattered in women's work under state socialism. Instead, researchers studying women's work in former socialist economies have either used homogenizing categories such as "employment in CEE (Central and Eastern European) countries"⁶ and "women in the (Yugo)plastic industry,"⁷ or they have focused on women in specific ethnic groups but have studied them outside of any relational paradigms connecting them to other groups of women both within the socialist economy and state and without.⁸

These limitations notwithstanding, researchers contributing to this field of study have generated important insights into the relationship between gender and socialist political economy emphasizing several distinct features. Gendered division of labour persisted under state socialism: women entered the public economy en masse yet they continued to bear the responsibility for domestic work and child care, resulting in a double and triple burden for women who worked in factories and offices full-time while rearing children, performing domestic work, and tending private and public agricultural plots and farms.[9] Despite the burden, some feminist scholars, especially in the West, highlight the emancipatory effects of work under socialist conditions arguing that women's access to education, professions, and full-time employment increased their independence and supported new and empowering modes of women's identifications and social relations.[10] Socialist states provided benefits that protected women from the devastating effects of the kind of unleashed capitalism and neo-liberalism we witness in the contemporary postsocialist moment. Gender discrimination, unequal pay, women's unemployment, feminized low-wage labour, and lack of health care and work safety are staples of the global economy that took shape after the Cold War and the demise of socialist states internationally.

Feminist scholars in the West have celebrated these accomplishments of the socialist economy but only after separating them from the political and ideological aspects of the socialist state. For example, American anthropologist Kristen Ghodsee's comparative study of women's improved health and lives under a socialist economy versus women's plight in capitalist and neo-liberal economies is conditioned by the author's explicit rejection of the authoritarian political nature of "state socialism" and embrace of "democratic socialism," the latter combining elements of a socialist economy with a Western-style democracy.[11] The ensuing hybrid politico-economic construct implies the cultural and social deficiencies of the peoples and societies who built and lived under a socialist economy. It presumes the political and cultural superiority of Western cultures and the capacity of Western-type of liberalism and democracy to sustain both an economy based on socialist principles and a genuine egalitarian society. Simultaneously, Ghodsee upholds a strong and activist state as a force able to provide and secure women's access to education, the professions, jobs, and thus independence.[12] Concerns about top-down, state-led socialist women's emancipation expressed by feminists from former socialist countries, Ghodsee suggests, should not obscure the fact of real material legacies and emancipatory effects that evidence women's improved lives and gains in former Eastern European socialist states – gains and emancipation not yet achieved in capitalist states.[13]

This chapter both extends and disrupts these arguments about women, work, and emancipation in a socialist economy. It argues that the economy is a major area of social and ideological interventions enacted by both socialist and capitalist states, hence under state socialism the economy was also a site of state force and violence that impacted how Muslim women, sex workers, racially and ethnically privileged women working in the creative industries and the caring professions, and women factory workers negotiated the meaning of work, womanhood, and socialism with each other, men, and the socialist state. In-depth examination of the power structures and violence underlining these negotiations in the Bulgarian socialist state reveals a mode of gendered socialist state governmentality pitting unequal groups of women against each other by tasking some with the reform of others and the distribution of wages, and access to education, the professions, and employment based on a woman's proximity to Eurocentric socialist modernity associated with development, civilization, and useful labour. By highlighting these aspects of women's work under the socialist state and economy, the chapter contributes a methodological approach inspired by transnational feminist theories, where socially and ideologically constructed differences between women are placed at the centre of the analysis of women's work and socialist political economy. The approach reveals that the socialist economy presented an important site where differently imagined and valued groups of women were both positioned and were self-positioning for relationships to other women, men, and the state. The chapter observes these positionings in the relationship between Muslim women in rural Bulgaria and the ethnic Bulgarian women teachers and social and health workers tasked by the state with their reform; the personal friendship between a sex worker known for her good looks and professionalism and a female journalist and communist who recorded her story in a moving memoir; and the mood of seminars facilitated by leaders of the state-sponsored women's movement whose work included lecturing other women on the value of motherhood and productivity in the home and the factory. Together, these stories shine light on the Eurocentricity, the patriarchal nature and violence of socialist state governmentality, and how women serving as leaders and reformers and those targeted by the reforms both cooperated with and resisted these socialist techniques of power.

Socialist Governmentality and the "Woman Question"

In Foucault's writing, "governmentality" refers to state practices of subjugation and techniques of rule over land and populations.[14] Yet state governmentality involves self-constitution, or processes by which men set up rules to govern their own conduct but also seek to transform their lives into something elevated and different. State governmentality further involves a modern and secularized form of pastoral power as the state takes on the role of a guiding force, leader, and shepherd of a gendered flock obedient to moral, legal, and ideological norms reflecting the needs and goals of the state. In the socialist context, state ideological commitment to speedy industrialization and fostering proper socialist subjects provided an important rationale for governing women's work in Bulgaria. Fast-paced economic development under socialism required moving women from the domestic and private realms to the public economy, where their labour would drive modernization. State Marxist and Leninist ideologizing also narrated women's participation in the pubic economy as an emancipatory mechanism: paid employment transformed women from subjects of exploitive and oppressive capitalist economy and bourgeois sociality into independent, free, and equal socialist citizens whose political and civic rights were secured by their equal participation in the collective ownership of the means of production.

Socialist emancipation of women, however, supported an ensemble of repressive socialist state policies and programs often carried out by ethnic Bulgarian women whose paid work involved surveying, reforming, guiding, and uplifting Roma women, Muslim women, sex workers, pregnant teenagers, divorcées, and other women who deviated from socialist moral, aesthetic, and behavioural norms. These controlling and governing mechanisms extended racialized, sexed, and gendered logics deputizing women belonging to the Bulgarian ethnic majority, associating itself with European civilization attached to racial whiteness, with the task of reforming and emancipating ideologically, culturally, and morally undesirable genres of women through lecturing, propaganda, training, education, membership in state-sponsored women's organizations, and personal mentoring and friendship. These soft and feminized techniques of socialist state power articulated a multipronged and complex higher order of punishment and power combining incarceration or harsh labour with an ideological conviction: punitive laws in socialist Bulgaria in the 1950s and 1960s intended punishment through imprisonment and labour camps only after the socialist state could not achieve its aims through propaganda, education, and fostering conviction.[15]

The Bulgarian socialist state did not invent this gendered technology of power. Women had already been mobilized for colonial, political, and racial projects by other state formations and powers. For instance, in the late 1900s, the British Empire dispatched nurses to West Africa to care for the medical needs of male colonizers while presenting visible examples of proper British and European womanhood to native women.[16] These female postings were so popular that the Colonial

Nursing Association had more candidates for the positions than were needed. In the 1920s, African American women travelled to countries in Africa to perform civilizing work there; many believed that the European presence in Africa would have modernizing and uplifting effects, so Black American women wanted to support these processes.[17] African American women participating in these missions had received their postsecondary education in Black colleges in the United States where they were taught that it was their duty "to Christianize and civilize" their ancestral land of Africa and its peoples. Hence, African American women served as nurses and teachers in community and missionary schools and hospitals in Angola, Mozambique, and South Africa, where they participated in civilizing schemes targeting local girls and women. Likewise, white European and American women committed to modernization in the twenty-first century have participated in modernizing and educational projects supporting war in the Middle East to save, protect, and emancipate veiled Muslim women perceived as victims of "backward" cultures, Islam, and violent terrorists.[18] A shared feature of these otherwise distinct feminized state and colonial projects is mobilizing educated, professional, and middle-class women as enforcers of European, Euro-American, and Christian power and control over subjugated men and women deemed inferior.

The socialist state exemplified by the Bulgarian case shared the Eurocentric cultural perceptions that inspired these feminized colonizing projects, but its objectives also differed significantly. Lenka Nahodilova, after Mary Neuburger, described the Bulgarian socialist state reforms of Muslims as "internal orientalism" inspired by a desire to affirm the nation and the socialist project as properly Bulgarian and European.[19] State campaigns mobilizing ethnic Bulgarian and Christian women for the modernization and assimilation of Muslim women drew a boundary between Europe and the Orient, and between Christianity and Islam; in much the same way, European and American women mobilized by colonial powers enforced racial, cultural, and religious boundaries maintaining the superiority and domination of Christianity and Europe. However, socialist state techniques exhibited the properties of socialist racialism as they simultaneously sought to erase racial, class, and ethnic boundaries in a gesture of inclusion in a socialist society, where equality was signified by homogeneity. Difference and internal borders – racialized, class, religious – impeded socialism and communism, which required erasing them internally, cleansing the nation of Muslim, oriental, and Asiatic influences and presence in order to foster a homogeneous national body of citizens dedicated to the ideas of socialist and European modernity, which were deemed a higher stage of human development. For socialist authorities, Muslim women's bodies and aesthetics represented "oriental darkness," "Turkishness," "impurity," and "danger" associated with racial non-whiteness. "Civilizing" them was a question of fostering cultural, political, and ideological unity upon which depended the success of the socialist project.[20]

Women's work and places of work became a major site for creating a homogeneous socialist nation. An extended work-based state apparatus supported the surveillance, uplifting, or punishment of women straying away: workers' juries, teams of volunteers, and peer committees watching over workers' discipline, moral behaviour, workplace hygiene, safety practices, and work performance used public shaming, wage reduction, and other forms of punishment to reform those workers who engaged in antisocial behaviour, misappropriated state property, missed work, dressed inappropriately, or did not perform their work duties accordingly. Communist Party units and members embedded in factories, plants, offices, and agricultural collectives selected and mobilized citizens and workers deemed to be of a higher ethnic, ideological, and moral constitution to serve on these peer-based forms of socialist jurisprudence located in places of work.

These techniques of socialist state power were gendered, racialized, and Eurocentric as well. Socialist state policies regarding women and their work rested upon ideological beliefs labelled the "woman question" and originally developed in the nineteenth century by influential European socialists. In this paradigm, capitalist relations supported monogamy and marriage, which extended the contractual and material logics of the capitalist economy. Capitalist material production kept women in the domestic realm, yet women's housework and child rearing allowed men to participate actively in the public economy, where they exercised their rights as citizens, made political decisions, and protected their property. In contrast, a socialist economy fostered women's emancipation and independence by giving women access to education, the professions, employment, and the opportunity of earning her own income. Socialist state ideologues also believed that as mothers and people who take care of the home, women serve society and men; therefore, they must be compensated for both their domestic work and the work they do outside the home. In socialist states, the compensation took the form of publicly funded food canteens, laundries, nurseries, kindergartens, and extensive maternity leaves meant to support women as mothers, workers, and citizens.

These formulations of women's emancipation in relation to the economy and material production have been highly influential among Marxists, socialists, and feminists the world over, yet their European genealogy has remained vastly unaddressed in the feminist literature exploring the issue. For example, central to the literature on women and work is the so-called woman question, defined as multiple important questions pertaining to citizenship, property rights, and access to the public sphere engaging intellectuals, political leaders, and members of the public extensively in the ninetieth century.[21] The "woman question" has become since then a foundational tenet of feminist theories related to women's political and civil rights, economic exploitation, and participation in public life. For socialist feminists, Marx's treatment of the question presents a critique of power and capitalism that remains unsurpassed in providing understanding of the ways in which women are positioned in society.[22]

The "woman question," however, originates in European ontologies and material realities. It was first articulated by August Bebel (1840–1913), an influential socialist in Germany in the earlier part of the nineteenth century.[23] Born into a working-class family and raised by a mother who lost two husbands, Bebel travelled to find work and, in the process, developed a strong class consciousness that propelled him to a leadership role in the German labour unions and service in the Reichstag, the German national parliament. In 1879, while in prison for socialist beliefs and activism, Bebel wrote the most influential book on the plight of working-class women titled *Woman and Socialism*. He argued that women's dependency on men could not be resolved without resolving the material organization of society, mainly economic relations. Importantly, Bebel's formulations of the woman question reflected the ontologies of women in his native Germany and industrialized Western Europe, more generally. His observations about women did not speak to the material and colonial condition of women in other regions of the world.

Feminist writers interested in women and their work also draw inspiration from the ideas of Fredrich Engels (1820–95), who first theorized the family as the outcome of capitalist economic and political relations. Engels was a German philosopher and a close collaborator of Karl Marx.[24] The son of a wealthy German industrialist, Engels developed communist ideas in the comfort of bourgeois material and social prosperity. Likewise, canonical feminist texts refer to socialist feminist Lily Braun (1811–90) as an early pioneer who understood the exploitation of women and their work and lobbied rigorously for maternal leave and increased social support for working and poor women in her native Germany. Braun was the daughter of a Prussian Army general and his wife, who provided private tutoring for their curious and highly intelligent daughter. Education and material resources propelled Braun to public life, where she became involved in social movements such as the ethical movement in Germany, which sought to establish a system of morality in place of traditional religions. Braun also worked as a journalist for a feminist newspaper and through this work embraced socialism and feminism.[25]

These extraordinary thinkers and writers whose ideas continue to shape contemporary debates about women and political economy perceived women's ontologies, formulated the "woman question," and developed visions of socialist and communist revolutions from within the local and international epistemological, cultural, and historical contexts of German industrialization and imperialism, Western European colonialism, capitalism, and gender roles and class struggles stemming from these conditions. Engels, for instance, explicitly named rising bourgeois, Protestant countries, West Europeans, and the Church as locations from where to observe the dissolution of traditional relations and the rise of family and marriage based on property relations. Yet Engels's writing on the family and capitalism informs foundational and highly influential universalized and globally applied critical, anti-colonial, anti-capitalist, postcolonial, and transnational paradigms involving gender, feminisms, sexuality, agency, and freedom.

Indigenous and Black feminists from the global North and South have noted the Eurocentricity of the "woman question" theories governing feminist and women's studies. Marxists, socialists, and feminists in Western academies, they argue, have perceived and assessed the status of women in colonial and postcolonial contexts in the global South in relation to a division of labour and the material mode of production specific to Western Europe. Feminists have thus placed Indigenous and Black women in Africa, Asia, and North and South America always in a hierarchical relationship to men, domesticity, and the economy. However, researchers from Africa reject these Eurocentric constructions of African women as perpetual victims of an underdeveloped social and economic order by highlighting instead women's social and economic empowerment on the African continent before European colonization.[26] Women in African societies served as political leaders and acted as justices in their communities; they participated actively in public trade and agricultural labour and were chiefs, queen-mothers, and holders of political offices. Indigenous African societies did understand men and women as having different roles but not in the hierarchical order related to division of labour and occupation implied by the Eurocentric paradigm constructed by thinkers such as Babel, Engels, Marx, and Braun. Likewise, in the North American context, white settler ethnographers and white feminists have been critiqued for analysing a Native woman's status in the United States or an Aboriginal woman's history in Canada through the lens of "work" and "profession," thus perceiving an Indigenous woman's degree of oppression or emancipation in relationship to the settler state, its capitalist economy, and women-settlers' participation in that economy.[27] These constructs naturalize racialized and colonial systems of thought by treating European and Euro-American women's ontologies, concerns, and struggles as those of all women and by celebrating feminisms, women's activism, women's achievements, and freedoms in the West but narrating women's perpetual oppression and victimization in "the Rest" of the world.

The next section illustrates how a Eurocentric socialist ideology related to women and their emancipation through education and participation in the economy rationalized and justified a socialist state governmentality involving Muslim and Christian women's work in Bulgaria between the 1950s and the 1980s.

Reforming Muslim Women: The Cost of Inclusion

The Rhodope Mountains have been the home of Muslim communities for over a century. These communities consisted of three ethnic and linguistic subgroups: Turks, Bulgarian-speaking Muslims (Pomaks), and Muslim Roma who, together, comprised the largest minority in the country. The region is also the site of important social history involving women's work. Beginning in the 1950s, the Bulgarian socialist state began mobilizing locally and nationally scores of women, the majority Bulgarian ethnic and Christian women in the caring professions – teachers, nurses, doctors, social workers, paid agitators, and so-called cultural workers (artists, writers, journalists) – whose professional activities involved penetrating Muslim families and communities, reaching the women there, and instilling in them modern and socialist ideals of work, domesticity, child rearing, beauty, and useful labour. State authorities and leading Marxist ideologues perceived the Bulgarian ethnic teachers and health workers involved in these reforming programs as state "agents" and "Christians [who] behave freely and in a friendly manner with the Muslims and influence them positively."[28] Therefore, health professionals encountering Muslim women in hospitals, maternity wards, paediatric clinics, and kindergartens abided by a work code tasking them with teaching and enforcing modern and European techniques of hygiene, child care, and nutrition. Women creative workers, including musicians, singers, artists, and writers, organized cultural campaigns and artistic events where Muslim women and children were introduced to Bulgarian folk music, dance, and traditions as

Fig. 8 A Bulgarian female teacher and her Muslim students in 1936. Thousands of ethnic Bulgarian women were trained as teachers carrying out modernizing missions among rural Muslim communities before and during state socialism (1944–89). lostbulgaria.com.

well as European classical art. Female teachers in small Muslim villages and towns taught Eurocentric sciences in the Bulgarian language and ushered in socialist morals, aesthetics, and values. Teachers' work further involved organizing and leading Muslim girls' visits to museums, cinemas, Sofia, and other large towns exposing Muslim female students to modern urban life.[29] Many of these caring feminized workers formed personal friendships with Muslim women, recruiting them for participation in public initiatives showcasing Muslims' increased literacy and progress under socialism.

Women's organizations commenced and controlled by the state and the Bulgarian Communist Party played a leading role in the campaigns, especially in the earlier years of the socialist regime. Nazarska's (2013) important research in the area revealed that, in the 1950s, the force of overwhelmingly Bulgarian female activists attempted to recruit Muslim women to the state and communist women's organizations established across the Rhodope region.[30] Some Muslim women joined meetings and cultural and literacy events organized by these organizations; however, the feminized arms of the communist party, the so-called National Front, did not attract much support from the Muslim communities. Socialist authorities responded to this lack of local interest by devising another technique for reforming Muslim communities: training Muslim women in modern domestic work, thus improving their skills in keeping personal hygiene, sewing, cooking, and child rearing was used as a way to penetrate the communities. The approach worked: imams, husbands, brothers, fathers and male community leaders did not object to efficient and improved feminized domestic labour. Gradually, the Bulgarian female instructors facilitating these programs focused on domesticity introduced in their curriculum ideological and political ideas explaining to Muslim women the meaning of socialism, Marxism, equality of men and women, and the merits of employment in the public economy.

These educational and propaganda activities managed to recruit a contingent of Muslim women loyal to the state, albeit a small one.[31] Their membership in the Bulgarian Communist Party and related political organizations provided state authorities with visible examples of transformed and emancipated Muslim females whose proximity to the echelons of power further gestured to privileges attached to such loyalty and aligning, including increased travel and mobility, social respect, employment in a managerial or leadership role, and improved lifestyle for the woman and her family.[32] In the 1970s, the state also demanded that Muslims change their personal names for Bulgarian and Christian names. Muslim women who were trained as schoolteachers, health and social workers, and manual labourers who refused to abide were fired or denied access to employment altogether. Those who refused to unveil or dress in skirts, knee-length dresses, and other proper modern attire could not work in the public economy; some women were forced into labour camps and imprisoned.[33]

For example, in 1974, the Nurse School established in Southern Bulgaria graduated its first cohort of Bulgarian-speaking Muslim nurses, who were asked to adopt Bulgarian names as a condition for their professional realization. A Muslim woman remembers, "One morning when I was at work, Yurukov, the party official of the hospital came to me; he had some document in his hand. 'Can you sign it?' he asked. I read the document and saw that it was related to the changing of names. 'You either agree to sign or you are fired!' It was really difficult for me. What decision was I supposed to make? I looked at the document and signed it."[34] Muslim women and men trained as teachers also had to change their names because their training was predicated on the ideological purpose of reforming and modernizing Muslim communities from within. A teacher remembers, "As usual, it all started with the teachers. They called us. It was 15/09/1971. They said we had to change our names. Those who refused were immediately sacked, as they were no longer considered qualified. I was one of them. It was really humiliating, they called us traitors who served foreign countries (Turkey), etc."[35]

Muslim women's access to education, professional training, and practice thus hinged upon their cultural death: the demise of their historical spiritual, linguistic, and cultural traditions and identities symbolized by their personal names was the condition for their personal, material, and social prosperity.[36] Archival records illustrated the mindset of the feminized workforce involved in these population-governing schemes. Eucators who are ethnic Bulgarians and Christians and communist activists facilitating and directing the vocational and academic programs targeting Muslim girls and women talked about their work as "a mission" rewarding them with professional prosperity, social prestige, and a sense of historical agency and importance. For example, Nadejda Marinova, an ethnic Bulgarian woman and former schoolteacher who worked among the Muslim communities of the Rhodope region for forty-four years articulated such self-fulfilment vividly. In 2011, Marinova penned a newspaper article that described her arrival in the city of Kardzali – the cultural and political centre of the Rhodope region – on her way to the small Muslim villages where she and a cohort of young teachers had been posted to work by the socialist state authorities:

> I will never forget the reception at the train station in Kardzali. I still remember the music playing and children rushing towards us with flowers. I can't forget the words of the adults: "Welcome, dear teachers! We are glad you came because we are implementing Bulgarian-language-based education and we need you. The Rhodope children are waiting for you. Good luck![37]

Marinova felt confused and lost on the first day of school. The Muslim children in the classroom did not speak a word of Bulgarian, but the innocence of their faces, the braids under the headscarves, and the long dresses covering the tiny bodies of the girls moved the young teacher. Her self-professed love for the children and dedication to their enlightenment carried her through hard times and good times, serving as an example for other teachers coming to work in the region. Yet Marinova's memories of successful and deeply satisfying professional work gloss over important ideological aspects of the paid worked she and other ethnic Bulgarian women performed on behalf of the socialist state.

Local archives and Muslim women's oral histories recounting state and social violence serve as an important counternarrative to public memories celebrating socialist emancipation and modernization of these women, without taking responsibility for the violence. The archives remind us further that nurturing socialist and Marxist society and consciousness involves violence against groups of women performed by other women as paid work, and at places of work. This gendered technology of state power led to Muslim women's linguistic, cultural, and spiritual demise and assimilation into a Eurocentric Christian socialist modernity whose completeness, expansion, and longevity depended upon social and cultural homogeneity achieved through the work of women. Socialist modernity further relied on women's work for absorbing and silencing racialized and religious prejudices in the country by using the case of reformed Muslim Roma and Turks as a proof for its overarching ideological thesis that all races were capable of culture and civilization given the proper material and social conditions. This kind of socialist anti-racism involving women and their work, however, embodied gendered violence that needs to be considered when analysing both socialist and capitalist realities.

Indeed, Muslim women tend to remember state socialism fostering material prosperity and emancipation as well as personal and state violence.[38] These seemingly contradictory memories capture a central feature of the socialist political economy where minority women experienced social and material uplifting but for many women the price was both state and domestic violence. Angry and abusive husbands and fathers from all ethnic groups in the country often resisted women's and girls' education and work outside the home. The socialist state did not collect or publish information on the scope of gender and domestic violence under socialism. Yet Muslim women's oral histories are underlined by memories of physical, emotional, and epistemological abuse at the home suggesting that Muslim women's access to education, professions, and jobs did not necessarily translate into their equality to men or other women.[39] Rather, the socialist state extended pre-existing patriarchal structures, effectively resubordinating Muslim women while supporting their personal and family's material uplifting. Women's education and waged work in addition to domestic work increased households' income, allowing families to build houses and buy land, automobiles, and agricultural plots. Yet the male heads of these families remained primary decision makers exercising authority over the women's public life and income. Socialist state campaigns pushing Muslim women into the public economy also pushed these workers into feminized and caring professions and occupations such as nurses, teachers, seamstresses, and cooks. The socialist state did not encourage Muslim women to enter prestigious professions reserved for men or take jobs involving decision making in state administration or politics. Rather, Muslim girls and women were groomed for jobs that allowed them to serve in their own communities and modernize these communities from within.

Muslim women's education and professionalization under socialism promoted women's literacy and education in the Bulgarian language and Eurocentric scientific and aesthetic values and ideas that further transformed these communities, drawing them closer to socialist modernity defined by cultural and social homogeneity, perceived as a condition for equality. Important contemporary archival research and oral histories collected by scholars from this community also analyse postsocialist subordination, veiling and forced domesticity of Muslim women in Bulgaria not as a disruption countering the effects of socialist state policies targeting Muslim women but because of these policies. These studies show that Muslim women in Bulgaria were never allowed to make their own choices and decide what to work, how to dress, where to live, or what to study; men and patriarchal socialist and later capitalist states have asserted their power in making decisions and choices for these women. This exemplifies the hegemony of patriarchal governmentality operating in the domestic and public realms both nationally and internationally. The undressing, unveiling, educating, and reforming of Muslim women through work and employment also empowered socialist state propaganda pointing to the education and employment of Muslim women outside their communities as socialism's victory over imperialist, capitalist, and Muslim states during the Cold War.[40]

Neither the ethnic Bulgarian women serving as reformers nor the Muslim women targeted by the reforms could openly refuse or avoid participation in these emancipating schemes because the socialist state controlled the public economy entirely. There were no jobs or employment outside of the state economy, and a woman's wages and placement in the economy depended on the state. The socialist state controlled the professional training and education of women, the work available to them, how women would perform that work, and the material and symbolic rewards distributed among women for work done. The state also attempted to control women's morality and behaviour, how they managed their time to perform efficiently both their domestic and public work, and the ways in which they raised their children. The degree of state control over women's lives in fact positioned the socialist state as a greater and untouchable patriarch whose rule over women and their work determined women's freedoms, choices, and equality under socialism. Despite the totality of socialist state governmentality, women resisted the roles and purposes assigned to them by the state. Muslim women in rural towns and small villages in socialist Bulgaria expressed their resistance to policies stripping them of their traditional clothing by adopting a mixed style incorporating pants associated with socialist workmen and women, but these garments were in bright colours, mismatching the crude blue working shirts worn by some women.[41] This aesthetic resisted socialist standards of Europeanized beauty; it also gestured to the possibility of change or modernization in ways chosen by the women themselves. The next section observes other forms of resistance enacted by two women also caught up in the gendered and sexualized local and international politics of the Cold War.

"Life under Men": Sex Work in the Socialist State

In the late nineteenth and early twentieth centuries when Bulgaria was building itself as an independent nation, prostitution was viewed as a social evil and moral degradation totally alien to traditional Bulgarian norms and customs.[42] Women engaged in the trade often came from foreign countries, which reinforced public beliefs about the un-Bulgarian nature of prostitution. The first official survey of prostitution in Bulgaria from 1895, for instance, showed that 447 women were registered as prostitutes in the country; 55 per cent of them came from other countries: Croatia, Germany, Greece, France, Italy, and Turkey.[43] State authorities viewed prostitution as a private matter, hence the state tolerated sex work but kept sex workers hidden. In the 1930s, state and city authorities took a more active approach to prostitution, which was linked to the spread of venereal diseases such as syphilis, especially in urban areas and the Bulgarian seaports where tradesmen, seamen, tourists, and locals used the services of prostitutes. As a result, prostitution became a state concern for public health leading to new legislation taking cues from liberal European moral and judicial frames subjecting prostitution to regulation by medical and health professionals and the police. Under socialism, the state approach to the phenomenon was informed by Marx's and Engels' notions of prostitution as caused by women's subordination and poverty, class inequality, and gender relations based on capitalist material production: sex for sale presented a commodity exchange that was not to be tolerated in the socialist society.

Importantly, socialist representational regimes of sex, women, and prostitution did not relate sexuality to work (i.e., sex work); rather, socialist discourses constructed women's sexuality and prostitution as related phenomena understood through ideological and moral paradigms. Sex work in socialist Bulgaria was perceived as a deviation from proper socialist morals, yet a prostitute was also a social parasite who engaged in work enriching herself rather than the society or the socialist project. A prostitute thus stood as the antidote of the proper socialist female subject depicted as a mother, a tool for socially useful labour and a public figure responsible for bearing proper socialist citizens building communism.[44] The Bulgarian socialist state utilized fully its repressive apparatus, the people's militia, to uproot prostitution, which had no place in a socialist society. Women engaged in sex work were sent to reforming camps where productive labour was supposed to instil in them a new kind of consciousness and socialist values. Simultaneously, the reforming institutions instilled fear among all women in the country, deterring sexual and moral deviance of any kind. These repressive measures were accompanied by socialist state campaigns that provided shelter as well as access to employment and education for those women who wanted to exit the sex trade.

In 1978, the Bulgarian writer and dissident Georgi Markov, who was killed in London after he fled the country, witnessed at first hand the socialist approach to prostitution. Markov penned a sharp-toned essay capturing the totality of socialist state heteronormative patriarchy. One evening, Markov and two other male writers found themselves in the police station at the heart of Sofia. They had responded to a state call to observe and write novels, stories, notes, and journalistic material to help the state in the fight against delinquency and prostitution. The head of the division dedicated to anti-social behaviour told the writers that about three hundred girls who were sex workers were listed in their roster. That night, Markov and the other writers met some of the girls in person. One of them angrily rejected the "help" offered to her by the state: "Go help your daughters! It is not much help forcing me out of the city or sending me to work in ... the mine," she yelled, refusing to be paraded in front of male writers on a field trip collecting notes about prostitution.[45]

A few years later, in another Bulgarian city, the journalist Todorka Nikolova also responded to the state call for reforming immoral subjects and producing writing deterring deviant anti-socialist behavior. Nikolova was a respected journalist trained in the Soviet Union and a valued member of the local branch of the Bulgarian Communist Party. One morning, Nikolova was walking to the offices of the local newspaper for which she worked when she saw a beautiful young woman sitting on a bench, her face bleeding.[46] The woman introduced herself as "Peppie Nedyalkova," a well-known local sex worker nicknamed

"Peppie the Hundred" because of the high cost of her services, which started at one hundred in any currency. Nikolova felt compelled to help the young woman leave the life of prostitution behind, hence she invited Peppie for a series of recorded conversations published as a memoir entitled *Life under Men: The Revelations of a Prostitute* (1992). The memoir reflected how both women negotiated state socialism and resisted its patriarchal order and morals.

Peppie was born in a small village in Southern Bulgaria. She described her father as a cold and violent man who abused both Peppie and her mother. At the age of sixteen, Peppie met a dashing young man who worked for the Komsomol, the youth organization attached to the Bulgarian Communist Party. It was that political and male privilege that involved the young girl in a sexual relationship with the young communist, who got her pregnant.[47] Peppie's narrative illuminated the physical, psychological, and emotional pain of the beatings she suffered in the hands of both her father and her lover upon the news of her pregnancy. Through sex work, Peppie felt she had taken power over her life and body, promising herself to never depend on men. Her professionalism as a sex worker was guided by the principles of "honest work" that defied both the morality and collectivism of socialism.[48]

Peppie considered prostitution a line of work similar to any other trade or professional occupation. Sex work, in her view, required skills such as understanding how to give and get sexual pleasure, practising safe sex, providing customer service, financial literacy, and good relations with neighbours, the people's militia, and state authorities. Hence, Peppie took very good care of her body and health, wore expensive underwear, studied foreign languages, and kept a log of her encounters and the payments she received. In sex work, she also found genuine emancipation in the form of the independence she believed was impossible in the socialist economy and job market. Wages and public employment subjected her to state and public control and determined her wages regardless of her talent or contributions. Having a "decent" or regular job would not save her from the patriarchal system of sexual favours that many women were asked to provide as the cost for getting a job, gaining access to a particular service, passing a university course, or claiming a benefit. In sex work, Peppie experienced freedom to choose where, when, how, and with whom to work, the cost of her services, and above all when to stop and retire. She also controlled her finances fully by operating outside formal patriarchal institutions such as heteronormative and patriarchal marriage and domesticity and the state-controlled banks. Peppie thus practised sex work as a form of resistance to socialism as both ideological and economic formation. Amid a planned socialist economy where the means of production were owned and controlled by the state on behalf of the people, Peppie practised commodity exchange typical of capitalist economies. She further defied socialist notions of womanhood that she experienced as domestic and state violence and male control. She believed that her sexual encounters and exchanges with men constituted moments where she exerted her own power and agency. These perceptions and experiences crystalized vividly in the young woman's stories about the local and international clients she met over the years.

Peppie worked alongside the international highways criss-crossing socialist Bulgaria, encountering clients especially in the trucking industry from various races, religions, and nationalities. "I love these adventures with foreigners a lot," explained Peppie, "I am learning a foreign language while filling my pocket with money"[49] Her understanding and hierarchy of men and the socialist and capitalist societies and cultures that made them was based on these encounters, specifically her clients' violence or tenderness, sexual prowess, fair and honest payment for services as agreed, and personal hygiene. In Peppie's narrative, men who could not "perform" but paid a prostitute in the hope of gratification irritated her the most. Men's sexual impotence or weakness in Peppie's bed signified for her a broader condition: men's entitlement and social, political, and economic domination was neither earned nor deserved but a performance of actual inner weakness and sexual and emotional impotence. She was very sensitive to clients from the West who wanted to try a Bulgarian girl like herself. She sensed their condescending attitude, for which Peppie would punish them with sex to spin their head off but also a steep price for the demonstration. She was kinder to Russians; they were "brothers" in socialism, so Peppie often gave Russian men a free ride and even formed a friendship with one of them. Her work was thus political, international, and deeply shaped by the Cold War. Her descriptions, comparisons, and reminiscences of Arab, Black, German, Bulgarian, Serbian, Austrian, Russian, Turkish, Greek, and Roma men reflected common public racial and ethnic perceptions about others and their place and meaning in the historical and geopolitical order of the Cold War. But Peppie's views also defied ingrained Bulgarian prejudice against Muslims and Roma in and outside Bulgaria. In her work, Peppie did not discriminate against such clients; in fact, she praised their humanity, kindness, honesty, and passion for life (and women).

By the 1980s, the winds of Soviet perestroika brought increased presence of domestic and foreign tourists and visitors to Bulgaria, transforming female sex work into a state-supported intelligence-gathering network using young and beautiful women to collect information on persons of state interest.[50] The Bulgarian sea and mountain resorts hosted the operations of hundreds of women sex workers who cooperated with state authorities in order to practise their trade. The socialist state used these young women and their bodies to collect information on corruption, political loyalties, trade secrets, and diplomatic relations among men in the highest echelons of local and international power. Young and beautiful Bulgarian girls accompanied communist leaders and statesmen at meetings and parties and while travelling. They also escorted and provided sexual services for Western and Eastern diplomats, bankers, traders, and military personnel. Throughout her international activities, Peppie also met Black men who were foreign students and visitors from African countries.[51] Her memoir documented the violence of these Black male anti-colonial activists who received Marxist and militarized training in socialist Bulgaria. Peppie Nedyalkova thus got to know socialism and capitalism through the men and modes of gender and sexual violence they produced. Narrating encounters with often confused, morally ambiguous, and violent men, her memoir stands as a testimony to the pervasive nature of patriarchal inequality and male violence in both socialist and capitalist cultures and societies.

For Todorka Nikolova, the writer and journalist who recorded Peppie's story, life as a sex worker opened an international and comparative avenue for perceiving both socialism and capitalism. Nikolova wholeheartedly responded to state and communist party calls to help the fight against anti-social behaviour and moral decay in the socialist society. She really wanted to save Peppie from the "evil men" and sexual predators exploiting her.[52] Yet the encounter changed Nikolova, who realized through Peppie's story the profound immorality and violence of socialist and capitalist patriarchies. As a result, Nikolova surrendered her membership in the Bulgarian Communist Party. She also surrendered her marriage to a man who kept her in a difficult relationship she described as a "cat and dog fight."[53] By breaking these unions to a man and political party, Nikolova felt liberated, appreciating further Peppie's struggle to control her own body, work, and life path.

The two women also became lifelong friends. Peppie left Bulgaria and settled in Greece, where she opened a restaurant with the money she earned as a sex worker. She married an older Greek man to reduce the chance of domestic and sexual violence and gave birth to two children. Nikolova continues to practise journalism dedicated to helping sex workers and girls and women who are victims of sex trafficking in the Balkans. *Life under Men*, the book she wrote, documented not just the life of prostitution under state socialism but women's ontologies of work and violence beyond a particular ideology and time. For other women, negotiating socialism and womanhood took a different form.

Increasing Women's Productivity in the Home and Factory

Varvara Kirilova was an educated woman entrusted by socialist state authorities with the education and uplifting of working-class women in the country. As the editor of the woman's magazine *Lada*, Kirilova had authored numerous columns providing tips for efficient household care. In 1982, Kirilova took the role of facilitator leading state-sponsored workshops aiming to teach women how to modernize and better balance their domestic and public work. The archived minutes from one of the workshops illustrated how a class of privileged socialist women attached to the state constructed a paradigm for understanding "woman's work" as the cost for female happiness under socialist conditions. In her lecture, Kirilova brought ideas of time management, organization of socialist production, and modernization and mechanization to the domestic realm, advocating for embrace of these principles as a coping mechanism for women's work overload.[54] She perceived the burden of work under socialist state conditions as a prerequisite for the good society. Yet women could learn to manage the burden by changing the culture. Kirilova proposed that women learned to manipulate patriarchal norms to allure sons and husbands into sharing domestic chores by using home appliances such as advanced vacuum cleaners and electric food mixers, which they would find amusing and interesting.[55] But she also proposed letting go of Bulgarian cultural traditions and customs expecting women to greet guests with elaborate meals or keep the house clean while maintaining a nice hairdo. Instead, she called upon the women gathered at the seminar room to feed the guests with semi-processed foods that were becoming available, use frozen ingredients to shorten the time of meal preparation, accept that their carpets do not need cleaning every day, and buy all the modern appliances that save time.[56] Socialist women should learn to use household technologies rather than follow their mothers' and grandmothers' examples of reaching for the broom when there was an electric vacuum cleaner in the house, she lectured.

For Varvara Kirilova, an ideologically and ethnically privileged woman, the domestic work performed by women in the socialist state constituted the cost a woman pays for her true happiness and emancipation. A woman's happiness, she explained, was in having children, a

Fig. 9 Female workers in the tobacco factory "Vasil Topalski" in the city of Pleven in the 1970s. Over a million women from rural Bulgaria left their home villages and towns to work in the industrial factories build by the socialist state in the 1950s and 1960s. lostbulgaria.com.

husband, and a beautiful home. And to be truly happy and fulfilled, a woman had to take good care of her children and keep the home clean. Women in the audience assembled for the seminar, however, had other concerns that challenged Kirilova's paradigm of female happiness. Some of the women in the audience complained about their low wages; others wanted to talk about the high cost of a proper wedding for their grown-up children, their lack of sleep, or the quality of food in the public and factory canteens. Kirolva silenced these narratives, calling on the assembled women to stop complaining and take responsibility for how they manage their time and household income, teach their children good and proper manners and habits, and balance domestic and public work.[57] In sum, Kirilova suggested that the problem of women's overwork yet insufficient supports and income was not a problem of state and social structures but an issue of a working woman's individual culture and lack of proper skills.

Yet not all women in the socialist state were willing to pay that cost for happiness. Women who chose not to have a husband and children or keep the kind of "beautiful home" described by Kirilova constituted kinds of womanhood that were bashed and rejected by other women, socialist mass culture, and the state. In 1984, another seminar organized by the state-sponsored Movement of Bulgarian Women and the Fatherland Front in Sofia identified these genres of women as a serious issue inhibiting the future of both the Bulgarian nation and socialism. The seminar's facilitator introduced state-collected data showing that the increased women's access to higher education had led to many educated women choosing not to marry and bear children, leading to a serious decrease in fertility and the rate of population growth.[58] The seminar also addressed the growing lack of stability in married couples due to access to abortions, prompting decisions against having children and lack of trust in the marriage partner. The growing number of women choosing to have a child out of wedlock was also attributed to improper education within the family and mothers not teaching girls to protect themselves from an unwanted pregnancy. Equally important, according to the seminar's facilitator, was the lack of consciousness and ideological education of youth in the family, leading to the spread of bourgeois values and capitalist propaganda among youth. Young people had not paid for socialism with their blood, so young women and also men lacked commitment. Yordanka Topolova, the speaker leading the seminar, was the deputy chair of the Bulgarian Women's Movement. She ended the event with a vivid example illustrating the kind of educated woman who was endangering socialism:

> I want to give you an example. I had the chance to speak to a gathering in the Pleven-city area, giving the same lecture ... A woman in the audience got up and said: "On March 8 [International Women's Day] this year, I was very upset. My son is serving in the army and for March 8 he sent home two telegrams. The one for his grandmother read: 'Dear grannie, happy holiday, be healthy and continue to warmly welcome me as I come and go.' The other telegram for me said: 'Dear mom, happy holidays, wishing you new achievements in your work ...' I was stunned and felt sad because [my son] sees me as a woman-worker striving for success ... The motherly warmth he thinks comes from his grandmother who stays at

home ... What did I do wrong ...? Maybe, when the child was in the age of puberty, I was writing my dissertation at the time, and somehow I put distance between us.[59]

Topolova's example of an educated and independent woman, who was also a failed mother and social subject seemingly out of control, illuminated the paradoxes of socialist state-led women's emancipation. Uprooting Muslim and non-Muslim women from the small villages and pushing them into feminized professions and the public economy created cohorts of "unfit mothers" unable to keep balanced and well-managed households and families. These women in turn endangered the well-being of the socialist nation in need of properly raised male workers with collectivist consciousnesses as well as soldiers ready to protect and die for it. In the 1950s and 1960s, socialist state authorities welcomed women into educational and employment programs; by the mid-1980s, the same state authorities subsidized extensive measures to bring working women back in line with patriarchal state ideology valuing heterosexual families where mothers and fathers played traditional roles and raised more children. What remained a constant was the class of women working for state organizations and offices who carried out lecturing, propaganda, and reform campaigns among the rest of the female population on behalf of the state. Yet these ideologically, socially, and culturally privileged women – women who enjoyed better jobs, greater mobility, and access to services because, in the eyes of the state, they embodied Christian and European socialist modernity – had become the primary source of postsocialist historiography of women, work, and emancipation in Bulgaria. However, viewed from within the historically racialized, ethnicized, sexed, and classed standpoints of different women, state-led women's emancipation was both incomplete and violent.

My reading of the role of ethnically privileged Bulgarian and Christian women enacting violent reforming and modernizing schemes targeting Muslim or Roma women, sex workers, factory workers, and other genres of devalued feminized types is countered by alternative interpretations demanding attention. For example, a study of women in leadership positions in state-supported institutions in Bulgaria considers these women a feminist socialist vanguard of women who played a key role in demanding more and adequate state services, protections, and policies that benefited all women in the country regardless of their ethnic background, religious beliefs, or sexuality.[60] Women like Varvara Kirilova and Yordanka Topolova who lectured other women pursued agendas defined by the Committee of the Bulgarian Women's

Movement attached to the Bulgarian Communist Party and the state. If their lectures presented "a revolution,"[61] that revolution reflected the aspirations of privileged women with close ties to state power.

In 1969, the women leading the organization and the editorial board of the popular women's journal *Zhenata Dnes* conducted a mass survey exploring the well-being of women in socialist Bulgaria.[62] The survey found that scarcity of material resources and lack of time due to domestic duties and full-time work in the economy informed women's decisions not have as many children as they wanted, leading to a serious decline of the national birth rate. The activists who organized the study engaged in a public campaign moving state authorities to organize and support new services and benefits supporting women. These events prompted some feminists in postsocialist Bulgaria and the United States to praise "state feminism" led by privileged and influential women married to communist leaders, or appointed to their positions by the Communist Party for being "successful at representing Bulgarian women's interests" and extracting resources from reluctant patriarchial and predominantly male state authorities that improved the lives of women.[63] These praises assumed that the interests of ethnic Bulgarian women or those attached to the state represented the interests of all women in the country. They also presumed that the mass survey led by socialist femocrats reached minority women in the rural areas, Muslim villages, Roma ghettos, or the resorts, highways, and state-owned luxury villas frequented by the thousands of female sex workers pleasuring international travellers or Marxist and socialist bureaucrats.

These women's experiences of work and the economy suggest that their needs might have been very different from those of the female editors and readers of the colourful journal *Zhenata Dnes*, where state feminists expressed their views and aspirations. Peppie Nedyalkova's memoir suggested that she needed protection from sexual violence and non-judgmental health care and social services so she could practise her trade. Peppie's greatest need was for social recognition of her humanity and her desire to choose for herself: "I am human, a woman, and want respect. At least by those who don't know yet that I am a prostitute," she stated.[64] Many Muslim women appreciated the access to education, professional skills, and employment they received under socialism, yet these gains did not stop the domestic violence they experienced or the anti-Muslim campaigns that robbed them of their identity, culture, and sense of self. To the contrary, the Bulgarian Women's Movement and the Committee of Bulgarian Women spearheaded educational and reforming programs leading to that loss.[65] And for those of us who worked on the floors of socialist plants and factories without choosing that line of work, the greatest need was for equity so that we were not pushed into vocational schooling programs because we were "ordinary" while opening the doors of universities, language training schools, and professional placement for those girls and women whose fathers, brothers, uncles, and husbands presided over the socialist state. Yet state-aligned feminists in leadership positions who campaigned for more supports for wives and mothers did not address the needs that underlined the lives of Muslim women, Roma women, factory workers, or the prostitutes exploited by the socialist state. Their demand for differently designed apartments, more disposable diapers, or pubs in apartment complexes where men could socialize but also watch over the children expressed an elitist and privileged feminist point of view and the needs of a class of women who equated socialist feminism with childbearing, heterosexual marriage, prosperous materiality, deeply satisfying and well-paid jobs appropriate for a woman, and Christian and European notions of beauty, womanhood, and freedom. Women and their work in socialist Bulgaria were not equal and equally valued, and that history demands historiographies that recognize how and why we worked, lived, and loved under socialism differently.

Women's Work, Emancipation, and Political Economy

Socialist state-led women's emancipation was not and could not be historically, racially, or morally impartial. Socialist state schemes for women's liberation active in Bulgaria took shape within local and global racial, ethnic, political, and economic formations, and therefore women gained access to education, professions, and employment under racialized and hegemonic terms set by local and transnational regimes of knowledge and power. The historically racialized, ethnicized and patriarchal aspects of the socialist state determining when, what, where, how, and if groups of women get to work is a reminder that state political ideologies and needs always shape the public economy and that historically devalued women experience even socialist economies as sites and processes of state and personal violence. Like the socialist state, a liberal democratic state with a socialist economy in a Western setting that some contemporary feminists envision is unlikely to shake off its racial, ethnic, and class lenses and lead women's emancipation embracing Black and white women, immigrant and refugee women, Indigenous, Muslim, Roma, poor and rural women, or those who profess ideological passions not shared by the state. Such visions of state-led gender emancipation through the economy extend Western feminist gazes and epistemologies that celebrate state socialisms in Eastern Europe, the Balkans, and the former Soviet Union as materiality emptied of the real women who lived it. The experiences of these women instruct a feminist paradigm that rejects the economy as a primary location of women's emancipation and equality.

Scores of Western feminists and activists have embraced the idea that greater access to education and jobs provide women with social mobility and material independence from men, which in turn allows them to live lives free of domestic and sexual violence. Hence, national and international programs targeting violence against women have operated under the belief that by educating poor girls in postcolonial Africa, providing employment opportunities for Indigenous women in North America, or absorbing Roma women in the employment markets of former socialist countries in the European Union would position these women for material prosperity and domestic and public life free of class, racial, and sexual violence. Indeed, education might allow these women to get desired jobs and enter professions historically reserved for men. Wages might further make minority and racialized women materially independent and free to make choices regarding domestic arrangements, marital and sexual partners, and childbearing. The history of socialist state-led emancipation of women, however, reminds us that educated and working women might be less likely to experience violence in the home, yet they might encounter equally damaging state and patriarchal violence within the public economy and the workplace, reaffirming their subordinate place and leading to their cultural death.

Chapter Four

Second and Third World Women: Socialist State Feminisms and Internationalisms

The concept of "state feminism" refers to women activists' and women-based movements' ability to move the state to support policies focused on women and gender equality. In former socialist countries in Eastern and Central Europe and the Balkans, state feminism also describes the activism of women attached to the state, the Communist Party, or men in position of power with connections to the state. In this chapter, I read two archives documenting the international engagements and relations of state feminists in socialist Bulgaria in the period between the 1960s and 1980s. The first archive consists of political projects, articles, images, and notes produced and curated by a group of women presiding over the popular and influential journal *Zhenata Dnes*. The journal was the official publication of the Committee of the Bulgarian Women's Movement, a state-sanctioned organization whose female leaders had close ties to the government. Between the 1960s and 1980s, the magazine published a great volume of articles narrating and depicting women's lives in countries worldwide, creating an extensive archive documenting international connections, activities, networking, and relations between socialist state feminists and women in Africa, Asia, and North and South America. The second archive consists of the writing and life experiences of Lydmila Zhivkova, the most prominent woman in socialist Bulgaria who was the daughter of Todor Zhivkov, the Bulgarian head of state for three decades. Serving as the Minister of Culture, Zhivkova initiated major changes in cultural production and mass education before her untimely death in 1981 under a cloud of suspicion that she might have been killed for her revisionist views and politics. Zhivkova had formed a strong relationship with India's prime minister Indira Gandhi, who, like Zhivkova, followed in the footsteps of her father's political career. Zhivkova left behind an important body of written work documenting her doubts about Sovietism and Marxism as well as ideas about socialist humanism and the relationship between materiality and culture that linked Zhivkova closely to the international revisionist movement emerging in the 1960s called the New Left.

I am not the first one to read these archives. Bulgarian and foreign researchers have analysed state feminism and women's internationalism in socialist states extensively, highlighting especially how these forms of women-based activism extended state agendas yet produced real material and symbolic gains for women under socialism.[1] But the popularity of these archives is also an outcome of unequal relations of power between women. These collections have preserved the voices and world views of the women whom the socialist state and the ideologues who governed it valued the most. We lack archival sources preserving and revealing how minority women, women factory workers, or those deviating from socialist moral and political norms understood the world, enacted forms of feminism, and related to other women internationally. For example, in 2015, by sheer chance I stumbled upon the story of Melina Andreeeva, a Muslim woman in socialist Bulgaria who spearheaded the campaign supporting African American feminist Angela Davis, leading to Davis's visit in the country in 1972.[2] I relied exclusively on a personal interview with Andreeva in 2017 to explore that feminist encounter because I could not find any archival data related to Muslim women's internationalism and feminism under socialism. Yet Andreeva's story was very important because it challenged claims that feminism hardly, if ever, existed in socialist states such as Bulgaria – a claim advanced by intellectuals who view "feminism" as a singular political or discursive form embodied by feminisms enacted in the West. This chapter challenges that claim further by utilizing an autoethnographic approach to read state feminisms and state archives in socialist Bulgaria. Through the autoethnography, I claim the self as a form of a feminist archive from within which to interpret women's identities, international relations, and activism under socialism. Specifically, I read these archives in the space between a woman and a socialist nation, where a myriad of discursive and ideological constructions and relations of power constitute imagined communities of women whose perceived racial, ethnic, religious, and sexual differences provide the international and local contextuality of women's relations and sense of self.[3] My reading of that contextuality focuses especially on the roles that race, culture, and ideology played in international state feminisms in socialist Bulgaria during the period under consideration. I want to suggest that socialist state women's internationalism and feminism left behind a mixed yet important legacy: state feminists readily and wholeheartedly embraced the plight of Black, Brown, Asian, Muslim, Hindu,

Christian, and postcolonial women in the global South but showed no consideration for the struggles of minority women and racialized bodies domestically. A similar disconnect between local and global feminist activism continues to shape postsocialist feminist internationalism in Bulgaria today, where women's activism reaches globally without taking responsibility for the plight of racialized and marginalized women domestically. Despite these limitations, state feminists in socialist Bulgaria forged connections to other women the world over. Studying that legacy is to encounter a rich reservoir of wisdom about the empowering aspects yet pitfalls of international feminism that fails to see how race, class, geopolitics, culture, religion, and power have shaped our relationships with others who are different and unequal.

Zhenata Dnes: Between a Woman, Race, and the Socialist Nation

The state-supported women's magazine *Zhenata Dnes* was the only publication of this kind in socialist Bulgaria. Published by the Committee of Bulgarian Women and attracting nearly two million readers, the magazine offered travelogues and information depicting the lives, struggles, and cultures of women in countries around the world. These stories played an important role in shaping the perceptions of its millions of female readers, the majority of whom could not travel abroad and see the world for themselves. Travel abroad in socialist Bulgaria was restricted and a privilege reserved for the men and women closest to the state and the Communist Party. For the rest of us, internationally minded publications such as *Zhenata Dnes* presented important sources of knowledge about foreign lands and peoples. Between the 1960s and 1980s, the magazine featured local and foreign women, some depicted in their homes and communities, others in their public roles as leaders, artists, educators, or mothers engaged in feminist, anti-war, and world-peace activism. The journal also featured women from various countries who visited Bulgaria as guests invited by the Committee of Bulgarian Women and othr state organizations. At the other end of the magazine's representational spectrum were stories about women in poverty, in misery, and under oppression; these women were overwhelmingly located in Africa, Asia, and, occasionally, the Middle East. Together, the narratives revolved around metaphors of "women victims," "women struggling," and "women prospering," which served to re-establish and reinforce symbolic and material international borders enclosing the socialist nation.

The socialist nation state, like all other modern creations of this kind, was defined by multiple borders, sometimes in contradiction, other times in alignment. A physical territorial border marked the spatial parameters of the Bulgarian socialist state and defined insiders and outsiders to the nation. Internal boundaries separating or aligning different groups signified by their degree of assimilation into gendered and racialized socialist modernity were positioned adversely or favourably to the political centre embodied by state institutions and public bodies. A third transnational ideological border divided the world into socialist and capitalist camps and drew a militarized ideological wall between these formations. Socialist state feminists editing the influential women's magazine *Zhenata Dnes* actively reified these borders by enacting gendered metaphors instructive of who stood inside and outside the socialist nation state. The metaphors of suffering and victimized women supported the normalization of state socialism as a superior social order by depicting women in Africa, Asia, and North and South America as victims or poverty, colonialism, male violence, corrupted politics, cultural barbarity, and capitalism. These metaphors, marking the "outside" of the nation, had enormous symbolic and political value domestically because against the images of suffering and struggling women abroad, *all women* within the socialist nation appeared as prospering subjects enjoying freedom and material and social safety. In turn, ordinary women's resistance or rebelling against socialism was kept at bay. Stories about women political activists disappearing in Chile, mutilated women in Africa, burned or stoned women in India, or struggling Black women in the United States created among the magazine's female readers a sense that although we were not in an ideal situation, we were much better off than those millions of women in other countries and we should be grateful for it. The depictions also created a sense of self. The magazine's constant comparisons between prospering domestic socialism and the oppression of women abroad further erased the struggles of women domestically. The editors and contributors wrote passionately and emphatically about the inequality of and violence against women abroad but remained silent on issues of repression and force experienced by Muslim and Roma women, sex workers, unmarried women, lesbians, or divorcées in socialist Bulgaria. Socialist feminist internationalism connected women's struggles globally but not domestically, and the repetitive metaphor of suffering women in developed and developing countries in the global North and South quietly entrenched the view that both majority and minority women in socialist Bulgaria enjoyed state care and protections. Whatever issues pertaining to women remained unresolved, the magazine suggested, would be resolved by a loving fatherly state and Communist Party.

The magazine displayed these inside/outside metaphorical gestures especially vividly in 1975, the United Nations' International Women's Year. It reflected the spirit of the year by publishing stories about internationally recognized feminists like the Chilean Gladys Marin, Portugal's "professional revolutionary" Maria Margarita Tengarina, and the German-Israeli pro-Palestinian attorney Felicia Langer. Reports reflecting on the UN women's conference in Mexico and the Berlin World Congress of Women also took centre stage alongside articles featuring the lives of women in Spain, China, Vietnam, Iceland, the Federal Republic of Germany, and the United States. The magazine also featured prominent female leaders of the state-sponsored Bulgarian Women's Movement who were active on the international scene: Elena Lagadinova, Rada Todorova, Tsola Dragoicheva, and Maria Zaharieva. The magazine further highlighted the conditions of women in socialist Bulgaria by publishing a lengthy analysis of the domestic life of Bulgarian women entitled "The Contemporary Wife."[4] The report celebrated the achievements of women under socialism in industry, politics, and education, yet it drew upon a survey among women to conclude that female professional achievements in socialist Bulgaria had not displaced the traditional ideals aspired by women, mainly dedication to husband, children, and family. And that, the report proclaimed, was the real "charm of the contemporary wife."

A few pages later, another story called on women in socialist Bulgaria to take responsibility for their own equality. Praising socialism, the Communist Party, and the socialist state, the female author named qualities of "the female personality" that inhibited women's careers and their advancement to managerial and leadership positions.[5] Gossiping, small talk, and lack of steady rationality prevented women in Bulgaria from commanding the kind of social respect afforded to socialist men; so did the lack of a cultured and politically informed "female personality," as many women did not find time to go to the opera or read the newspaper. Women's strife for self-perfection, the writer concluded, was the missing component for achieving fully gender equality in the socialist state. State feminists contributing to the magazine imagined a socialist nation state that was "responsible" for women whom the magazine constructed as a mass of people defined by their biology and their relationship to work and to men. One discursive event, however, ruptured the brand of socialist feminism displayed by the magazine during the International Women's Year.

In May 1974, an eighteen-year-old Roma girl had written a passionate letter to the magazine, sharing her distress, sadness, and pain caused by the prejudice and discriminatory attitudes she faced by her peers in school and the community for being Roma.⁶ In September of the same year, the editors published excerpts from readers' letters responding to the girl, written by young women, married women, and men from all walks of life, including readers who self-identified as being of Roma and Turkish ethnic origins. The responses manifested the wide scope of the magazine's readership and its significance as a social platform at the time. More importantly, in the letters, readers condemned the attitudes and encouraged the Roma girl to keep her head high. A female reader wrote: "I am Roma too. My husband is a Bulgarian, with higher education and interests. I have never been offended by him or his parents. Thus, with time, I understood many things. I am sure you will understand too. You need patience and seriousness. Don't despair ... try to be jolly and friendly ... and have a higher goal in life."⁷ Another reader praised the industriousness of Roma youth with whom he worked and reminded the Roma girl that she "is a Gypsy in a happy country."⁸ Responses by other readers praised socialism for "equality between all nationalities" and "black and white" and attributed anti-Roma attitudes to the ignorance of the Roma girl's schoolmates and their parents.

Responses to the Roma girl's letter further displaced responsibility for the elimination of historically racialized prejudice against Roma onto the shoulders of its victims. The magazine's female editors made editorial choices suggesting that they shared that view. In January 1975, opening the UN International Women's Year, they published in its entirety a letter addressing the Roma girl penned by a prominent male essayist. The letter, they explained, served as an important "conclusion to the spontaneous discussion" about the anti-Roma attitudes in Bulgaria on the pages of the magazine. Responding to the issue with someone else's brief letter also exposed the feminist editors' own lack of commitment to sustained and purposeful public conversation about the issue. In the letter, the male essayist encouraged the Roma girl to keep her head up but to recognize as well the "negative things among [her] people" so "we can overcome those together." "The socialist society," he added, "needs nothing more than the rapid uplifting of citizens from Gypsy origin."⁹ He invited the Roma girl to find her life purpose in the cultural and moral uplifting of her people, assuring her that such dedication was "necessary and noble," dovetailing social respect with "state support." The narrative thus tasked the Roma girl with the reform and uplifting of "her people"; it also linked social acceptance and equality of Roma women and girls to their commitment to socialist modernization.

Between the 1960s and the 1980s, the publication also presented dozens of stories about struggling and oppressed women in other countries. The travelogues describing women and life in lands far and near were authored by women active in the state-sponsored women's organizations as well as women who accompanied statesmen in their official travels abroad. For example, Eugenia Kiranova's rich notes from her visit to Senegal and the African continent were generated during her state-sponsored visit attending the pan-African Congress of Women hosted in that country.[10] Kiranova depicted the hard lives of Senegalese women, their labouring from dawn to dusk, wearing heavy loads on their heads and working behind the walls of small yards and private residences. Kiranova explained that Senegalese men had multiple wives but defined Senegalese women's attitude toward polygamy as "accepting." Much like the responses to the prejudice experienced by the Roma girl, Kiranova's narrative was underpinned by a colour-blind empathy that saw Senegalese women, and African women in general, not as racialized Black, sexualized and gendered subjects of European colonial projects and local patriarchy, but as members of a homogeneous mass of "women victims" in developing countries who could be saved by socialism.

The magazine's textual depictions of women in Africa reflected the material relations between Bulgarian state feminists and Black women in the global South. The leaders of the Committee of the Bulgarian Women's Movement who published the popular magazine forged close relationships with women's committees in African countries, especially Angola and Zambia. These relations were encouraged by the Soviet authorities as well as the Bulgarian Communist Party, which provided financing and legitimacy to Bulgarian female-led programs and educational campaigns in Africa.[11] Soviet involvement in Africa during the anti-colonial struggles actually used state women's organizations and foreign military interventions as indirect methods to penetrate African countries. The Soviet Union authorized the sending of Cuban troops in Angola, for instance, and used softer feminized "troops," such as the Bulgarian women's activists, to organize women's socialist movements on the African continent.[12] Bulgarian state feminists' outreach to Black women in the global South was thus prompted by Soviet and socialist state foreign policy and a Cold War agenda focused on expanding socialism and communism globally. Not surprisingly, Elena Lagadinova, who chaired the Committee of the Bulgarian Women's Movement, viewed the Bulgarian-Zambian women's friendship and collaboration as "solidarity" rooted in Lagadinova's own belief that socialism is a superior political and economic system and that African women had much to learn and gain from their more advanced socialist sisters. The relationship between Bulgarian and Zambian women also manifested unequal power and dependency that actually defied the very notion of international women's solidarity claimed by state feminists. The inequality was especially apparent in the dependence of African anti-colonial movements and postcolonial nation-building on material support and know-how supplied by socialist states. In fact, exchanges and relations between Bulgarian women and women activists in Zambia, Senegal, Angola, Kenya, Mozambique, and other countries were underlined by African women's hope that socialist states, including Bulgaria, would aid their countries as they struggled with poverty, illiteracy, lack of organized agricultural production, and know-how in engineering, banking, mining, education, and other areas of tremendous social and economic importance. The Kenyan international activist and leader Oginga Odinga, for example, described the education of thousands of Kenyan men and women in Bulgaria, the Soviet Union, Cuba, Yugoslavia, and other socialist countries as vital support in fighting illiteracy, developing health care, constructing bridges, and building schools, which in turn helped sustain emerging democracies in Africa.[13] Interviews with Zambian women who worked with the Bulgarian state feminists back in the 1970s also confirmed the importance of Bulgarian aid in Zambian independence.[14] In all, by 1982, socialist Bulgaria had invested 1.2 billion dollars in thirty-one so called developing countries, most of the funds going to Ghana, Nigeria, Mozambique, Lesotho, Tunisia, and Zimbabwe.[15]

African Students and Vietnamese Guest Workers in Bulgaria

Amid these international state activities, state feminists producing the popular women's magazine *Zhenata Dnes* brought "Africa" and its women to the Bulgarian public consciousness in significant ways, yet they failed to translate that presence into a meaningful conversation about the role of race in African women's plight. Bulgarian state feminists failed to take responsibility for the muted racialized and Eurocentric aspects of socialist subjectivity. These feminists solidified the symbolic and material borders separating self and national territory from those racial and cultural African and Asian Others who came to work and study in the socialist state. Beginning in the middle of the 1960s, more than seven thousand young men and women from African countries came to socialist Bulgaria as international students and anti-colonial activists funded by Bulgarian state institutions or by their native governments. The majority were men who enrolled in engineering and medical university programs as well as military schools preparing foreign activists for partisan struggle, armed mobilization, and ideological and anti-colonial warfare. Their greeting by local people, however, suggested mixed sentiments. Persons of African descent remembered their stay in Bulgaria with warmth and nostalgia for the kindness of educators and colleagues who supported their training.[16] They also recalled with humour the instances where their presence in rural Bulgaria caused locals to gather and stare at them with curiosity because they had never before seen a Black person in the flesh. Others, however, remembered socialist Bulgaria as a racist country that crushed their faith in socialism and communism.[17]

In December 1962, African students in socialist Bulgaria attempted to organize an All African Student Union in order to deal with student grievances related to housing, services, and the curriculum. The Bulgarian authorities tolerated the union for a few months but then crushed it. As a result, on 2 February 1963, a reported group of two hundred African students organized a public demonstration in Sofia that was countered with state repression.[18] Students who left Bulgaria for other countries due to the events described the "racism" they encountered in socialist Bulgaria: "We have been called monkeys and jungle people and were treated like dirt," a Ghanaian student complained. A student from Nigeria explained that he left socialist Bulgaria because he did not want to be in a country "where black and white people are not treated equally." The ambassadors of Ghana in Bulgaria and of Ethiopia in Belgrade who intervened on behalf of the students expressed openly their shock by the events. The leading Ghanaian newspaper, the *Times*, reacted to the Bulgarian treatment of Black students strongly: "If we condemn the need for armed soldiers to ensure James Meredith's admission to the University of Mississippi, we are entitled to condemn any form of prejudice against African students in Bulgaria. Too many nations are under the illusion that they can come to Africa, screaming friendship and equality, while in their own home the black man is an object of scorn."[19]

The nearly thirty-five thousand Vietnamese students and guest workers who arrived in socialist Bulgaria between 1968 and 1985 also felt the sting of local prejudices. The presence of Vietnamese workers in socialist Bulgaria was the result of an agreement formally signed by the two countries in 1973, and extended again in 1980. The agreement brought Vietnamese labour to socialist Bulgaria as a form of repayment of Bulgarian state aid provided to North Vietnam during its war with South Vietnam and the United States.[20] Some of the Vietnamese workers coming to Bulgaria were, therefore, also veterans from the wars whose work as builders, electricians, metalworkers, and other industrial activities, contributed to the socialist economy. Postsocialist reports suggested that Bulgarian attitudes towards the Vietnamese were not outright negative or racist; rather, Vietnamese workers were welcomed at the construction sites where they were assigned to work and the university programs they attended. But political corruption in both Bulgaria and Vietnam began producing tensions with racialized overtones. Bulgarian authorities became aware that many of the Vietnamese workers coming to Bulgaria had no experience or training in the jobs for which they were invited: electrical engineering, construction, operation of heavy machinery, or plumbing; they had paid a substantial fee to socialist authorities in North Vietnam to join the program. Documents suggested further that many of the students coming from North Vietnam were the sons and daughters of Vietnamese communist leaders who benefitted from the bilateral agreements directly. Vietnamese nationals in Bulgaria also received lower wages than their Bulgarian counterparts, unleashing a black market of material goods organized by Vietnamese networks that bought large quantities of medicines, especially antibiotics, clothes, and other goods in Bulgaria and selling them back in Vietnam for profit. Although the illegal Vietnamese trade was also caused by ill-equipped housing complexes and insufficient support for the guest workers, rumours and stories fuelled Bulgarian negative attitudes and racialized views of barbaric Asiatic migrants who abused the privilege of being in Bulgaria and stole from it. Reflecting on this history, a Vietnamese migrant noted in 2005 that "there are still nationalists and racists in Bulgaria" who despised the Vietnamese although, according to this migrant, things had improved in the postsocialist period.[21]

The popular women's magazine *Zhenata Dnes* never addressed the presence of racial and cultural difference in socialist Bulgaria and the racialized tensions that the guest workers' presence invoked. Instead, the state feminists editing the publication constructed colour-blind narratives depicting non-white women and men in Mozambique, Vietnam, Bangladesh, South Africa, Angola, and other countries as masses of oppressed non-white subjects who could be elevated and saved. The magazine further invited women in socialist Bulgaria, including this author, to feel empathy, connection, and solidarity with the struggles of women the world over without any meaningful discussion of how racialized images and imaginations created unequal groups of women and men within the socialist nation and internationally. The discursive race-blind mode of socialist feminism enacted by the magazine suggested awareness that race mattered in European and US imperialism and capitalism; however, racialized thinking was part of the Bulgarian social consciousness as well. Yet the state feminists producing the popular magazine failed to translate that awareness into a meaningful relation or action domestically or internationally. They failed to engage and interrogate the meaning of race and racial difference in the lives and experiences of women and men inside and outside the socialist nation. In so doing, the influential socialist women who contributed to the magazine extended the racially ambiguous postures of socialism: all races were equal and would flourish culturally and economically if given the opportunity. Socialism provided such prosperity so that racial, ethnic, or cultural differences would be irrelevant to the socialist project, yet all was about such social differences and what kind of difference should be allowed to endure or die. The socialist state silenced race inside the nation, as did state feminists who gazed at African, Asian, and Latin American women outside the nation, producing thus a feminized spectacle of non-European women's difference and using the oppression and violence they endured to reify the superiority and economic safety of state socialism. Ideological and social superiority intersected with other axes of privilege, especially Bulgarian ethnic and majority privilege anchored in claims to European racial and cultural origins and what Abby Ferber called "Christonormativity" – the normalizing and domination of Christian values as the foundation of state and society.[22] In socialist Bulgaria, formal religions were suppressed, yet Christian character and values remained foundational through Eurocentric cultural and epistemological systems of thought positioned explicitly against the barbarism and underdevelopment, especially of Muslims who were "Asiatic," therefore racialized as non-white.

Socialist women-based discursive formations that silenced race and difference performed the political role of drawing and reifying borders enclosing the nation, socialist citizenry, and European civilization against others and difference that did not belong. However, labelling the state feminists publishing the magazine "racist" would not capture the complex ways in which that brand of women's activism also used the pages of the influential magazine to awaken and keep alive over the decades ordinary women's curiosity about women in Africa, Asia, and the Americas, inviting desire for travel, exploration, and connections with other women who were different. I myself was an avid reader of *Zhenata Dnes* and claim its pages as an important force in my own awareness of global systems of patriarchy and gender inequalities. A prominent Bulgarian female historian condescendingly qualified the magazine as "unpretentious ... and intellectually halfway between a romance and a cookbook," suggesting that neither it nor women's voices before or after socialism in Bulgaria constituted "a feminist discourse."[23] Instead, women factory workers like myself "basked" in the popularity and vulgar socialist populism emitted by the magazine, unable to grasp the meaning of true "feminism," which the historian located in "Western Europe and the United States after the Second World War."[24] Elsewhere, the same historian proclaimed that the Balkans and Bulgaria had always been in "Europe" and "white."[25] Much like the state feminists vocal in the 1970s and 1980s, this historian's pronouncements regarding feminism and Bulgarian racial belonging erased the multitude of identifications and women's relations that existed in the socialist national space. It erased the lives of women like myself.

Upon entering in 1980 the three-year vocational school that trained a female-only cohort of students in soldering, electrical wiring, and power circuits, I became friends with the out-of-wedlock daughter of a Bulgarian woman and an international student from Cuba, whom the women running the children's home that took the child named "Fidelia" after the Cuban president Fidel Castro. Not yet sixteen, Fidelia and I tried to make sense of the gazes and crude remarks her dark body caused everywhere we went, while my own swarthy skin invited comments about the "natural" connection Fidelia and I shared. Four decades later, my body still remembers the fear we both felt navigating the social spaces we inhabited and my worry about Fidelia's future as a lone Black woman in a society that at best treated corporeal difference with amusement and pity and at worst bashed dark-skinned bodies as mental and physical aberrations to be tolerated only if they absorbed dominant local values and world views. I needed my favourite magazine, *Zhenata Dnes*, to see race and speak about racial difference and racism before and during socialism, positioning my budding feminist consciousness for solidarity and relating in the form of taking responsibility for the oppression of others who were not like us. But that need was never fulfilled. Instead, *Zhenata Dnes* advanced a form of ideologically short-sighted state feminism that placed women's inequality and needs back in the hands of a fatherly state – European, Soviet, and African alike. Be common, not different, the magazine advised, and embrace socialism as the only true emancipatory reality existing in the space between a woman and her nation – a nation consolidated upon its refusal to see and accept difference.

However, another mode of state feminism fractured that space between myself and the socialist nation in the late 1970s and early 1980s, dislocating and quietly subverting Bulgarian socialist Eurocentrism by locating the principles of the good society and women's prosperity in the spirituality and knowledges of the non-white and the oppressed bodies residing in the global South. That kind of gendered international and revisionist socialism was embodied by Lyudmila Zhivkova, the most prominent stateswoman in socialist Bulgaria, whose intellectual and political legacies far exceed the spatial and temporal tropes of the socialist state.

Humanism, Internationalism, and Feminism: Indira Gandhi and Lyudmila Zhivkova

Lyudmila Zhivkova was a highly educated woman who spoke English and Russian fluently. An intellectual with a doctorate degree in history, Zhivkova was also an avid reader and was well aware of European and world knowledge systems. According to her father, Zhivkova was an open-minded person better received by politicians and intellectuals in the West than those in the Soviet Union.[26] Some acquaintances also described her as "a communist princess," yet friends and those close to her remembered her as kind, tolerant, and a good listener able to take in critical opinions even by those working for her. By 1973, Zhivkova's political choices and activities were dedicated to two goals: establishing a national policy for the cultural and aesthetic education of all citizens, and sharing with the world Bulgarian culture in all its forms.[27] These goals were the political culmination of Zhivkova's ideological and spiritual views rooted in a paradigm described by Zhivkova herself as "the best of West and East."

Lyudmila Zhivkova developed her notions of "East" through her international travels, friendship with Indira Gandhi, and immersion in the teachings of Agni Yoga or "Fiery Yoga": a philosophical tradition established by the Russian painter and philosopher Nicholas Roerich (1874–1947) and his wife, Helena, a spiritualist and clairvoyant. The Roerichs left Russia soon after the October Revolution in 1917, disapproving of Soviet rule and treatment, especially of Russian cultural heritage and arts. Subsequently, the Roerichs travelled to China and Tibet and lived and worked in Great Britain, the United States, and India, where they drew a circle of followers practising Agni Yoga. The practice involved daily meditation using focused and directed thought to connect to nature and the universe thus bringing wholeness, beauty, and creative energies to human consciousness. Lyudmila Zhivkova travelled to India in 1975, where she met Roerich's son Svetoslav (1904–93) and his wife, the Indian actress Devika Rani. Zhivkova also met India's prime minister Indira Gandhi, whose father had a good relationship with the Roerich family. Svetoslav Roerich had painted the portraits of Nehru and Indira Gandhi that adorn the Indian national parliament until this day. Zhivkova found in Indira Gandhi her political idol and an extraordinary stateswoman whose visions for a society and world build

Second and Third World Women 115

Fig. 10 Indira Gandhi and Lyudmila Zhivkova during Zhivkova's official visit to India in 1976. lostbulgaria.com.

upon humanism, equality, and peace inspired Zhivkova greatly. In 1989, the Indian magazine *Hinduism Today* celebrated the "deep friendship" between the two stateswomen and the "Hindu influence in communist Bulgaria" resulting from the relationship.[28]

Indira Gandhi and Lyudmila Zhivkova shared political views and spiritual beliefs evoking the ideals of socialist humanism and, from their positions of women state leaders, translated these beliefs into deeply gendered national and international initiatives that helped shape India, Bulgaria, and the Cold War world. Both Gandhi and Zhivkova defied power by rejecting Soviet and American hegemony. Indira Gandhi and India led the so-called non-aligned countries formation that refused to take sides with the Eastern or Western camp in the divided Cold War world. Both women also aspired to a new socialist order supprting the full unfolding of the human personality.

Zhivkova embraced a revisionist view of Marxism and socialism rooted in human emotional and spiritual needs rather than materiality. She believed that human consciousness determined social relations and history, therefore human creative and cultural productions stimulating and shaping social consciousness rather than the economy presented the pathways to a better and just society.[29] The material realities of work, and the physical environment of the factory, she suggested, deprived socialist workers of beauty and creativity. Work in the socialist economy, therefore, did not resolve the issue of workers' alienation from the processes of production, a central issue debated by Marxist and leftist intellectuals worldwide.[30] Rather, socialist materiality seemed to have actually deprived subjects of spiritual and creative roots and understanding of their own history, hence the socialist project was stumbling and losing steam. But Zhivkova did not abandon hope for a good society build on the principles of collectivism, relationship with nature, and the universe. Zhivkova attributed tremendous political importance to cultural production that fosters creativity and beauty – a political approach for cultural "management" she began implementing at the state policy level in the mid-1970s. As a result, knowledge and conversations about ideals and beliefs attributed to Hinduism, Agni Yoga, Buddhism, and humanism imbued the public sphere with images, visions, sounds, ideas, languages, and theories originating in the experiences of non-white and non-European societies and cultures.

Zhivkova's political influence, for example, resulted in the inauguration of a graduate program in Hindu culture and language at Sofia State University in 1983. Yoga and marshal arts clubs, previously forbidden, also opened their doors. Indian movies came to socialist movie theatres, attracting crowds of Bulgarian viewers in the 1970s and early 1980s.

Moviegoers in socialist Bulgaria marvelled at the colours, sounds, dance moves, and love stories created by Bollywood cinema masters. Exhibitions of Aztec and contemporary Mexican art filled art galleries in Bulgaria, decentring further the Eurocentrism of Marxism and Bulgarian socialism by locating civilization, achievement, beauty, and the good society in the epistemologies and humanity of the non-white, the colonized, and the oppressed. Bulgarian artists, musicians, painters, engineers, and scientists travelled to India, Sri Lanka, Vietnam, Nigeria, Saudi Arabia, Iraq, Mexico, Venezuela, and other countries in the global South, sharing their knowledge there yet bringing back novel ideas and cultural forms that enriched Bulgarian socialism tremendously.[31]

The archives in postsocialist Bulgaria lack documents shining light on how ordinary people received these cultural events, but the following anecdote from my own life might convey the spirit of the Indian-Bulgarian cultural exchange. One of the most memorable events of my childhood was the premiere of the Bollywood movie *Elephant My Friend* (aka *Haathi Mere Saathi*, 1971). The movie hit the cinemas in my hometown of Sofia in 1974, drawing millions of viewers, many of whom saw the film multiple times. The love for humans and animals conveyed by the movie, its depictions of human suffering and triumph, its beautiful landscapes, and its splendid music appealed to socialist viewers who stood in line for hours to obtain tickets to see the film. A big story surrounding the film was the thousands of Roma viewers who embraced the movie; a recent newspaper article confirmed that many Roma boys born at the time were given the names of characters from the movie.[32] My own father was so mesmerized by the movie that he took a loan to buy a small Japan-made cassette recorder that he sneaked into the movie theatre in order to record the music. He took me with him all four times he went to see this movie, which we loved. My father's dream was to travel and see the world – something he could not do being from a poor family and a citizen of a socialist country that restricted travel abroad. He took two major loans in the 1970s: one for the tape recorder and the other to buy a Soviet-made automobile with which we criss-crossed Bulgaria. Both items enabled my father to "travel," so he did not mind working every weekend over the period of two full years in order to pay back the loans. His "travel" was enabled by a stateswoman who firmly believed that cultural production and spirituality were more effective than machines and materiality at awakening human consciousness to collectivist and socialist social and economic forms that transcended national borders.

Therefore, Zhivkova also promoted vigorously Bulgarian art and history in countries around the world, celebrating especially Bulgarians as "the heirs" of ancient Thracian art and civilization. She took an archeological exhibition of Thracian artefacts around the world, putting the country on the global map of "civilizations." Interestingly, Zhivkova's narration and depiction of "Thracian art and civilization" positioned that civilization, and Bulgarian culture as its "heir," simultaneously inside and outside Europe. In her speeches related to the exhibition, Zhivkova depicted Thracian art as the expression of an ancient people occupying territories across Greece, Bulgaria, and Turkey that were the precursor of "Europe," and a springboard for what would become the culture of the Continent. She thus alluded to the Thracian civilization as an explicitly Balkan civilization that made "Europe." Zhivkova further connected Thracian ancient culture to "great civilizations" located in the global South: Hindu, Egyptian, Babylonian, Thracian, Persian, Jewish, Greek, and Buddhist civilizations, she explained, shared symbolic languages expressing a human imperative for self-evolution and a desire for knowing the universe.[33] Opening the Thracian Treasures Exhibition in New Delhi in 1981, Zhivkova drew strong cultural, political, and spiritual links between Indians and Bulgarians, stating that in India, the exhibition was especially "at home" because of the "organic closeness" between Thracian and Indian art and cultures.[34]

Zhivkova's policies and public speeches had an important gendered edge as well. Lyudmila Zhivkova and Indira Gandhi shared an understanding that a truly socialist and good society would be the making of women. Women were bearers of beauty, Zhivkova wrote; they were creators of spiritual values but as mothers, they also created life itself.[35] She further suggested that women in socialist Bulgaria had not yet realized fully their role as creators of a novel society built on the principles of justice, equality, and harmony with nature. And that, wrote Zhivkova in 1976, was not an issue of female psychology or physiology, but a question of social conditions.[36] Cultural and social policies in the advanced socialist society, therefore, had to support women's participation in cultural and artistic productions, supporting further social appreciation of women in all spheres of life. Zhivkova's views on women echoed those of her political idol Indira Gandhi in India. In the 1960s, the Women's Department of the All India Congress Committee led by Indira Gandhi published a newsletter called *Women on the March*. Indira Gandhi was the publications' chief editor, and in that role she shaped both the content and overall direction of the journal dedicated to the political issues of the day: nation-building in independence, food shortages and developing the agrarian and industrial sectors of the Indian economy, and international relations. Yet the journal published essays on the life of women in socialist countries such as Poland, Bulgaria, Yugoslavia, and Czechoslovakia while also tackling pressing questions concerning the education and participation in political life and the economy of the women of India. Indira Gandhi wrote several articles dedicated to the role of women in building independent socialist India. In her mindset, women's role in the nation was best defined by her own father's teachings, wherein womanhood embodied the Hindu code and a natural social evolution. Indira Gandhi rejected "feminism" as constitutive of Indian women's emancipation, attributing instead expanding women's rights in independence to "a great social revolution" won not by women's movements but by the culmination of a 150-year-long social evolution changing India's laws and opening doors for women in the country to role in education, politics, and the economy. Yet the problem for Indira Gandhi was that progressive laws were much ahead of social patriarchal practice; moreover, women themselves were not fully aware of their own rights and perpetuated their own subordination to men. Indira Gandhi assigned special roles to "educated housewives" and "university women" in India, upon whose self-induced evolution depended the education and expansion of women's freedoms especially among the rural and "backward" classes.[37]

Indira Gandhi called upon all women of India to play their "constructive role" in India's modernization and development. And that role resembled closely the views of Bulgaria's rising political stateswoman Lyudmila Zhivkova, who had a personal relationship with Indira Gandhi. Both stateswomen charged women with preserving world peace and fostering non-violent societies and relations, and with spearheading their country's modernization and development. Women's role of mothers determined the future of the nation; in the case of Bulgaria, a "mature socialist nation" of citizens striving for self-perfection, and in the case of India, "a socialist pattern of society" led by progressive women and men. Children were assigned special meaning as well. The Indian newsletter *Women on the March* dedicated special pages in every issue to "our children" drafted under the slogan: "Today's children, tomorrow's promise."[38] Zhivkova's cultural programs revolved around children as well: she considered them the future and believed that creating national and international environments stimulating children's creativity, spirituality, and imaginations was the key to fostering non-violent adult citizens and workers locally and globally. The pinnacle of Zhivkova's political activities was the inauguration of a special International Children's Assembly, for which she was known around the world.

However, much like the state feminists publishing the influential women's magazine *Zhenata Dnes*, Zhivkova's gendered writing and politics constructed "Bulgarian women" as a category devoid of difference – a universalized biological and political group that subsumed the different and unequal groups of Roma women, Muslim women, lesbians, women factory workers, and those ethnically and economically privileged women who shared the socialist national space. In fact, Zhivkova's biographers noted her compliance with state policies forcing Muslim women and their communities in changing their names for Christian names or facing no access to jobs, education, and services. Zhivkova never spoke against the racialized state programs aimed at Roma women either, thus witnessing in silence the violent disciplining, reforming, and modernizing of Roma women and their communities. Her ideas about the role of culture in building a socialist society provided a powerful rationale for political programs initiated by her father, Todor Zhivkov, who believed that protecting and allowing the flourishing of already existing cultural, ethnic, religious, and other differences in Bulgaria bred "divisiveness" that greatly inhibited the socialist project.[39] Lyudmila Zhivkova did not object to the erasure of cultural differences within the nation, while embracing the cultures and spirituality of others internationally. Her international feminist relations and activities contradicted her domestic compliance with oppressive politics targeting the bodies and cultures of women who were different.

Contemporary observers have also interpreted Zhivkova's politics as comprising nationalistic and elitist impulses reflecting the objectives of a peripheral country asserting itself internationally and building relations with other marginal "developing" countries in the global South to promote socialist state economic and ideological agendas.[40] Described as a "red princess" and often ridiculed for her spiritual beliefs and, at times, impenetrable writing, Zhivkova has been dismissed by native and foreign social scientists and pundits as a privileged woman and a pseudo-intellectual whose attraction to the mystic and occult presented a peculiar aberration of the Bulgarian state and Communist Party line amid the Cold War. As much as these critical interpretations capture aspects of Zhivkova's life and legacy, they fail to see her as a woman in a position of state power who *dared to defy* domestic and foreign masculinist and scientific modes of socialism, articulating instead a woman's view of life, culture, and society. Zhivkova displayed political courage and independence of thought that marked the lives of younger women like myself whose vocational education and hard labour on the factory floor were disrupted and redirected by artistic, spiritual, and knowledge events that were the outcome of Zhivkova's policies. From the institutionalization of foreign-language studies in public education and emphasis on the humanities to the free access to the opera, theatre, and art galleries, the increased abundance of translated literature at the bookstores and libraries, and the influx of Western and Eastern music, films, television programs, and printed material, the policies and visions of one stateswoman set the stage for the flourishing of consciousness and desire that would soon change not just Bulgaria but the world.

Zhivkova's feminism was also in her daring to be defiant, different, and open to the world. She embraced what she thought was good in West and East despite Soviet threats and political surveillance of her activities by domestic and foreign agencies suspicious of her international relations and activism. Her feminism was also in her close relating with non-white women and the global South. Her friendship with Indira Gandhi rejected notions of white and European racial and cultural superiority. Zhivkova called racism, colonialism, classism, ideological dogmatism, and ethnic and religious intolerance "ugly" and "destructive" forces harming humanity and the Earth.[41] According to one of her biographers, witnesses to her speech delivered to the United Nations Assembly in 1979 condemning hegemony, colonialism, racism, and apartheid while asserting "equality of sovereigns" in international relations "stunned" those gathered at the meeting.[42] Zhivkova exhibited feminist agency by further refusing to succumb to the discursive and material violence of socialist patriarchy present in her private and professional life. Her biographers noted her claim to a woman's self and point of view in the midst of political and professional men who mocked her ideas as "female eccentricity" and tolerated her only because she was the daughter of the chief ideologue and head of state. But Zhivkova, like Indira Gandhi, took the protective mantra of her father's political position to enact politics articulating an independent and womanist political self that understood how to use political privilege for purposes supporting a greater good. For a young woman like myself, Zhivkova opened doors and windows and served as a powerful example of a female politician at times when few dared to be critical of the Soviet line or share unconventional world views. Her politics also provided educational and cultural environments where generations of young women achieved university degrees and professional status. In fact, much of the women's historiography currently published in Bulgaria is authored by women who grew up and received education in institutions and with curricula whose broadened and enriched epistemologies and worldliness were the result of Zhivkova's politics and activism. These women's fluency in foreign languages, access to foreign literatures, and exposure to cultures in West and East enabled their own scholarship and participation in social scientific debates that are global.[43] My own internationalism and feminism were marked by the legacies of strong stateswomen like Zhivkova and Gandhi, whose political alliance during the Cold War transcended racial, cultural, and religious differences. Lyudmila Zhivkova showed us that making the spiritual needs, aspirations, and struggles of others the centre of the relationship to that other is the key to an international feminism that works as a strong political force nationally and globally. Yet Zhivkova, like other state feminists in socialist Bulgaria, reached out to women in the global South but did not acknowledge the struggles of underprivileged women in her own country who worked to protect their cultures, languages, and traditions in the face of a powerful socialist state that declared their difference an obstacle to the future of socialism and communism.

Stateswomen in the Global New Left

Despite the shortcomings, Lyudmila Zhivkova and Indira Gandhi's political alliance should also be viewed as an important feminist political alignment expressing the ideals of an international revisionist leftist movement that dominated much of the 1960s and 1970s global debates about socialism and capitalism. Intellectuals and radicals in different corners of the world were envisioning "socialist humanism" against the centralized and militarized styles of socialism implemented by Soviet authoritarian and repressive communist regimes. Socialist humanists were also critical of post–Second World War capitalism whose form and shape manifested the equally oppressive tendencies forming in Western liberal democracies. Intellectuals and activists sought instead a democratic form of socialism where human needs, creativity and participation in social governance stood at the centre of socialist political and material relations and forms. The critical movement began in Eastern Europe and the Balkans, where starting in the 1940s and continuing all the way to the 1980s, political thinkers and activists in Poland, Hungary, Czechoslovakia, and the former Yugoslavia developed an intense critique of Soviet interpretations of Marxism. Soviet international hegemony entrenched power-laden and authoritarian notions of Marxist theory and science and socialist governance that solidified a strong revisionist left in the newly established socialist states in Eastern Europe and the Balkans. The Hungarian uprising in 1956, Yugoslavia's defiance of Soviet power and desire for an independent socialist path beginning as early as 1947, the Prague Spring of mass protests against communist repressions in Czechoslovakia in 1968 all expressed anti-Sovietism and resistance to the kinds of socialism pursued by communist parties and states in the Soviet sphere of political and economic influence. The so-called Praxis Group established by philosophers and university circles in the former Yugoslavia was especially influential in the movement, publishing a special journal featuring the works of prominent intellectuals such as Herbert Marcuse, Jürgen Habermas, and Gajo Petrovic, who was one of the Praxis Group founders. From 1964 to 1974, the Yugoslav Praxis Group also organized the Korčula Summer School in Croatia, where an international group of Marxist theoreticians and scholars debated the past, present, and future of socialism.

In the West, socialist humanism manifested itself though the emergence of the so-called New Left. Open letters penned by E.P. Thompson in 1959 and C. Wright Mills in 1960 marked the birth of the "First New Left" in Great Britain. Cultural theorist Stuart Hall described the tradition as an intellectual critique of "the violence and aggression latent in the two systems that dominated political life at the time – Western imperialism and Stalinism."[44] In the United States, New Left politics drew inspiration from Maoist Marxism in China refusing Soviet domination and Third World politics of radicalism and anti-colonial revolutions defying both Soviet and US hegemony and power. The student and civil rights movements in the United States further embraced New Left ideology refusing hierarchies and bureaucracy and producing an extensive critique of oppressive structures and authoritarian politics. Marxist humanism in former socialist countries in Eastern and Southern Europe and New Left politics and activism in Western countries thus emerged as internationally shared expository analytics rejecting political oppression, imperialism, and Cold War violence by both communist and capitalist hegemonic states and powers and calling instead for socialist societies based on democratic principles.

The historiography of socialist humanism of East and West has been pronouncedly masculine and heteronormative, naming distinguished men as the intellectual and political pillars of this critical school of thought: German sociologist Karl Marx, Hungarian Marxist philosopher Georg Lukács, the circle of philosophers publishing the dissenting journal *Praxis* in the former Yugoslavia, historian E.P. Thompson and Black cultural theorist Stuart Hall in Great Britain, German-American intellectuals Herbert Marcuse and Erik Fromm, and the leader of the student movement Tom Hayden in the United States have been identified as primary figures who defined the intellectual and political directions of Marxist and socialist humanism and New Left politics the world over. The exception is Raya Dunayevskaya, a Russian émigré of Jewish dissent who founded the Marxist humanist tradition in the United States in the 1950s.

Socialist Bulgaria has been viewed as an obedient satellite and vassal state to the Soviet Union: a small and insignificant socialist country where dissent was rare, and if appearing, it was quickly squashed by a repressive state. But that was not entirely true. Lyudmila Zhivkova in socialist Bulgaria was a unique female political figure who carried humanistic and Buddhist ideas all the way to state policy regarding the so-called cultural front. While men in Europe and the United States philosophized and theorized what societies based on socialist and humanistic principles might look like, Zhivkova tried to implement these visions, albeit imperfect and not always successful, through a series of policies aimed at fostering inspired and culturally elevated workers and citizens by tending to both their material and spiritual needs. In the process, Zhivkova's political initiatives displaced European modernity as the ground of socialist culture and located a truly humanistic society in the "East" and the cultures and spirituality of colonized peoples. She failed, however, to form a similar alliance with Roma and Muslim women in socialist Bulgaria, whose humanity, spirituality, and rich cultures and histories remained ignored by Zhivkova's radical international visions for a new and peaceful world. That failure to see race and difference locally and globally as central to the conversation about socialism, women's well-being, and societies built on collectivist principles limited her politics significantly.

Yet Zhivkova dedicated her thinking and writing to the issues that preoccupied the international New Left. Her theorizing of the relationship between socialist (or capitalist) economic production, cultural production, and social relations and consciousness tapped into major critical aspects of Marxist theory and praxes that continue to be debated today. Privileging the role of culture in forming social relations and human identities rather than class struggle, Zhivkova's thinking aligned with the so-called post-materialist, post-Marxist, and post-structuralist intellectual school emerging at the time where the premise of social change lay in tradition, myth, stories, discourse, spirituality, imagination, and human emotion: in a word, elevated and collectivist human consciousness was more likely an outcome of culture rather than economic class and material redistribution as Marx had argued. Zhivkova arrived at this conclusion shared by major theoreticians East and West in her own way and via Agni Yoga, Buddhism, and Indigenous cosmologies she encountered through her travels and relations. It was also likely that her thinking was inspired by her residence at Oxford College in London in 1976, where she did research for her dissertation amid burgeoning student movements and polemics spurred by the British New Left. In any case, her political views bravely crossed East and West and the result was a progressive and revisionist female intellectual and politician who dared to claim her own spot in the international polemics about socialism, communism, and the future.

It is true that Zhivkova's standpoint and influence were possible because of her privileged position as the daughter of the head of state. In fact, those close to her joked that the daughter of Bulgaria's chief communist ideologue was "dissident number one" in the country: a woman who felt that Russian and Soviet history embodied violence and that Marxism-Leninism was an epistemological dictatorship over Bulgarian social life.[45] Millions of other women in socialist Bulgaria had their own opinions about socialism and Marxism but did not dare share them in public due to fear of repression and violence. Importantly, Zhivkova used her privilege to think critically and engage with various epistemologies, using them to instigate change and open socialist culture to the ideas, values, languages, and images of others who were different. Her policies fractured and globalized socialist culture, bringing to it progressive Western and Eastern non-European ways of knowing that inspired the thinking of ordinary women and girls like myself who, in the 1980s, began dreaming of another kind of society and future.

Like Zhivkova, Indira Gandhi embraced politics of national and personal independence, refusing to align with either Soviet-style socialism or American-style of liberal capitalism. As India's prime minister, Gandhi invited economic resources and know-how especially from socialist countries: between 1953 and 1973, socialist countries' trade share in India increased from 0.5 to 18 per cent, helping India to deal with the poverty and food shortages.[46] Yet Indira Gandhi embraced ideals of equality, peace, and respect for the Earth and the natural world that deviated greatly from the socialist and Marxist ideologies seeking full mastery over nature. Indira Gandhi further supported women-centred political initiatives in education, agricultural, entrepreneurship, and the law that could easily be called "feminist." But the Indian prime minister explicitly rejected the feminist label in 1980: "To be liberated," she stated, "a woman must feel free to be herself, not in rivalry to man but in the context of her own capacity and her personality."[47]

Above all, Indira Gandhi and Lyudmila Zhivkova left behind "a history of doing" extending long traditions of women's movements and activism in their countries, and a legacy of "Second World" and "Third World" women in leadership roles whose political and spiritual alliance impacted their societies and the world.[48] Lyudmila Zhivkova died suddenly in 1981 at the age of thirty-eight. Soon after her death, Indira Gandhi travelled to Bulgaria in a deeply moving gesture honouring her ally as another stateswoman who searched for that good society devoid of poverty, oppression, violence, and destruction. Using a metaphoric language describing Bulgaria as a land of roses and India as the land of the lotus, Indira Gandhi announced the inauguration of the Lyudmila Zhivkova Professorship in Bulgarian Studies in New Delhi. Other international collaborators with whom Zhivkova had relations also founded the Lyudmila Zhivkova Foundation. In 1984, soon after her visit to Bulgaria, Indira Gandhi was assassinated. Bulgaria honoured the fallen Indian prime minister with a special monument and a sheet of stamps depicting the charismatic Indian leader who inspired generations of women around the world.

In the years following Zhivkova's death, the liberalization of Bulgarian culture, the massive push for artistic and spiritual life, and the promotion of radical writers, poets, painters, and thinkers in Bulgaria supported by Zhivkova declined steadily. The return to masculine and centralized Marxism-Leninism slowly gripped the country and its people. But the cultural and ideological liberation initiated by Zhivkova had already sparked a fire, especially among youth, shaping a youth black cultural market of American and Western European music, films, and videos that would play an equally important role in Bulgarian socialism and postsocialism: a role I will discuss at length in the next chapter.

Learning from the Past

For those of us building on the legacies of state internationalism and feminism in socialist Bulgaria, the relations forged by Lyudmila Zhivkova and the women publishing the popular magazine *Zhenata Dnes* pose the important question of meaningful ways in which to stand in political solidarity with other women who are historically racialized as non-white, non-European, underdeveloped, and different. Feminist internationalism in postsocialist countries such as Bulgaria would not extend the bridges, connections, and alliances forged by these women under socialism by narrating our own historical pain and suffering as victims of Balkan patriarchies, foreign domination, authoritarian communism, or contemporary victims of global capitalism. The histories of state feminisms in socialist Bulgaria teach us that political collaborations and working relations with non-white women in the global North and South would happen if we learn to make racial, sexual, class, religious, and geopolitical difference and unequal relations of power the centre of our feminist conversations with women in Africa, Asia, and North and South America with whom we want to stand in solidarity against patriarchy, violence against women, racial oppression and marginalization, and ideologies to the right and left wherein women and their needs and struggles remain secondary to the needs of nation states and global neo-liberalism. We also learn from the shortcomings of state feminisms in socialist Bulgaria that women's internationalism should begin at the local level by acknowledging and addressing the oppression of those women whose racialization, religion, and culture stand between them and their full membership in the nation. In postsocialist Bulgaria, international feminists belonging to the privileged Christian and ethnic majorities are yet to seek political alliances with the Roma girl, the Muslim woman, the lesbian, the transgender person, the refugee woman, or the Black immigrant and her child who are within the borders of our postsocialist nation states. Upon such meaningful relating to others at the local level depends the strength of our political togetherness as women at the global level.

Chapter Five

Challenging the Modern/Postmodern Duality: Race, Socialist Masculinity, and Global American Culture

In his rich descriptions of "modernity" and "postmodernity," renowned Polish-British social theorist and philosopher Zygmunt Bauman charted the economic, ideological, and historical aspects of two kinds of cultures dominating the second half of the twentieth century. Bauman associated socialist states in Eastern Europe and the Balkans with "streamlined" and overtly rational modernity, producing a "communism" whose cultural and economic essence was its refusal to satisfy human needs.[1] Highly planned socialist economies as well as state-managed mass cultures deprived socialist subjects of both material and emotional choices, including choice of the kind of person one wished to be. State socialism thus constituted "dictatorship over needs" and modern realities "purified of the last shred of the chaotic, the irrational, the spontaneous, the unpredictable."[2] While socialist states stood on the path of Reason, Western capitalism, taken to an extreme, transcended its own modernity by turning "consciously, explicitly and joyously to the production of new needs."[3] The proliferation of needs and choice redefined human happiness in the West as one's consuming capacity. Therefore, while socialist states devoted their energies to a self-sustaining Eastern bloc, capitalism in the West went global, seeking new territories where it could reproduce the cycle of creating needs and gratifying them. The expansion produced postmodern effects visible in capitalist cultures void of final truths, standards, or ideals.[4]

American literary critic and political theorist Fredric Jameson marked the beginning of Western cultural postmodernity sometime in the late 1950s and early 1960s.[5] He qualified it as a depthless, superficial, fast-paced, highly individualized commercial culture that reflected the logic of transforming, maturing, and globally expanding capitalism. From film and literature to high visual art and advertising, Jameson lamented, postmodern culture produced "aesthetic populism" robbed of historical consciousness and social commentary, resulting in "impersonal intensities" rather than deep feelings. Unlike socialist modernity dedicated to collectivism and the erasure of economic and social difference, postmodern capitalist culture lacked a sense of "any great collective project"[6] mobilizing instead individualism and material consumerism mistaken for political choice and democracy.

Zygmunt Bauman and Fredric Jameson captured important features of the cultures produced by state socialism and globalizing capitalism; their theorizing also constructed clearly defined, demarcated and mutually hostile socialist/communist East and capitalist West as well as modern and postmodern cultures signifying contrasting ideological milieus. This chapter undermines these binaries. It highlights the travel and intertwining of globally diffused American popular culture, especially films, and local cultural production sponsored by the Bulgarian socialist state in the 1980s. It argues that these related cultural flows signify crises of masculinities in capitalist and socialist locales illuminating further important intersections between socialist and capitalist and modern and postmodern cultural forms during the Cold War. My analysis of these intersections is rooted in a transnational feminist cultural studies paradigm centred on crossing spatial, material, and epistemological boundaries.

Writing in 1993, postcolonial theorist Gayatri Spivak described "transnational feminism" as feminist interventions using cultural lenses "to complicate" degendered and deracialized economic and philosophical theories of social forms and relations, highlighting their intersections and cross-cultural nature.[7] Spivak's notions inspired the intellectual formulation of "transnational feminist cultural studies," defined by Caren Kaplan and Inderpal Grewal as "a practice of resistance and critique that transforms the traditional divides in ways that are crucial to ongoing and emergent cultural theories and practice."[8] Kaplan and Grewal were referring to feminist deconstructions of epistemological divides and battling theoretical approaches in the Western social sciences and humanities: Marxist scholarship privileging class over race or gender; feminist intellectuals centred on gender but not race; so-called postmodern theorists studying narratives disconnected from material structures; and structuralists inspired by Marxist theories insisting on the foundational properties of the economy but failing to recognize the role of cultural production in the formation of identities and social relations. Transnational feminist cultural studies cross these divides, thus resisting binary thinking and masculinist lenses depicting entities as authentic, pure, and self-contained forms.[9] Simultaneously, transnational feminist cultural studies privilege gender and difference, seeking to understand how raced and sexed male and female subjects receive and interpret global cultural flows penetrating their societies and how these flows enhance or disrupt local patriarchal, racialized, and hegemonic forms. Such local situating of globality enables an understanding of people's *agency*, the varying individual local contexts that shape male, female, or transgender interactions with and appropriations of globally diffused cultural texts as well as cultural amalgamations, performances, and counter-productions that defy, resist, or change hegemonic local and global cultures.

This chapter questions the modern socialist East/postmodern capitalist West duality of cultures constructed by Zygmunt Bauman's and Fredric Jameson's conceptualizations of socialist modernity and capitalist postmodernity. Questioning the duality involves resisting the raceless, genderless, and universalized masses of Western and Eastern citizens reduced to "consumers" of capitalism or "subjects" of state socialism that Bauman's and Jameson's influential theories also presumed. The transnational feminist cultural interpretations presented here displace such horizontally moving theorizing by thinking *vertically*, thus linking local to national to global, and by using "gender" as a category of multiple intersecting formations demanding questions about multisited cultural practices encoding masculinities, femininities, and adjacent racial and sexual hierarchies across state socialism and capitalism. The chapter highlights the connections between entities appearing as disparate in Bauman's symbolic autopsy of socialist modernity and Jameson's deconstruction of capitalist cultural postmodernity depicted at the moment of its birth.

These connections, the chapter suggests, reveal an important yet understudied gap in theories about building "good societies" associated with collectivist sociality and non-oppressive economies. Specifically, Marxist and liberal philosophers and social and cultural theorists have rightfully argued that the emergence of egalitarian, democratic, and solidarity-based social relations requires cultural production fostering consciousness that positions individuals for novel relations conducive to collectivism, and hence, social responsibility for others. Richard Johnson articulated the idea succinctly, insisting that culture is not a category but "a reminder" that the historical formation of consciousness and subjectivity begins with culture.[10] Myths, stories, literature, music, films, and other cultural products present a powerful tool for normalizing and diffusing novel ideas, and making them common sense. "Culture" thus presents the contextual space and temporality where a social subject becomes a political agent who acts consciously towards change. Thinking about that transformative moment, American philosopher

Richard Rorty argued that social and political solidarity among people is not discovered but created by the literary novel, the theater play, the cartoon, the film, or the docudrama which propel social thinking supportive of collectivism and togetherness upon which both liberal and socialist "good societies" depend.[11] Socialist builders in Bulgaria and other former socialist states understood the key role of art and culture in building socialist forms. Lenin's famous phrase that "of all the arts, the most important to us is film" encapsulated the central role of visuals and stories in fostering socialist subjects. The Bulgarian case of socialist cultural management, discussed in this chapter, however, highlights the limits of such commonly perceived relationship between culture and social innovation bound to local or national space.

The rest of the chapter illustrates the ways in which the cinematic images of US-based popular culture penetrated socialist Bulgaria, creating in the 1980s a powerful visual undercurrent that exacerbated socialist racialism by supporting Bulgarian heteronormative masculinities revolving around resistance to state and desire for autonomy and economic power and by supporting social imaginations linking Roma in Bulgaria and African Americans in the United States to each other and to biologized racial constructs originating in the United States. These gendered racial forms provided an amalgam of local, national and global cultural tropes upon which socialist subjects could imagine themselves, others and the future of socialism. Yet American popular culture also brought to socialist Bulgaria images of empowered women which invited women and girls in socialist Bulgaria to ask questions about womanhood under socialism and capitalism. American representations of material and individual prosperity and freedom also added fuel to already existing desires for transformed social relations and complete economic and political change.

"Uncooperating" Socialist Film Audiences

Throughout the 1970s and 1980s, socialist Bulgaria was in a state of perpetual crisis. Economic ineffectiveness, shortage of goods and services, decreasing labour productivity, low wages, social alienation from authority, alleged manifestations of "capitalist anachronisms," and doubt in the future of socialism marked the Bulgarian landscape. Despite the cultural liberalization and influx of cultural products from India, Mexico, African countries, Western Europe, and the United States instigated by the cultural policies of Lyudmila Zhivkova, with her untimely death and loosened grip of the so-called cultural front, a highly ideologized, Soviet-style culture rose back to power alienating especially young people who found inspiration and self-fulfilment in a black market of Western, mostly American, films and music.[12] Therein, socialist youth found an alternative world that provided escape and happy endings as well as stable grounds for social identifications amid economic uncertainty and ideological doubt. Socialist authorities acknowledged the economic shortage, widespread corruption in all levels of government, low labour productivity, and attraction to Western cultures but attributed the crisis to exhaustion of the present model of socialism and failure to foster the kind of consciousness needed to support the socialist project. To address the problems, the Bulgarian Communist Party introduced economic reforms, institutional and labour restructuring, and changes in what the Party called the "cultural front."[13] The state created new structures and cultural policies believed capable of enabling mass culture that inspires productivity, morality, elevated citizens' consciousness, and loyalty to state and ideology. The black market of Western, especially American, popular culture undermined that objective by deepening the cultural distance between the state and its subjects. State documents acknowledged that "movies [were] the most popular form of cultural activity" among Bulgarians, hence reformers called on the Bulgarian film industry to produce new and exciting cinema centred on "the contemporary theme."[14] Mastering of that theme was an "outstanding task" because only mass culture that reflected the "advantages, ... virtues and contradictions, aspirations and hardships" of the socialist personality could meet "both the new and much higher needs and requirements of society and people."[15]

Creators, experts, and bureaucrats in the Bulgarian state film industry took the task of the new cultural policy seriously. In 1977, experts in the field gathered at a conference titled "Cinema and Audiences: Problems of the Aesthetic Education." Prominent film expert Ivaylo Znepolsky presented the conference participants with a report on the changing tastes of Bulgarian audiences and their distaste for socialist native films.[16] Surveys showed that the majority of viewers watched films for fun and entertainment. Socialist audiences also preferred the "light genres" of comedy, crime adventure, and musicals. "Only a small percentage of those polled wished to see films about the village, the working class, or current political issues," the report concluded. The data further showed that most popular were "films that offer good conditions for identification ... and happy endings." According to Znepolsky, socialist audiences paid more attention to the music in the film than to its directorial achievements; some viewers even confused the cinematic depiction with actual reality.[17] In terms of Bulgarian films, Znepolsky reported that 85 per cent of those surveyed did not think "the problems of our contemporary life find sufficient place in Bulgarian films." Sixty per cent of those surveyed also told pollsters that "the heroes in Bulgarian films did not exist in real life, and if they did, films idealized and exaggerated them." Viewers also complained that socialist films lacked brightness, force, and action. Moreover, the survey showed that the higher the education of the viewer, the lower their interest in Bulgarian films. "Our cinema," Znepolsky concluded, "is least respected by university students ... [and] viewers between the ages of 19 and 24."[18]

Indeed, younger socialist audiences disdained native socialist films and preferred Western, especially American, movies that satisfied their desire for fun, entertainment, action, happy endings, and characters with whom Bulgarians could identify. Znepolsky, however, interpreted these preferences as markers of an "inadequate," "cinematically illiterate" audience and "not very high level of cinematic culture" among the masses.[19] By seeking "strong excitement, entertainment, and escape" in Western films, Znepolsky argued, Bulgarian film audiences neared "the status of the irresponsible viewer." In the spirit of the newly implemented policy for "mass aesthetic education," he proposed cultural education that would breed a sophisticated and "responsible" Bulgarian viewer who could read and appreciate native socialist films and their problematic. Simultaneously, Bulgarian viewers so elevated would be able to engage and critically assess Western films. As Znepolsky put it, "it is time to talk about the responsibilities of the [Bulgarian] film-maker, but also about the responsibilities of the public ... [and] the need for one good, active, cooperating public."[20]

The popularity especially of American action films among Bulgarian youth was evident in the writing of another cultural expert. In 1977, this pundit suggested on the pages of the state-sponsored film journal *Kinoizkustvo* (Cinema art) that native socialist cinema could attract back young audiences by adopting the formulas of the American "crime/adventure" genre. The genre, Vladislav Ikonomov explained, was very important in fighting the Cold War because it depicted the characters and works of detectives and spies, who were at "the barricades" between the socialist and capitalist worlds. More importantly, the United States used the genre most successfully "to demonstrate the superiority of the American way of life, to construct the myth of their society and the values of their social order." The United States won viewers around the world by implementing in the genre "strict realism" and "photographic, requisite realism where attention was paid to the smallest detail, from the street and the small town to the Arizona desert and the bachelor apartment of the policeman and detective." Above all, Ikonomov stated, American films in the action genre attracted

Bulgarian audiences with the realism of their characters, who were complex and embodied the features and feelings of the "common person." That was the reason why the characters played by "Gene Hackman, Marlon Brando, Al Pacino … Charles Bronson, Clint Eastwood" in films such as *Dirty Harry*, *Magnum Force*, *The French Connection*, *The Godfather*, and *Death Wish* "will remain memorable" and "historians of cinema will write many scenes [from these films] in the handbooks of professional mastery." But Bulgarian cinema and television were slow in appreciating the genre, Ikonomov complained. Many observers rushed to label it "pseudo art" although the genre was responsible for "all real successes achieved among our audiences." Therefore, creating characters of socialist fighters and detectives using the realistic formulas of American crime-adventure and its empowered masculine heroes was the "first and primary condition for winning the viewer. Or, the first condition for winning [the Bulgarian] viewer for our cause."[21]

The issue of alienated Bulgarian youth persisted and continued to worry state authorities in the 1980s. Socialist managers of culture realized that their loss of control over audiences and youth indulgence in Western culture was related to new and revolutionary communication technology. The videocassette recorder (VCR), specifically, became a significant problem for the socialist state because the technology resisted policing yet it propelled local dissemination of uninvited foreign capitalist culture penetrating and undermining socialist values and order. Through the VCR, socialist audiences engaged in private and therefore uncontrolled consumption and exchange of cultural products. In 1985, an observer called the fears surrounding the VCR "a mass psychosis that links it solely to watching films at home. Hence, commentaries target either the supply of videotapes (of course in an unofficial way!) or the legal penalties that go along with such supply of films." Another observer noted that the VCR was "identified with a wave of pseudo-culture, violence, pornography, and whatever else is coming at us. The VCR is also implicated in pure criminology: illegal [film] séances with entrance fee, theft, re-recording, and making of easy money. Videotapes circulate irrepressibly in the so-called black market."[22]

Problems associated with the black market and the VCR technology intersected with authorities' concern about increased Western anti-communist propaganda. Throughout the first part of the 1980s, writers for the state journal *Kinoizkustvo* spoke of a "crisis" and an "ideological war" and pressure staged by increased American propaganda under the presidency of Ronald Reagan, and a "loss" of Bulgarian youth to foreign films. Some called for action against the "film/TV imperialism" and the "psychological war" against socialist countries developing in the United States. In 1984, the Chair of the Union of Bulgarian Film Creators suggested "increased ideological-educational work with films to address youth interests that are realistically in danger to fall captive to entertaining cinema and to increase activities related to discussions of Bulgarian and Soviet films."[23] Male youth, a prominent Bulgarian film expert added, "experiences strong thirst for a cinematic hero who embodies moral qualities and persists in fighting for his goals and ideals ..."[24] The young socialist audience "readily identifies" with this hero and "accepts as its own his victories and losses." "There is a thirst," the expert explained further, "for monolithic, goal-driven, fighting characters who are ready to sacrifice themselves in the name of higher justice and socially significant ideas." Those were heroes who "go through losses and severe impacts" but remained "uncompromising."[25] The expert was describing movie characters embodied by international Hollywood male stars such as Sylvester Stallone, Charles Bronson, Chuck Norris, Clint Eastwood, Steven Seagal, Al Pacino, and Robert De Niro, among other American cinematic heroes who had captured the imagination of socialist youth, especially boys and young men.

Cinematic American Racial Modernity Penetrates Socialism

Indeed, videotapes were rolling into darkened rooms where Bulgarian male youth gazed at the captivating cinematic images of powerful, racially white, and masculine American characters. The character "Rambo" played by Italian-American actor Sylvester Stallone was a cultural icon among young Bulgarian men: depicted as a one-man army, a "perfect killing machine," and a Vietnam War veteran, the character's serial reproductions in national and international stories travelled from a Small Town USA to Vietnam, Thailand, and Afghanistan. In Afghanistan, Rambo fought the Soviets. In Vietnam, he did what a cinematically constructed weak American state and divided politicians and society could not: win a victory by saving American soldiers from the tortures of Vietnamese depicted as barbarians. Another popular character, Colonel James Braddock (Chuck Norris), was a Vietnam veteran as well. His blond and muscled body trained in martial arts exerted physical strength and moral authority that commanded the screen. Like Rambo, Colonel Braddock would save American soldiers "missing in action" in Vietnam – men left behind by a country unwilling to fight the war to victory. And like Rambo, Colonel Braddock crossed international and domestic political theatres as versions of the character would take law and order into his own hands to catch and punish dark-skinned criminals, who, according to these films, were not effectively policed by US law enforcement agencies.[26] Another cinematic protagonist, also a Vietnam veteran embodied by Sicilian-American and master of Japanese aikido police sergeant Nico Toscani, portrayed by Steven Seagal, had to stand "above the law" because corrupt US government intelligence agents protected non-white delinquents and their drug operations poisoning urban America.[27] Tall and handsome "Dirty" Harry Callahan (Clint Eastwood) pointing a big gun at a Black man at his feet also followed his own laws and rules to bring justice to innocent victims.[28] So did the characters played by Charles Bronson, a white male vigilante who restored order and justice from New York to Los Angeles.[29]

These cinematic depictions centred Euro-American white male identities amid their displacement, disorientation, and loss of privileges propelled by political and social transformations also portrayed in the action films, which were popular in socialist Bulgaria. Within the national domain, the civil rights movement, the gay liberation movement, the feminist and women's movement, expressions of ethnic pride, and Indigenous struggles challenged white male supremacy in the United States in the 1960s and 1970s. Amid the social and political uncertainty and ruptured racial, patriarchal, and ethnic orders, Hollywood was producing action movies organized around the symbols of racial whiteness and desire for the kind of American nation state before civil rights, feminism, Vietnam, and advanced capital. These films captured the displacement, confusion, and losses felt by white men. Action movies constructed stories commenting on American moral and political "disorientation" due to the loss of stable identifications, final truths, and grand narratives on progress, racial superiority, and civilization provided by modern culture and knowledges. The American action heroes depicted in these films embodied the fractured, disoriented, and confused Western subjects described by Frederic Jameson's theory of "postmodern entrapment," marking the emergence of globalized industries like Hollywood and cultural productions devoid of stable meanings about the social order where men, women, whites, non-whites, Indigenous people, and others occupied a determined place in the once stable social hierarchy.

For example, the first three *Rambo* films (1982, 1985, and 1988) exemplified American male subjects' displacement and inability to map their relative position inside the nation state and a divided Cold War world. These were anchorless, immobilized, and disoriented Western men who were no longer capable of distinguishing between "friend" and "enemy." A profound sense of confusion organized the story in *Rambo: First Blood* (Ted Kotcheff, 1982), which depicts a post-Vietnam local war between white American men, all of whom are soldiers and servants of the nation state. John Rambo (Sylvester Stallone) is a decorated Vietnam War hero who arrives in a small American town to look for a "lost" war comrade. A banner overarching the town's main street reads: "Welcome to Hope! Holiday Land." The banner cues the viewer that Rambo has returned to a United States that was supposed to be full of hope, enthusiasm, and a sense of celebration after a long war, and one ready to embrace those who fought for it in Vietnam. But the reality appears different because it is cold, dark, and rainy. The town's sheriff does not like Rambo and takes him for "a drifter" invading the public space, where everything looks orderly and under control. The sheriff arrests Rambo and takes him to the local police station. There, Rambo refuses to identify himself, but a background check conducted by the sheriff reveals that Rambo was a decorated war veteran from the special forces. This information does not lead to an apology and Rambo's release. Instead, the sheriff and the other policemen at the station subject Rambo to violence and beatings. Rambo escapes into the woods, and his hunt by the local police escalates to a war, now involving the US Army and the National Guard, all against one man: an American war hero.

The parties engaged in this chaotic and violent manhunt express deep animosity and resentment for each other. The sheriff of the small town hates the army colonel, who is there the get back Rambo, his "perfect killing machine." The National Guard, whom the story underlined as civilian part-time soldiers, does not take orders either from the police or the army. Meanwhile, Rambo kills anyone who goes after him. These American men, who have so much in common, as they are all racially white, all with authority and power, all working for the state, and all militarized and holding weapons, fight and kill each other over a cause that the film never makes apparent. Neither does the story explain the motivation that drives these men. Rather, these American men appear totally incapable of recognizing their commonalities. They also seem to act to protect a society and a state, yet all express alienation and discontent with this state, which brought them into the Vietnam War but did not "give [them] a chance to win," as the colonel tells the sheriff while discussing "these confusing times."

Rambo and the other cinematic action heroes, however, take on the state and its repressive apparatuses – the police, the army, and the judicial system – by staging local wars against these authorities. The characters constructed by these movies take the law into their own hands and act as private soldiers, judges, and executors all at the same time. Armed with weapons, skilled in martial arts, and parading on screen their muscular, well-trained bodies, these one-man army characters portrayed by Stallone, Seagal, Eastwood, Norris, Bronson, and others restore order, kill evil non-white villains and criminals, and save sexy, beautiful blonde women from trouble. The action movies celebrate these men as morally superior yet powerful citizens who can topple a weak state and win a war. These men have earned their privileged place in the social and racial order called USA; hence these cinematic representations counter the political demands of non-white citizens, women, gay people, immigrants, and others to whom the American state, under the pressure of the civil rights movements, was extending services, rights, and liberties – ones traditionally reserved for white men. In the 1970s and 1980s, such self-produced images of a turbulent United States penetrated socialist Bulgaria.

Crises of Masculinity East and West

The struggles and victories of the heroes constructed in Hollywood action films embodied the "monolithic, goal-driven, fighting characters" that had become highly popular among viewers in socialist Bulgaria. One reason for the appeal was that action films advanced the images of "hegemonic masculinity" embodying traditional, modern, and idealized ways of being a man in the world.[30] American geopolitical hegemony manifested itself on screen through images of muscular, physically strong men armed with weapons or trained in martial arts who exerted power. US action film heroes were seductive masculine ideals to emulate because they acted independently, took control of their fate, and articulated simple but firm notions of right and wrong, good and evil presented to viewers as timeless universal truths. US-based hegemonic masculinity allowed Bulgarian men to fantasize and enact their own independence and freedom against a controlling socialist state that deprived them of space to compete and accumulate personal wealth, exert full control over women and minorities, retain their privileged social status, and choose what they wanted to be. Instead, socialism created a political male elite of socialists and communists who indulged in lifestyles and privileges not available to the mass of men under the thumb of the state. The continuous threat of international cold and hot wars as well as long compulsory army service, which ordinary men under socialism dreaded, exacerbated a thirst for liberated masculinities played out in darkened rooms where private VCRs rolled American action movies.

Bulgarian males entered the army at the age of eighteen for a two-year period of compulsory service and military training aimed at crushing their sense of individuality, while instilling loyalty and readiness to die for the socialist nation state. These soldiers of socialism, however, had neither elected nor necessarily believed in socialism or communism.

Through characters such as Rambo, young Bulgarian men fantasized about and experienced their own victory and liberation from an oppressive army and state. In 2003, I interviewed eighteen men for a study of the impact of American popular culture in socialist Bulgaria. One of the study informants told me the following story from his life. While serving in the army in 1981, which he "hated," he was put on a plane in the middle of the night and dropped off with his unit in a remote wooded place. The soldiers were ordered to shoot at the enemy, which was supposedly on the other side of the trenches. It was dark and my study informant could not see that enemy but he knew it had to be the Westerner from "the capitalist block." This Bulgarian soldier held his weapon up but could not shoot. He wondered: "Who is the enemy here?"[31] The communist army officers and generals standing behind him who humiliated, crashed, and terrorized him "during two long years" preparing him to fight and die in the name of communism that had proven unworthy, or the "West" that fought the communists? The informant pointed his weapon toward the Bulgarian officers but did not shoot. This person watched *Rambo: First Blood* (1982) seven times. He and his male friends spent long weekend nights discussing the *Rambo* films, "want[ing] to do to the communists what Rambo did to the Americans and the Soviets." Young Bulgarian males identified with Rambo and the other cinematic male characters who were disoriented, could not distinguish between "friend" and "enemy," and fought each other. And the state for which Rambo sacrificed himself in Vietnam hunted and imprisoned this soldier much like the socialist state diminished, abused, and immobilized its men through material shortages, low wages, and heavy policing yet demanded men's loyalty and lives in fighting Cold War enemies. Socialist men found in Rambo a brave and strong masculine character who defeated state and army. Amid fear and subjection under a socialist state, Rambo's character and experiences tapped into Bulgarian male anxieties and desire to be that brave and strong character able to counter an oppressively strong and controlling socialist state.

Other personal interviews I collected between 2000 and 2003 revealed similar male enthusiasm for American action films in the 1980s. In the words of another male interview subject, American action heroes supplied his adolescence with "role models" and visions of masculinity he shared with a group of friends who spent long hours watching movies together:

> Back then, in my time, I mean my high school years and military years and thereafter, my heroes were action film actors like Arnold Schwarzenegger, Sylvester Stallone, Chuck Norris, Van Damme, Seagal ... ah ... What

I liked about them was that these were men who had taken the law into their own hands, in the sense that, there was the idea that the law did not work well. They had taken law and order into their own hands and exercised it, in the sense that they brought justice. I told myself, if this were the case, why not. Sylvester Stallone says something in *Cobra*, something I will always remember: "You are the tumour and I am the surgeon!" and boom-boom-boom, three bullets between the eyes ... I also liked their physique. I liked that they were strong muscled men but this is part of the image, part of being an action hero. You gotta be masculine ... I wanted to be like them, at least physically. I identified with them somehow; they were models for me about what a man should be like.[32]

Socialist authorities were aware that the alienation of youth that worried them was actually a loss of trust among the young males who supplied the state with labour and soldiers. The cultural policies seeking to bring back socialist audiences specifically targeted male audiences by creating native films that emulated those featuring the American action heroes they admired. Between 1981 and 1983, for instance, the state film company released a series of motion pictures starring Ivan Ivanov – a handsome, masculine Bulgarian ethnic actor often compared to the French cinema sex symbol Alain Delon, who was one of the most prominent actors in Europe in the 1970s. The Bulgarian movie *Kombina* (1983) was the first Bulgarian socialist action thriller, and it cast Ivan Ivanov as a mule in an international drug ring, who at the end of the movie reveals himself to be an active agent of the socialist state secret service. Other movies casting Ivanov from the period depicted equally strong and driven characters: a member of a team of tough mountain climbers swept by an avalanche but saved by their collective spirit; a masculine and protective character revenging the rape of the woman he loves; and a young man who escapes a youth reform school to be with the girl he loves despite the disapproval of her parents and the severe punishment for breaching the rules of the reformatory. These characters embodied a kind of socialist masculinity constructed to emulate yet counter the popular American action heroes seducing young Bulgarian men. Tough, physically strong, smart, independent, and at the margins of the law, socialist masculine movie characters exuded moral superiority and commitment to ideals of collectivism, cooperation, order, heterosexual love, and family surrounded by the wonders of socialist science and Eurocentric modernity.

These commitments were illuminated further by socialist visual constructions of womanhood from the same period. Socialist movies and mass media celebrated women's participation in the public economy and political life. For instance, the number of women with university education in the period increased significantly, even surpassing that of highly educated men. Women's employment in the public economy reached 93 per cent; female decisions over fertility and bearing children were enabled by state services and legalized abortions.[33] Yet visual "symbolic glorification" of socialist womanhood solidified the patriarchal order by constructing women as mothers, lovers, workers, carers for others, and objects of male love, sexual desire, protection, ideology, and needs.[34] Simultaneously, socialist mass culture portrayed women as masculinized girls who could perform "men's work" and jobs: the press, literature, and movies in Bulgaria depicted socialist women as tractor drivers, builders, mechanics handling heavy machinery, and soldiers in uniform holding weapons. But these masculinized genres of women symbolizing socialist emancipation did not appeal to all ordinary men. In fact, women's access to male professions, higher education, and political life under socialism was viewed as ideological gender redistribution led by the state. Men resisted such reorganized gender relations; this resistance was signalled by unabating sexual and domestic violence against women by men asserting male control, especially in the domestic realm.[35]

Much like Hollywood movies, socialist cinematic representations were reacting to women's changing roles. In the United States, ruptures of the patriarchal order were caused by feminist activism and the women's liberation movements; in socialist Bulgaria, cinematic masculinity rejected women endowed with men's qualities and access to education, professions, and politics. Similar male resentment of changed gender roles took place in other socialist countries. A study of Soviet-style masculinities, for example, considered postsocialist attitudes towards women to be the outcome of such gender reordering under socialism, causing "emasculated" and "effeminized" socialist men seeking restored privileges during and after socialism, often violently.[36] In other Balkan socialist countries, violence against women, especially minority women, also expressed a backlash against "those members of the population who had gained much from socialist rule and laws – women."[37] These male anxieties mark the 1970s and 1980s as a shared moment of ruptured and changing patriarchal forms articulated by local and global cinematic representations of masculinities in crises and men alienated from state ideology in both socialist and capitalist countries. This male destabilization and anxiety was racialized as well.

Like Roma, Like African American

American movies entering socialist Bulgaria pictured racial non-whiteness in the United States as un-American and dangerous. Black men in rags by barrel fires on urban streets at night, Black pimps over-accessorized with gold jewellery, Black drug lords in bright velvet fedoras, Black youth dancing on streets and carrying loud boom boxes, and idle African American characters roaming neighbourhoods in the middle of the work day contrasted sharply with the fashions, mannerisms, and industriousness of American whites. Images of scary-looking Asian villains who rarely spoke English and resided in dirty urban Chinatowns woven by dark secretive passages protruded on the background of clean and bright suburban neighbourhoods populated by white people. Ruthless Asian characters marked as un-American, for instance, crowded the martial arts films (popular in Bulgaria) starring Jean Claude Van Damme: *No Retreat, No Surrender* (1986), *Blood Sport* (1988), *Kickboxer* (1989). So-called serious American films extended racialized hierarchies of worthy and unworthy human races. In the work of American film-makers such as Arthur Penn, Francis Ford Coppola, Sidney Pollack, and Martin Scorsese, Bulgarian state guardians of socialist culture and morality saw "serious," "political," and "progressive American cinema" that "attacked" American social realities, as one film expert put it. Bulgarian film authorities understood that the works of these progressive film-makers constituted a critique of capitalist America from within; hence, these films served as a powerful ideological tool against the United States during the Cold War. Thus, through movies depicting American countercultures, the socialist state invited Bulgarian audiences to see for themselves the violent and corrupted social and political realities of American capitalism. Yet these films also centred on the stories, struggles, feelings, alienation, values, and hopes of either US-born or immigrant Euro-Americans. From the small-town power relations in *The Chase* (1966), the inhumane dance competition in *They Kill Horses, Don't They*? (1969), the bombardier's attempts to escape the insanity of the Second World War in *Catch 22* (1970), the brave firefighters in *The Towering Inferno* (1974), the outerspace adventures of Luke Skywalker in *Star Wars* (1977), the federal agents' capture of Al Capone in 1920s Chicago in *The Untouchables* (1987), the love triangle in *Cabaret* (1972), the physically tough but emotionally self-destructive boxing champion in *Raging Bull* (1980), the brotherly love in *Rain Man* (1988), the feelings of a divorced couple in *Kramer vs. Kramer* (1979) to the saga of an Italian mafia family in *The Godfather* (1972) and *The Godfather Part II* (1974) and the fall of a union organizer in *Prizzi's Honor*

(1985), those were the stories of Euro-Americans portrayed by Hollywood stars such as Jane Fonda, Marlon Brando, Robert Redford, Alan Arkin, Liza Minnelli, Steve McQueen, Paul Newman, Dustin Hoffman, Meryl Streep, Al Pacino, Robert De Niro, Jack Nicholson, Kevin Costner, and Tom Cruise.

The racial superiority of white characters portrayed by these stars rested on their complexity imbued with moral dignity, sense of justice, and determination as well as strength and ability to face and overcome life challenges. The racial superiority of white characters was also evident from their privileged position as social, cultural, and political critics who made a difference in both social and individual terms by unmasking and fighting social ills and helping victims of injustice and corruption, all the while undergoing inspiring personal transformations. These constructions of racial whiteness in "serious" and "quality" American films complemented the images of delinquent and violent non-whites in the action movies; while action crime dramas marked members of racial minorities with delinquency, "quality" American films suggested that non-whiteness in the United States was socially, culturally, and politically irrelevant. "Quality films" selected by socialist authorities depicted non-whites as secondary and marginal characters and/or racial extras who, if present at all, did not affect the lives, emotions, plights, and transformations of the white people around whose stories these films revolved.

Eager and thirsty young Bulgarian audiences actively interpreted these racialized texts. Socialist audiences decoded African Americans' filmic depictions in terms of the Bulgarian Roma minority. For example, Bulgarians attributed to Roma similar qualities of criminal propensity, laziness, and lack of morals that American action films attributed to African Americans. In a survey of public opinion published in 1991, just a couple of years after the socialist state collapsed, 89 per cent of Bulgarians defined Roma as "thieves," 70 per cent as "liars," 76 per cent as "bullies," and 67 per cent as "drifters."[38] The personal interviews I conducted in the early 2000s to study Bulgarian reception of American films illuminated further parallelism between Roma in Bulgaria and African Americans. In the fashions of African Americans depicted in movies, Bulgarians perceived cultural characteristics that bespoke Blacks' difference from American and European whites and their deviation from tastes and aesthetics ethnic Bulgarians considered "high culture." From a Bulgarian perspective, African Americans mixed and mismatched colours and overdecorated their bodies with large golden ornaments as did the Roma. For many Bulgarians, Roma fashions presented "kitsch," or style and colour appropriations that defied Eurocentric cultural standards of harmony and beauty. Commonly used Bulgarian phrases such as "dressed like a Gypsy" and "decorated like a Gypsy," which Bulgarians I interviewed applied to African Americans depicted in movies, illustrate these perceptions. Even today one can hear in Bulgaria opinions about Roma and Black Americans as being "really good" in one area only: singing and dancing. In the 1980s, Bulgarian audiences excitedly received televised streaming of the American music industry Grammy Awards, Hollywood's Oscar Awards, and occasional weekend presentations of NBA basketball broadcast by the state-owned Bulgarian National Television company. These globally disseminated American programs celebrated singing and dancing Black bodies on stage or star athletes competing in games. These depictions intersected with domestic socialist images of Roma celebrated as entertainers and working bodies but not minds.

Not surprisingly, a male respondent I interviewed in 2003 expressed deeply racialized views and attributed those directly to American movies, citing these cinematic narratives as "proof" that Black people in the United States and Gypsies in Bulgaria were equally "unruly."[39] Another respondent, however, interpreted these films in relation to state power and order; he admired the psychical strength, athletic bodies, and mental resilience of both white and non-white action heroes depicted by the Chinese American Bruce Lee, Austrian American Arnold Schwarzenegger, Italian American Sylvester Stallone, and African American Wesley Snipes. These actors embodied agency: they restored order where the state appeared weak and incapable. He was very aware of the racial messages suggesting Black's subordinate position in these films, but he also asked questions about why all the bad guys in the American action movies were non-white since he recalled admirable Black men who were very talented; in fact, his favorite musicians included Prince, Michael Jackson, and the all-Black pop group Kool & the Gang, who created the soundtrack of his socialist adolescence.[40] A third respondent identified American movies as "the basis" of his dreams to leave Bulgaria, go to the USA, and see the world. He absorbed American film narratives with gusto but his attention did not seem fixed on the racial representations of men and masculinities, as was the experience for other respondents. Instead, this young man focused on the background of the stories, soaking in visuals of the wealthy material life depicted in these films. For him, US movies presented a comparative site where he assessed, judged, and resisted socialism, dreaming instead of an American-like social life where he could be whatever he wished to be, make a lot of money, and travel the world. Yet he rejected American notions of "happy endings"; films always ended on a happy note, but real life was different, he observed, making these films "just stories."[41]

Female respondents to my inquiry about the influence of American popular culture back in the 1980s also shared different stories. One interviewee explained that she disliked shallow American action movies but indulged in the quality films shown in the movie theatres. She found those stories powerful as they examined deep human feelings and relations but also showed strong female characters that inspired her. Laughingly, she pointed to the leading female character of a sex worker portrayed by Julia Roberts in the movie *Pretty Woman* (1990), explaining that she was mesmerized not only by the character's beauty and glamour but also by the fact that the character chose that line of work herself, gesturing to how women in the United States were much more liberated than socialist women.[42] Another female respondent articulated her dislike for "stupid American films" and their racial overtones, which she contrasted with other American texts, like her favourite childhood book, *Uncle Tom's Cabin*.[43] The book illustrated to her the plight, suffering, and kindness of Black Americans. These memories stood in stark contrast to a third female interviewee in my study who grew up near the "Gypsy ghetto" in Sofia. In a racist rant, she explained her dislike for both Gypsies and Blacks from anywhere, pointing to the delinquency of Black men portrayed in the American movies she watched growing up.[44] Another woman who indulged in American action movies with her boyfriend back in the 1980s recalled these stories as cheap entertainment; she felt much more influenced by American music, especially jazz. Her musical heroes were Black Americans, especially women like Tina Turner, Diana Ross, and Ella Fitzgerald as well as Michael Jackson, Barry White and black rhythm and blues artists in general. She fondly remembered the Euro-Caribbean disco group Bony M, formed by a German producer, which was a cultural phenomenon in socialist Bulgaria.[45] The group's popularity was equally high in other socialist countries, leading to Bony M's visit to the Soviet Union in 1978. The popularity of Western European and American pop music in socialist Bulgaria rose further with the opening of disco clubs in the early 1980s. Discotheques opened at eight and closed at eleven in the evening and at least 30 per cent of the music played had to be Bulgarian or from other socialist countries. But these rules did not prevent the spark of a vibrant youth disco culture revolving around historically Black music genres and performers, like those strong Black female entertainers who inspired some of the women I interviewed. My own teenage years revolved around disco and American popular culture. Later in life, when I was asked to identify that which sparked my own feminism, I realized the profound influence of American female artists, intellectuals, and educators, many of whom I first encountered in the American cultural stream penetrating socialism.[46]

Globally diffused American cultural forms articulated gendered and racialized messages but their interpretation and effects differed among socialist subjects depending on the specificity of individuals' social location. Yet these racialized messages exacerbated socialist racism by supporting Bulgarian heteronormative masculinities fashioned after Euro-American cinematic characters revolving around resistance to state control and desire for autonomy and economic power, and by supporting social imaginations linking Roma in Bulgaria and African Americans in the United States to each other and to a biologized racial hierarchy originating in European and American colonial conquests. A vivid manifestation of a shift from socialist racialism defined by state policies of forced inclusion to policies defined by violent exclusion occurred in 1989. In May of that year, the Bulgarian Communist Party's unabated campaign to change the personal names of members of the Turkish and Muslim minority with Bulgarian and Christian names culminated in the push of these communities outside the national borders into Turkey. The forced exodus of more than three hundred thousand Bulgarian, Turkish, and Roma Muslims leaving Bulgaria stunned the world, yet the events played out a new socialist state ideology born out of doubt and desperation: where the ideology of socialist economy and society could not succeed, nationalistic and racist policies would still secure the loyalty of male citizenry on the edge of revolution against a failed ideology and state. A few months after the purging of Muslim Roma and Turks, in November 1989, that citizenry took down the regime. Young men and women marched the streets with dreams for a new future inspired by globalized cultural streams celebrating freedom of a different kind. Not surprisingly, the decade thereafter saw another kind of exodus of young Bulgarians immigrating to the United States in pursuit of that dream inspired by racialized cinematic images that had captivated the hearts of a generation of Bulgarians on the move.[47]

Postsocialist Masculine Globality

The popularity of American cinematic masculine heroes continues today. Socialism ended over two decades ago but the production and dissemination of masculine US-based racial whiteness has made postsocialist Bulgaria its production springboard. The former state film studios used for the production of propaganda and special filmic materials targeting the nation's consciousness are now owned by a multinational company catering especially to Hollywood, providing low-cost technical personnel, movie extras, and sets. Amazingly, the recent sequences of the Rambo movies that so inspired socialist youth are now shot and produced in the outskirts of the Bulgarian capital. Actor Sylvester Stallone is a frequent visitor to the country and a personal friend of Bulgarian prime minister Boyko Borisov, who tweets intimate photos of the two men embracing each other.[48] Borisov admires Stallone but is also grateful for the business and employment the Hollywood action star brings to Bulgaria. Sylvester Stallone praises Bulgaria in media interviews, confessing his love for the local wine and people.[49] Other action movie starts are also filming in Bulgaria, where adoring male fans and media outlets follow their latest productions and private lives.

Mel Gibson, Arnold Schwarzenegger, Dolph Lundgren, Wesley Snipes, Chuck Norris, and other now aged stars of the action genre came to Bulgaria to film the American action thriller franchise *The Expendables* (2010, 2012, 2014). Sylvester Stallone is the writer, director, actor, and/or producer of four films in the franchise (either completed or anticipated), whose main story revolves around the adventures of a mercenary group of masculine heroes who fight against and punish evil and rootless characters and enterprises. Back in the 1980s, these same actors inspired a generation of young Bulgarians with their strength, moral claims, and above all defying powerful entities such as the state and the army, drug dealers, corporations, and terrorists. Yet these contemporary iterations of white American masculinity do not take themselves as seriously as in the past: *The Expendables* franchise pokes fun at the aged action heroes. Its discursive and visual parameters, however, continue to position a Western and Euro-American masculinity and point of view as pivotal and key to the survival of a US-centric democracy, capitalism, and a moral order seeking to dominate the world. Ironically, these claims are staged from within postsocialist Bulgaria and the Balkans signalling the new world order, where former socialist enemies are now embraced in the family of civilized and democratic nations. And that symbolism is not lost on generations of Bulgarians invited to bask in the power of a globalized American gendered and racial neo-liberal empire with which postsocialist Bulgaria collaborates.

Postsocialism is the stage of other and equally important stories produced by another and still rising power: Indian Bollywood movies are also shot in Bulgaria. Spectacular productions travelling with cast and staff members of over two hundred people come to Bulgarian small towns and villages to film love stories and dance sequences that spin the imagination yet glamorize traditional patriarchal relations, female sexuality under a male gaze, and light-skinned beauty.[50] These productions even bring their own cooks and home-grown food ingredients so they feel comfortable in the postsocialist space.[51] The presence of Hollywood and Bollywood productions in postsocialist Bulgaria illuminates the neo-liberal and multicultural logic of the global cultural flows that are marking our world today. "East" and "West" now mix freely and peacefully in postsocialist locales where they continue to inspire identifications, and meanings related to gender, racial, and cultural difference. The next chapter addresses these meanings and offers concluding remarks mapping locations of anti-racism after state socialism.

Conclusion: Postsocialism, Anti-racism, and Transnational Feminisms

The Bulgarian socialist state collapsed in 1989. The decades thereafter have been described by social scientists and laypersons as "postsocialism" – an era marked by cultural, social, political, and economic realities after state socialism along with "nostalgia" for the communist past;[1] desperation in the face of political corruption and impoverishment;[2] a state of being stuck on the road to democracy and economic growth;[3] and "Euro-Atlantic integration," referring to former socialist countries' assimilation into international organizations such as the European Union and NATO, political models of liberal democracy, Western-style multiculturalism, and free markets.[4] Postsocialism in Bulgaria and the Balkans has also been defined as the "re-Europeanization" of Balkan states that have been accepted as members of the European Union (Bulgaria, Croatia, Romania, Slovenia) or seek EU membership (Albania, Serbia, North Macedonia, Montenegro, Bosnia and Herzegovina). The postsocialist Balkans has also been described as a social territory witnessing the raise of "mug masculinity," neo-Nazism, racism, and extreme cultural/ethno-nationalism.[5] Reports of prejudice and discrimination against Roma, Arabs, Syrian refugees, queer and Black people as well as Islamophobia in Balkan countries, including Bulgaria, have become an international and national concern.[6]

In the case of Roma women, rampant discrimination and intolerance amid rapid neo-liberalization and social ruptures in Bulgaria positioned these women at the social bottom.[7] They are among the majority of the poor, the uneducated, and the unemployed. They are also the majority of victims of sex trafficking, child labour, and sexual and domestic and intimate partner violence not just in postsocialist Bulgaria but across former socialist states and the rest of Europe. Roma women on the move in Sweden, Spain, Italy, France, and other European countries have been deported en masse, discriminated against, and excluded.[8]

In Canada, the stream of Roma refugees arriving between 2010 and 2013 prompted changes in the country's immigration and refugee laws in order to prevent Roma from Eastern Europe from coming to and settling in Canada.[9] The political narratives accompanying the events depicted Roma women especially as idle subjects whose children and needs would have to be supported by the Canadian welfare system and the state. Ironically, Roma women have also become the subject of special national and international polices designed to uplift them. International women's NGOs originating in Western Europe, Canada, and the United States have rushed to Bulgaria and other former socialist countries to advocate for Roma social inclusion through programs funded by the European Union, individual governments, and wealthy donors such as the George Soros Foundation based in the United States. These organizations campaign for education and employment of Roma women and girls, stronger social programs to enable their participation in the formal economy, and access to education, adequate housing, credit, land, and other resources that support Roma women entrepreneurship.[10] This multipronged approach to Roma integration is presented as a way to liberate Roma girls and women from domestic and social violence, poverty, racism, and sexual exploitation. Incorporation in the waged labour market is also perceived as a mechanism to free Roma women from traditional family roles and transform them into autonomous subjects of liberal European states and capitalist economies. These contemporary Western neo-liberal international projects for addressing anti-Gypsism and racism in the Balkans have failed, however, to recognize Eurocentrism as a root cause for Roma oppression and marginality for over a century and throughout state capitalism and socialism. In other words, these European Union programs have failed to see how the intense support for developing supranational and pan-European consciousness in "United Europe" breeds Eurocentricity and racial thinking, which has been a historical root cause for prejudice, exclusion, and violence in Eastern, Western, and Central Europe and the Balkans alike. Yet critical reviews of these initiatives by intellectuals and activists in former socialist states in united Europe and the Balkans are yet to take up Eurocentrism as a kind of ideology rooted in intertwined local and global colonialism and racialized patriarchies responsible for identity formations and social relations in the Balkans. Instead, scholars from the region have highlighted the homogenizing tendency of European anti-Gypsism policies treating the Roma in Europe as a universal category erasing the differences between Roma subcultures, languages, and experiences. An especially poignant assessment of "European Policies for Social Inclusion of Roma" from 2015 stresses the paradoxical focus of these programs on Roma health, education, and housing – the same areas of Roma life targeted for reform by socialist state authorities and the Bulgarian Communist Party two decades earlier.[11] Yet the authors suggest further that contemporary European policies related to Roma integration take cues from socialist state policies whose approach to the Roma "largely mitigated" prejudice and discrimination against them. Socialist policies integrated the Roma more successfully by treating them as members of the larger population instead of a group of special interests requiring affirmative action approaches that exacerbate racism, prejudice, and discrimination against them in Bulgaria and other countries with large Roma populations. Stop treating the Roma as exotic other, Elena Marushiakova and Vesselin Popov urge, and enact policies for integration addressing Roma as "all other citizens of the European Union."[12]

This recommendation presumes that "integration" is a straightforward positive process leading to equality. However, one of the most important lessons from our socialist past is that "integration" has a high cost for those who are the object of this policy. In socialist Bulgaria, those targeted for "integration" were overwhelmingly Roma and Muslim women over whose bodies, labour, childbearing, and culture claims were staked by both men in their communities and those governing the socialist state. As chapters 3 and 4 in this book suggest, pushing these women into the collectivist socialist economy and workplaces controlled by the state, unveiling and redressing them, policing their morality and increasing their productivity were all state programs rationalized as emancipation, redistribution of privileges, modernization, and inclusion of oppressed and backward peoples whose liberation and equality necessitated their cultural death. Pushing Roma women into jobs and the neo-liberal economies of former socialist states also serves economic and social needs that have little to do with anti-racism and fostering Roma equality.[13] Providing education and training for Roma women and girls, thus preparing them for taking jobs in the formal economy actually, relieves both national and EU bodies from providing resources supporting Roma women and their communities. For example, a European Commission initiative from 2013 called "Equality Pays Off" presented itself as a gender equality program aiming to deal with the anticipated shortage of labour in the EU by "securing qualified labour" and supporting "large companies to diversify the pool of (potential) employees by getting better access to the female labour force." Incorporating and forcing millions of Roma women across Eastern and Central Europe and the Balkans in the labour force is key to the success of these neo-liberal schemes. Similar objectives inform the

European Union's "Framework for National Roma Integration Strategies up to 2020" where of "crucial importance" is educating Roma girls so as "to allow them later on to successfully enter the labour market." Properly educating Roma children and youth, according to the document, is "crucial" because these girls could be a substantial burden on the economies of struggling postsocialist countries in the European Union as unemployed subjects or single mothers.[14]

However, the economy is not a safe place for women, especially minority women. Pushing Roma or Muslim women into the public economy in the socialist state opened these women to state violence and close surveillance by managers, administrators, and representatives of the ruling political party, the majority of whom were men. It also forced them into a power relationship with ethnic Bulgarian women tasked with the surveillance and modernization of Roma and Muslim women. Indeed, postsocialist studies show that despite the force and violence, Roma and Muslim women gained access to education and jobs in the public economy; hence, they achieved greater financial and social independence. But these successes should not obscure the fact that forcing groups of women into adopting Eurocentric cultural views and values, forcefully dressing and redressing them as "modern European women," or herding them into boarding schools where they surrender their cultural and spiritual heritage, language, and traditions is neither socialist feminism nor female emancipation but control and domination exercised by state and patriarchal agents who are making decisions for these women. Likewise, contemporary EU and national initiatives that do not make space and provide resources for Roma women to make decisions for themselves, their children, and their communities but push educational and economic schemes designed by European and national administrative classes belonging to racial and ethnic majorities is not really minority and women's emancipation but Eurocentric neoliberalism disguised as equity. The underlining reason for these linked socialist and neo-liberal schemes is the racialized notion of Roma cultural inferiority and inability to function properly in the modern nation state where citizens perform useful labour benefiting the state and socialist and capitalist economic and political elites.

Not surprisingly, special educational and employment projects have been adopted by socialist and capitalist states and international bodies the world over as primary means to address the violence, poverty, and marginalization of Roma, Indigenous, and Black women. State policies and even some women's organizations in Canada, the United States, Bulgaria, Hungary, Brazil, Mexico, Italy, and other countries have all proposed or implemented employment projects as solutions to the problem of racism, sexual violence, murder, marginalization, and poverty experienced by minority women such as the Roma. Extending the racial and recolonizing logic of these schemes, the World Bank and the International Monetary Fund (IMF) have become vocal supporters of women's rights and gender equality measured as economic and financial gain.[15] The IMF has dispensed millions of dollars supporting research and NGOs dedicated to female employment, entrepreneurship, and financial prosperity. Yet sexual and other violence against all groups of women the world over has not decreased but has actually raged in the last decades unabated, illuminating yet again the fact that economic empowerment of women is not necessarily emancipation or liberation. This is a lesson many women learned as workers in the socialist economy where full access to education, work, and the professions *did not* lead to dismantling of the patriarchal symbolic and material foundations of state, society, and nation.

Anti-racism and Europeanism in Postsocialism

Domestic and international initiatives targeting racism, prejudice, violence against women, and homophobia in Bulgaria and other former socialist states further fail to recognize that they both originate in and advance cultural and political Europeanism, which, ironically, extends the Eurocentricity that has been historically a root cause for Roma and Muslim racialization, oppression, and marginality in countries such as Bulgaria. In the 1930s, leading Bulgarian scientists and intellectuals debated passionately the racial origins of the human groups present in the newly formed post-Ottoman liberal constitutional Bulgarian nation state. Their polemics illuminated the powerful ways in which Bulgarian scientific claims to genetic and cultural membership in the group of "European races" emerged within a globalized epistemological context shaped by inequal relations of power. Bulgarian ideas of racial and cultural origins and "Europeanness" have taken shape in relation to external Western and Northern European perceptions of their non-whiteness, barbarity, backwardness, and "oriental" cultural properties that made the Balkans dangerous, hence the object of external political power games. A scientifically backed claim to European racial and cultural origins was also a claim to self-humanity, self-respect, and independence in the face of hegemony as European and colonial state powers – Germany, France, the United States, Britain, and Russia – have repeatedly made decisions about how Bulgaria and the other Balkan states will be territorially determined, organized, and governed. Fascist and Nazi actions against Balkan Slavs and impure racial "mongrels" manifested the marginality and dehumanization of the small peoples in the Balkans, further prompting local scientific and political projects where racial sciences and racist vernaculars borrowed from European and American science served as a shield against power by seeking racial and cultural origins in the same Europe that consistently excluded Bulgaria and the Balkans. The construction of that epistemological shield, however, produced Roma, Jews, Armenians, Turks, and other others present in the Bulgarian state as Asiatic races whose farther distance from Europe and civilization provided the very proof for the European racial and cultural genealogies of ethnic Bulgarians.

Bulgarian state socialism further deployed "Europe" and "civilization" as platforms to assert the modernity and evolutionary capacity of socialism and communism amid the Cold War. The domestic and international visibility of Roma and Muslim minorities perceived as non-European and Asiatic smears on the socialist project presented an ideological problem as well as an issue of identification prompting violent policies targeting these groups for assimilation and eradication. The globalizing cultures of United States racial modernity re-energized racialized thinking in an ideologically and economically weakened socialist state, where racialized cinematic texts invigorated both male subjectivities and masculine claims to the kind of freedom, privilege, private property, and independence enjoyed by European and Euro-American white men. Not surprisingly, socialism collapsed soon after, making this kind of neo-racialized masculinity bolder and more visible. In the postsocialist period, Bulgarian claims to genetic and cultural Europeanness have been equally important in the face of external hegemony and power; much as in the early twentieth century when European and Euro-American powers decided who and what was "human," "European," and worthy of respect, these same powers decide who and what belongs to new and united Europe today, in the twenty-first century. Bulgarian and Balkan self-assertions of racial, cultural, or national pride function as political mechanisms for asserting both membership in Europe yet self-agency, self-direction, and the status of equal within that "new Europe."

These historical trajectories of racialized cultural identifications driven by geopolitics and unequal power in Bulgaria would not abate under the force of political anti-racism and anti-Gypsism programs designed by the European Union and controlled by the same Western powers against whose hegemony Bulgarian and Balkan perceptions of self and other have taken shape. These programs should be supported and resourced by European Union bodies and Western NGOs, but the design and delivery of these programs must be rooted in the experiences of local communities and placed in the hands of Roma, Muslim, and Bulgarian groups and individuals who live together. Instead, these initiatives are more often entrusted in the arms of state institutions, English-speaking foreign and domestic activists, and ethnic majority groups. These externally designed programs also stretch that modern geopolitical body named Europe and European planetary consciousness where race and culture continue to perform the work of major principles of differentiation within and outside "Europe." Such extended consciousness organizes EU-funded research platforms, special conferences, and surveys probing the degree to which the peoples living in the member states of the European Union show attachment to "Europe."[16] The visions of and desire for a "pan-European" entity and ethnicity behind these probes seek something more and different from a union of diverse nation states. Indeed, the idea of "Europe" is different from the idea of a European Union as some countries like Bulgaria are still constructed and referred to as members of the union but not really "Europe" in the sense of association with material prosperity, democracy, multiculturalism, tolerance, civil rights, functioning governments, cultural achievements, advanced judicial structures, and technological advancement – in a word, "civilization." In contrast, small postsocialist countries like Bulgaria are members of the EU but are associated with "traditional cultures," political and financial corruption, intolerance, violence, lack of gender, sexual, and racial equality, gross violation of minority rights, backward laws that are slow in adopting European principles and values, a struggling economy, poor infrastructure, and poverty by Western standards. In fact, these associations are shared not just by the "real Europeans" to the West but also by refugees and migrants from Syria, Afghanistan, Iraq, Nigeria, and China, who do not come to Bulgaria, Serbia, or Hungary because they want to stay. In media interviews, refugees have shown their distaste for the "poverty" of these countries, which refugees want to pass through on their way to the "truly developed land of opportunity" they see in the Europe north of Bulgaria, Serbia, and Hungary.[17] These attitudes feed natives' resentment and mobilization against migrants from Africa, Asia, and the Middle East: "It is hard to break an already thin slice of bread with someone who despises you," an old Bulgarian woman told me in a conversation about the refugees crossing the border near her small village.

Yet the Balkans have been associated further with "cultural racism,"[18] a recent term coined by social scientists in the West and North of the EU describing how and why societies in Eastern and Central Europe and the Balkans discriminate against Muslim natives and migrants. The "cultural racism" of former socialist societies, according to the scholars developing this concept, is evident in surveys showing that Bulgarians, Poles, Hungarians, and other former socialist peoples in the EU are less likely to accept a Muslim in their families, and exhibit more pride in their cultures than those in Western Europe.[19] Bulgarians thus have been identified as "racists" who discriminate based on biology and "cultural racists" who discriminate based on culture they consider backward or incompatible with their values. If forms of Islamophobia are modes of racism, one may argue, then Buddhists and Hindu in India and Sri Lanka attacking and purging Muslim groups are also *racists* rather than postcolonial subjects whose perceptions of self and other absorbed the values and ideals of their European colonizers and masters who considered them inferior both biologically and culturally. The debatable soundness and usefulness of the term "cultural racism" notwithstanding, its explicit attachment to Balkan, East European and former socialist subjects describes a difference between violent, intolerant and backward East and cosmopolitan, multicultural, tolerant and superior West Europe.[20] Media, social scientific and political discursive productions of "East European racism" of a particular type have prompted some pundits and intellectuals to suggest that lack of shared "European values" between these geo-locales threatens the very existence and idea of "united Europe" and "European Union."

Other scholars and observers have challenged countries like Bulgaria to "face up to its multiethnic reality" and admit that racism and xenophobia are serious problems in the country.[21] Of particular issue is the so-called Bulgarian ethnic model to which members of the Bulgarian political elite gesture in order to counter EUs, NGOs, and other international institutional claims of racism in Bulgaria. Specifically, Bulgarian political figures have asserted Bulgarian tolerance embodied in a parliamentary democratic system where the Movement for Rights and Freedom (MRF) – a political party representing explicitly the interests of the Muslim minority in the country – has played a major role in state politics after socialism. The MRF has been a key force in the design and implementation of judicial, social, and political initiatives that form the basis of the emerging democratic postsocialist state. Bulgarian claims to tolerance have also emerged in contrast to the fracturing of former Yugoslavia, where Muslims faced much violence and death. Countering Western claims of rampant East European xenophobia and cultural racism, intellectuals from the East of Europe have began documenting prejudice and discrimination experienced by students and migrants from Bulgaria, Albania, Poland, and other former socialist countries in the United Kingdom before, during, and after Brexit, calling British attitudes towards these "Europeans" racist views valuing a specific kind of "racial whiteness" that excludes Balkan and East European subjects.[22]

In the rush to compare who is more racist, Eastern or Western Europeans, we are forgetting that identity formations are fluid, changeable, fluctuating, and unstable. We also forget that identifications in regions like the Balkans are not the result of personal choice, as some scholars funded by the European Union insist.[23] Rather, these formations are what Foucault calls "subjectivities," in this case Balkan subjectivities that are the outcome of intertwined local, national, and transnational forces and relations of power. We also forget that the relations of power between what is referred to as the "East" and "West" of Europe are not the same as those between Western Europe and the Balkans: lands and peoples continuously governed and directed by hegemonic states and peoples considering themselves the norm of historical evolution and civilization. Indeed, "race" is a social construct, so spending much time debating its meaning misses the point that the function of race is not to describe the social reality in countries such as Bulgaria or the United Kingdom but to comprehend how race and power, or the lack thereof, has assisted in the constitution of these social subjectivities, which are deeply sexed and gendered as well.

"Woman" and "Race" in the Postsocialist Political Left and Right

The postsocialist political spectrum in Bulgaria consists of left and right flanks, with the Right represented by the openly nationalist political party Ataka (Attack), whose capture of parliamentary seats in 2005 announced the rise in popularity of openly nationalistic, populist, and anti-establishment movements in the country. The leader of the party, Volen Siderov, skilfully employs a narrative that speaks to Bulgarians' deepest emotions and fears: strong Christian identifications and traditions, anxiety over a never-ending perceived Muslim and foreign threat undermining the country's sovereignty shaped by a history of five-century-long Ottoman domination, and mistrust of both communist/socialist and liberal, middle-class Eurocentric politics and ideologies. Ataka and its followers also share a belief that Roma are delinquent, lazy, and undeserving of state and social support and that Muslims in the country are actual Bulgarians who converted to Islam under the historical oppression of the Ottomans. Yet Ataka and its famous anti-Semitic leader Siderov appear as milder and calmer ideological versions of the neo-Nazi and ultranationalist groups that have formed the far-right fringe of Bulgarian politics. These masculine, racist fractions, often attached to football fan clubs, have attracted mostly younger Bulgarian men, who profess fascist beliefs and preach in favour of a "white" and Christian Bulgaria and Europe cleansed of all others who are different. Followers of these groups were among the "private soldiers" who rushed in 2013 to "defend" the Bulgarian and EU borders from the thousands of Middle Eastern refugees and migrants at the Bulgaria-Turkey border who were en route to Germany. In the 2017 parliamentary elections, a coalition of these right-wing groups called "United Patriots" won 9 per cent of the popular vote, thus taking on the role of a broker in the country's governing coalition.

The left of the postsocialist political spectrum is occupied by the Bulgarian Socialist Party, the successor of the former Bulgarian Communist Party, which governed the country for over five decades. The membership of the party is ideologically diverse as newly emerged democratic socialists mix with old-style leftists who feel that Bulgaria's cultural affiliations are with Russia rather than Europe. The party's popularity in the country is apparent in its consistently high membership, yet the Bulgarian socialists have formed only two independent and two coalitional governments since 1990. Spending most of its parliamentary time in opposition, the Bulgarian Socialist Party has developed a distinctly leftist discourse that embraces traditional (read Christian) Bulgarian values and European identity. Since 2007, the Bulgarian Socialist Party has been a member of the Party of European Socialists (PES) composed of national-level socialist parties in EU member states. From that traditional national yet pan-European location, the Bulgarian Socialist Party has enacted a political agenda that embraces women and feminist issues but only as far as these issues do not violate what the female leaders of the party consider "traditional family values."

Eurocentricity, Christianity, and heterosexual patriarchal cultural values connect the ends of the political Left and Right in Bulgarian politics. Whether inclusive or deeply racialized and exclusivist, the Bulgarian socialist Left and populist Right have used "woman" and "queer" as tropes to mobilize a racialized, heterosexual, patriarchal national formation whose purpose is the preservation of Bulgaria as European and Christian and, for the political Right, a "racially white" country as well. The narrative depends on the prior belief that Bulgaria was once upon a time such a nation, hence its return to a presumed original form spurs the Right into action. For example, in December 2014, Valeri Simeonov, the leader of the Right who was also the deputy prime minister, made the following statement:

> The undisputed fact is that the majority of the Roma ethnos lives outside any laws, rules and human norms of behavior ... For them, theft and

robbery are a way of life ... The question is what turned the Roma into destroyers of the state and the laws ... Why do people, who during the socialist times twenty-five years ago worked, sent their children to school, and contributed to the social good have turned into insolent, cocky, and enraged anthropoids, demanding the right to wages without having laboured, demanding health care benefits without being sick, child support benefits for children who play with pigs in the streets, and maternal support benefits for [Roma] women with the instincts of street bitches.[24]

Simeonov's rant against the Roma was actually his way of addressing the Movement for Rights and Freedom, a centrist political party representing the interests of the Muslim minority in Bulgaria. According to Simeonov and the supporters of the Right, that political party served Turkish and foreign interests and manipulated the Roma population in the country into membership both in the party and Islam. Importantly, it was the image of a not-quite-human and idle Roma woman bearing unwanted and uncared-for children that carried Simeonov's message of postsocialist Roma degradation. In fact, Simeonov's speech praised, albeit indirectly, the assimilationist modernizing policies of the socialist state against the Roma, thus implying further the need for a forceful action in governing this "population." The rhetoric pointed to Roma, and Muslim women, as especially dangerous because their fertility and child rearing posed the most serious threat to a unified European modern Bulgarian nation of rational citizens engaged in work and labour that contributes to the economy and is thus worthy of state and social support.

In other public spaces, representatives of the political Right have bashed the queer community in the country fighting for recognition of sexual rights. In 2013, members of the populist political party Ataka initiated legislation that forbade expressions of sexuality and sexual orientation in public spaces. The legislation did not pass, but that did not prevent self-described defenders of "traditional Bulgarian values" from seeking other political, judicial, and cultural means to prevent a meaningful public conversation about sexual and transgender self-identifications and political equality. Like the political Right, the female leadership of the Bulgarian Socialist Party has not extended support for the queer community, although its recent platforms embrace the fight against gender violence, at least rhetorically. Kornelia Ninova, the leader of the socialists, wrote an open letter where she wished queer activists "good luck" in their struggles but declined to participate in pride parades; she also led her party to a vote rejecting the Council of Europe's Istanbul Convention mandating state actions against violence targeting women and domestic violence. The political Right rejected the convention as well, presenting it as a "gender ideology" forced on Bulgaria by external EU and Western European activists seeking the legalization of gay marriage and adoption of children and institutionalizing a transgender category. According to ideologues of both the Left and the Right in Bulgaria, a gender between "man" and "woman" did not exist and its institutionalization would violate traditional Bulgarian values. Ninova drew upon her training as a lawyer in 2018 to praise the decision of Bulgaria's highest court declaring the convention unconstitutional.[25] In the spring of the same year, Ninova publicly congratulated women in the country for March 8, International Women's Day: "Women, we give birth and bring new life," stated Nivova, "We take care of home and family. We work and prove ourselves in our professions every day. Bless you and be happy with the men next to you."[26]

These political stands to the political Right and Left in Bulgaria extend and emulate twentieth-century local, national, and transnational events. They echo socialist state rationalizations of policies targeting both minority and majority women's child rearing, work, values, and behaviours so that women breed and foster proper socialist subjects on the path of communism. Like the Communist Party state, present-day socialists take the strides and advancement of women in politics, law, cultural production, and science as symptoms of already present gender equality that does not need special conventions to deal with women's inequality and the violence inflicted on them. Women like Ninova often take their own ascent to the heights of politics and society as a mark of the opportunities that exist for all women in the country … if only they choose to take advantage of them. Yet both the Left and the Right in postsocialist Bulgaria are inspired by and enfolded within greater trans-European polity formations from which they take cues much like their earlier twentieth-century predecessors whose political views relied overwhelmingly on European, American, and Russian colonial modern sciences and ideologies to form domestic agendas. The leaders of the contemporary ultra-nationalist and racist fractions in Bulgaria rely on the same European racist science and popular texts for their present agenda guarding an imagined pure Bulgarian racial and cultural stock much like leading Bulgarian politicians and scientists in the late 1930s evoked German, British, French, and American racial sciences to campaign for a nation imagined as a "beehive" where only the same kind of bees could live and prosper. And much like the Marxist and leftist scholars and intellectuals of the early twentieth century, the modern postsocialist socialist party in Bulgaria evokes ideas of equal races but inequal cultures as a platform for envisioning a new Bulgarian

European nation; queer, transgender, non-traditional women without men, Syrian refugees, and Muslims from the Middle East in general do not and cannot belong to that nation. Both the Left and the Right in Bulgarian politics are motivated and stimulated by cultural and ideological exchanges within pan-European political networks solidified throughout the twentieth century by German, French, and Italian fascist and Marxist movements.

The heteronormative, racialized, and patriarchal politics of the Left and the Right in postsocialist Bulgaria have been rigorously scrutinized and deconstructed in a stream of critical literature and media stories domestically and internationally. However, today, as much as in the past, racialized identity formations and social relations in Bulgaria are uneven, fractured, fluid, and unstable; the racial aspirations of the economic and political elites have not been always shared by the middle classes, or the men and women who laboured in the socialist factories and agricultural fields. Neither is the racism and ultra-nationalism observed in Bulgaria today shared by the new urban wealthy classes, women and feminists, queer people, residents of small towns and villages, or youth. The problem is that an overwhelming focus on the deficiencies, excesses, ruptures, corruption, and violence of postsocialism in the Balkans has obscured the events and forces embodying humanity, goodness, cosmopolitanism, hybridity, tolerance, and anti-racism that are also Bulgarian. The chapters of this book have narrated both the violence of Eurocentricity and race-thinking under Bulgarian state liberalism and socialism as well as positive Roma, Bulgarian, and Muslim community relations, international feminisms forming meaningful alliances with racialized women, solidarity between women against the violence of sex work, domesticity, and ideology, and opening of cultural spaces embracing the spirituality and world views of the colonized, Indigenous, and non-white. These historical alliances and the individuals and groups that forged them have not been fully appreciated, studied, or utilized by foreign and native activists, who seem to believe that racial and cultural self-determinations in Bulgaria poised against external hegemony and power would abate and embrace "European values of tolerance and multiculturalism" under the force of political programs designed abroad. Anti-oppression activism in Bulgaria must locate and nurture instead the postsocialist cultural "third space" where artists, intellectuals, educators, and ordinary people have created and supported postsocialist cultural productions that reject global and local claims to racial, national, or sexual purity thus mobilizing a myriad of anti-racist vernaculars and imaginations that are a potent site for transformative politics not just in Bulgaria but in the rest of Europe as well.

The remainder of this concluding chapter explores this "third space" in relation to local art production and transnational feminist concepts of "borderlands."

Locating the Postsocialist Cultural "Third Space"

In his influential work on the "location of culture," postcolonial scholar and critical theorist Homi Bhabha (1994) began his inquiry with a story about his own journey as a young middle-class person from Bombay (Mumbai), India, in pursuit of a university degree in literary studies in England in the 1970s.[27] Bhabha reflected on his interest in the English literature he encountered as a colonialized subject but also stated his love for the vernaculars and richness of his own Indian culture. But nothing moved Bhabha as deeply as the prose of Indo-Caribbean author V.S. Naipaul, whose fiction constructed characters full of life and even laughter in the midst of despair.[28] These characters, Bhabha suggested, were "cosmopolitan" because they could be read "against the ideology and intent" of their author who wrote about the slums of London populated by immigrants in boarding houses ruled by heartless and often racist English landlords.[29] Bhabha used the term "vernacular cosmopolitanism" to refer to literary work embodied by immigrant, diasporic, and dispossessed individuals whose claim to equality and freedom was not anchored in a nation state but in experiences associated with a cultural "third space."

The "third space" is a territory of postcolonial cultural forms and subjectivities whose main feature is "hybridity:" discursive representations (speech, text, visuals, sound) which are political because they occupy a space that is not exclusively delimited by the history of either one country or ideology. Rather, it is a space that sits in between ideological and political polarities producing representations of things and people in the world who do not align with either the epistemological power and hegemony of the First World or the struggling, colonized, and counter-authoritarian Third World. However, the purpose of such a space is not to play with and experience free-floating signifiers; in the third space, discursive production functions in a non-linear temporality because it acts as "translation" of ideological and social symbols while delaying indefinitely a state of either unity or antagonism. And such a moment of translation in between distinct signifiers manifests the agency, energy, creativity, and struggle of the marginalized, the exploited, the postcolonial, and the non-white. The political novelty and power of the cultural representations produced in the third space are not in their refusal to align, or their counter-positioning to both left and right ideologies; rather it is in their ability to "overcome the grounds of opposition" between dualities. Bhabha describes the overcoming as cultural hybridity: a subject position which embraces identities that are always in the making and never finished thus countering modern Eurocentric and colonial notions of fixed racial, gender, sexual, and cultural categories and signs. And that location *between* sites and signs of origin and originality is a space of possibilities, of things emerging or not yet come into being.

Interestingly, Bhabha's explication of the "third space" contains multiple references to socialism, Marxism, and "left and right" ideologies as well as Serbian and Balkan "nationalism" used by the author to exemplify strife for "pure" and "ethno" national formations against which Bhabha's theory of a hybrid, non-white, and agentic cultural third space and subjects takes shape:

> The very concepts of homogenous national cultures, the consensual or contiguous transmission of historical traditions, or 'organic' ethnic communities – as the grounds of cultural comparativism – are in a profound process of redefinition. The hideous extremity of Serbian nationalism proves that the very idea of a pure, 'ethnically cleansed' national identity can only be achieved through the death, literal and figurative, of the complex interweavings of history, and the culturally contingent borderlines of modern nationhood. This side of the psychosis of patriotic fervour, I like to think, there is overwhelming evidence of a more transnational and translational sense of the hybridity of imagined communities.[30]

Against the "psychosis" of Serbian nationalism, Bhabha articulates the emerging transnationalism and hybridity of Sri Lankan theatre, Aboriginal cinema, African American prose, South African literature, and Muslim diasporic poetry. Bhabha's gestures to the Balkans and socialism and postsocialism thus serve to illustrate the singularity and violence of the opposing sides in the dualities that a postcolonial third space defies.

A gender and sexuality lens, however, complicates Bhabha's notions of cosmopolitanism and hybridity. It also challenges the situating of socialism, postsocialism, and the Balkans signified by "Serbia" within Bhabha's concept of the locations of culture. In feminist thinking, cultural, racial, and political "hybridity" is understood in relationship to racialized but also deeply gendered and sexed ideas of nation state and "national culture," where citizenship and belonging are tied to blood, land, language, class, and male heteronormative privilege. Therefore, gendered subjects do not experience hybridity in the same way.[31]

Women, transgender and queer hybrid identities, and cultural forms transgress national, racial, sexual, and patriarchal borders simultaneously, and these transgressions, and the local and international differential power relations that shape them, mark the postsocialist "third space."

Postsocialism is thus more than the ento-nationalism, racism, political hooliganism, corruption, and narrowly defined identifications rooted in space, borders, and territoriality. Postsocialist culture is productive yet fractured, uneven, varied, and heterogeneous, encompassing cultural forms that embody hybridity especially vivid in minority cultural productions that sit between East and West, between European, Euro-American, and "oriental," between socialism, Marxism, liberalism, and capitalism, between racial whiteness and non-whiteness, and between woman and man. In the postsocialist third space, identities are open-ended while meaning-making shifts rapidly, presenting an unstable and liquid terrain where subjects resist a final destination and move across and between ideologies and epistemologies, alternating between embrace and rejection and between hope and despair. These moods exemplify epistemological doubt expressed in public evaluations of the social realities while experimenting with novel social forms. Culture in the postsocialist third space is thus highly productive and potent as it deconstructs the racial, ideological, and sexual polarities that undergird Eurocentric socialist and capitalist/neo-liberal modernities. In so doing, artists and cultural producers occupying a postsocialist third space act out modes of anti-racism, transgenderism, and hybridity that could inform anti-racist programs in former socialist countries such as Bulgaria, from where my examples come. The life, art, and politics of the transgender Roma music artist Azis, who has become one of the most influential cultural figures in postsocialist Bulgaria since the early 2000s, embodies that cultural third space.

Azis: Hybridity and Cosmopolitanism in the Third Space

Azis, born Vasil Trayanov Boyanov in 1978, is a Bulgarian recording artist of Roma origin born in a prison for women in a small Bulgarian town where his mother was incarcerated for illegally trading small goods. Azis dropped out of school in grade 4 but without regrets as he felt he was born to do greater and more important things in life. Beginning in the early 2000s, Azis's music, image, dance moves, fashion, personal interviews, and public gestures, meant to outrage and move people, have inspired millions of fans in Bulgaria, Turkey, Serbia, Russia, Azerbaijan, Romania, Iran, the United Kingdom, Germany, the United

Fig. 11 Roma Bulgarian music artist Azis in *Erotic*, 2014.

States, Pakistan, and other countries from where followers post on-line messages of admiration, embrace, and sheer joy caused by the powerful transracial, transgender, and trans-Balkan, Roma-Bulgarian music genre "chalga," which Azis helped invent. The reason is that chalga is a genuinely transnational music mixing Roma, Turkish, Arab, and Bulgarian folk and pop sounds and beats creating thus a uniquely Bulgarian and Balkan grammar of aesthetics and rhythms that are highly popular among ordinary people in Bulgaria and throughout the world. Azis and his larger-than-life persona epitomizes the mixing and creativity of the genre, but he also stands out with his highly political imagery and allusions, social commentaries reflecting important current issues, and media interviews where the artist shares his own views and transformations. Within the span of two decades, the artist Azis has been a man, a woman, and a transgender person who married a man, had a child with a woman, identified as Gypsy, but painted himself "white," all the while mixing, blending, and performing musical and visual forms that crossed orientalism, European modernism, and American radicalism.

His style is thus profoundly postsocialist in the sense that it presents a cultural and social space of experimentation with multiple ideologies and social forms, some of them novel, others already existent but borrowed – in a word, a productive and open-ended space where subjects ask questions about their socialist past, neo-liberal and capitalist present, and the direction of their future. But these explorations do not always lead to "Europe" or the "West." To the contrary, chalga fans in postsocialist Bulgaria embrace both East and West as their cultural, ethnic, and racial origin, accept the ambiguity of these ontologies, often refusing to determine if one or the other is truer, or authentically "Bulgarian." These postsocialist identifications demarcate class lines as chalga fans face newly influential urban classes who call the genre and its followers a cultural underclass showing Bulgaria's "sinking to the bottom" and overtly sexualized kitsch featuring lyrics ranging from the lewd to the profane and vulgar. Two female critics wrote an impassionate essay calling for a more Shakespearean style of narratives and classical European art as a tool against "chalga."[32] An important critique of the chalga genre and culture is related to its patriarchal representations diminishing women, which, ironically, are constructed and performed by semi-clad female singers with enlarged silicone breasts and Botoxed lips who are the stars of the genre. Feminists and women critical of the genre demand that these stars take responsibility for perpetuating a neo-liberal logic where a woman is a sexual commodity making her own body available for exploitation. More important to the Bulgarian political and economic elites, however, is the genre's open affiliation with non-Christian symbolism associated with the Orient that reminds Bulgarians of their linguistic and cultural links to the Ottoman Empire. Yet these elites see their future in the "new and united Europe," and that requires erasing the Eastern, the "oriental," and the peculiarly local so that Bulgaria stands as truly European. But chalga and Azis are not really "oriental." Azis embodies a hybridity that embraces both Europe and the Orient and treats them as cultural, religious, and geographical entities locked in a dialogical and dialectical relationship where one is shaped by the other.

Azis writes his songs and often conceptualizes and directs his own music videos incorporating visuals of India's landscapes and culture to where he traces his Gypsy heritage, Muslim minarets, and lyrics in the Turkish language as well as Western urban landscapes where he (re)lives queer sexual encounters like those portrayed by American pop star Madonna and British gay idol George Michael. Azis also identifies with American "King of Pop" Michael Jackson because he believes that, like Jackson, he is "dark-skinned, discriminated against, talented … and feminine."[33] Azis also identifies himself as both "Bulgarian" and "Gypsy" and sings with whole heart and tremendous tenderness traditional Bulgarian folk songs and Roma romantic music mixed with sounds originating in Turkey and the Middle East. Sometime after 2010, Azis started dressing in the style of urban hip hop African American artists, peppering his musical and visual appearances with references to gay, feminist, and anti-racist activism in the 1960s and 1970s United States. "I love the United States," he explained in an interview about his musical inspirations.[34] Yet in his more recent music and public life, Azis has embraced a look associated with heterosexual masculinity: gone are the high heels, glamorous drag clothes, the ultra-blond hair, long lashes, and leopard-skin bikinis. Azis wears shirts and trousers, his videos are shot in darker and simple colours, and they carry social messages calling for acceptance of difference and love. Throughout, Azis insists on being called "Gypsy" and not "Roma" and referred to as "he" instead of female or plural pronouns. These self-references do not foreclose further transformations but suggest that a "man" could actually become and be something new, feminine, and very different.

Azis's new image and persona, much like his previous incarnations, is outright political as he has also embraced a new vocabulary of difference evoking the racial history of the United States. Azis began publicly describing himself as a "black Gypsy" and "dark-skinned man" while referring to Bulgarians as "white people," thus redirecting public and state discourses on "ethnic issues" in Bulgaria to a distinctly racialized terrain.[35] In so doing, Azis and his art have renamed Roma oppression and marginalization as racialization that must be recognized and consciously and publicly debated and interrogated. "I believe God created me to sing and unite people," says Azis, who has collaborated with a plethora of artists, intellectuals, and musicians from all walks of life and faiths.[36] In a recent music video, Azis collaborated with Bulgarian actress Tzvetana Maneva, an icon of Bulgarian film and theatre loved by generations of ethnic Bulgarians for over five decades. In the video, Azis sings in front of a band of tattooed shirtless male musicians while images of gay, straight, and interracial couples convey love amid difference. The lyrics, authored by Azis, allude to the marginality of women and the violence they endure, passionately delivered by Azis styled as a man who narrates the story using female noun endings. The words "audacity," "strength," "colours," "ambition," "reflection," "connections," and "survival" flash on the screen leading to a final monologue by the actress Tzvetana Maneva asking: "Are we evil or just people who have forgotten they are good?"[37] The question is clearly directed to the ethnic Bulgarian majority, where the actress claims membership.

The collaboration between Azis and Maneva spurred a public debate about difference, racism, and marginality that did more for raising social consciousness in Bulgaria than externally funded and designed EU and state campaigns. The video of the song has generated over eight million views on YouTube while media appearances by Maneva and Azis responded especially to those who bashed the beloved actress for "appearing in chalga, considered low-brow entertainment." More importantly, the collaboration between the two artists embodied a Roma-Bulgarian relationality and togetherness that bridged ethnic, racial, and cultural borders, connected high and mass culture, and referenced goodness that also defines the history of Bulgaria. The collaboration shows the productiveness and tremendous potency of political solidarity. Such solidarity is still scarce in feminist and women's politics in Bulgaria, where women's historiography is written by Bulgarian ethnic women who view their needs and experiences as representing those of all women in the country. Likewise, ethnic Bulgarian feminists and educators lack locally developed yet cosmopolitan language about "race," "gender," and "ethnicity," thus inhibiting possibilities for much-needed public conversations about difference, history, social relations, unequal power, ideology, and identity. Whatever conversations are taking place in the postsocialist public sphere are dominated by political figures, media pundits, and externally funded local activists who are translating concepts of difference originating in European and US contexts from the English into the Bulgarian language and local history. However, neither race, nor gender, nor ethnicity have easy translations: these concepts are not native to Bulgaria and their relatively recent appearance in the Bulgarian vocabulary manifests the epistemological gaps between the "East" and "West" of Europe as well as their unequal power relations where meanings travel unidirectionally to the Balkan margins of "Europe" and the world. In Azis's music, embodying that cultural postsocialist third space, however, translation is not needed because language in that space is not foreign and abstract but ontological, personal, and intimate, relating local and global and looking not back but forward to things that could be made to happen.

His music video "Motel" (2017) depicts a moving bus where Muslim refugees, Christian Bulgarians, Roma, and straight and queer people sit together travelling to a destination that is not geographical but temporal.[38] Passing a bottle of water to each other, migrants and natives in the bus are moving in time to a possible future. The video imagery and messages are reminiscent of what Paul Gilroy, in the context of black intellectual and cultural traditions, calls an antiracist "planetary humanity" connected to democratic and egalitarian forms of togetherness that have been all but expunged from contemporary imaginations fixed on social evil but forgetting that goodness also exists.³⁹ In the Bulgarian and postsocialist context, this imagery of social good that has been and that could be is located in cultural productions: fantasies, images, stories, cinema, music, myths, and literature supporting novel and different ways of being in the world. Nurturing such cultural space, crossing all kinds of borders while connecting past and future requires love for self and acceptance of one's own cultural and racial genealogies and past. Azis articulated such need to love self in order to love others powerfully in a song released in 2019 titled "Ciganche" (Gypsy). The video of the song has been viewed over eight million times since it was posted online. In it, Azis sings to a woman portrayed by another ethnic Bulgarian music star, Ruth Koleva, whom Azis chose for the video because she was "white and beautiful":

> Hear me out girl.
> Why do you hide your love for the Black, shabby, poor boy?
> Hear me out girl.
> Don't be ashamed of the colour of my skin and what people will say.
> Do you know how to love?
> A small death it is the way a Gypsy loves.
> He is ready to burn alive.
> A bridge I will become for you so you can walk on me
> My lungs I'll give to you so you breathe through them.
> I am not mad at you and I am not judging you
> But even if you spend the night with me
> You are someone else in the morning.
> You are with your friend and pretend I don't exist.
> Why do you hide me as if I am but a horrible crime?⁴⁰

Indeed, why are we rejecting and hiding our roots in and passion for East, West, North, and South? And who says we ought to be ashamed by our cultural transgressions and crossings? These questions are central to the Bulgarian postsocialist third cultural space where anti-racism, anti-oppression, and cosmopolitanism already exist and flourish. Nurturing that third space further is the work of artists, educators, activists, storytellers, writers, transnational feminists, and other persons who, like Azis, transcend the national and ethnic territoriality of culture and refuse to look only to the past but dare to imagine and thus make a different future. That future, much like in Azis's music, is neither socialist nor capitalist but a place and time of human freedom – freedom to claim and love one's history but also freedom to be whatever one wishes to be and above all freedom to change and be something new and different.

"I am the face of democracy," Azis told a reporter. "You are in the Balkans! You are in the middle of Gypsy land," where movement, mixing, and change rule.[41]

Postsocialist "Nepantla:" Anti-racism and Transnational Feminism

Azis's musical and visual depictions of culturally mixed Balkans, cosmopolitan democracy, and a Bulgaria that is also a "Gypsy land" should not be mistaken for the liberal, Western versions of "multiculturalism" that are the subject of public debates and policies in the United States, Canada, the United Kingdom, and Germany.[42] Rather, Azis's depictions echo transnational feminist knowledges originating at "borderlands" that have been the bedrock of women's anti-oppression work locally and globally since the 1960s. Bulgaria and the Balkans, I believe, embody such borderlands between political, epistemological, and cultural modern entities such as West and East; socialism, capitalism, and liberalism; Europe, Asia, and the Orient; and the First and Third Worlds. Peoples in the Balkans are therefore "border people" who live their lives in what transnational feminist and poet Gloria Anzaldúa calls a state of "nepantla," which is a Nahuatl word for the space between two bodies of water and between two worlds.[43]

Anzaldúa, a self-described Chicana dyke-feminist, tejana patlache poet, writer, and cultural theorist, was born into a family of sharecroppers in 1942 in South Texas, USA. Anzaldúa worked in the fields near the Mexico-United States border with her parents, who migrated to Arizona in search of work. She pursued higher education as well and became an influential scholar and feminist artist whose work captured the meaning of culture and identities of peoples living at material and symbolic border regions. Anzaldúa's concepts of the borderlands reflected her experiences of marginalization and her mixed cultural and racial heritage that did not fit into modern categories and types. She lived her life as a floating entity embodying the liminality, fluidity, and crossing of cultures and spaces: a "Shiva, a many-armed and legged body with one foot on brown soil, one on white, one in straight society, one in the gay world, the man's world, the women's, one limb in the literary world, another in the working class, the socialist, and the occult worlds."[44] Life in that space is marked by uncertainty: for border people, wrote Anzaldúa, ambiguity is actually a way of life "in-between" borders, boundaries, categories, and types. Knowledge based on hierarchies and types like those developed by European modern science and diffused through colonial conquests "splits us," preventing those of us at the borderlands from embracing all that we are historically, culturally, politically, our mixtures and crossings. Therefore, we at the Balkans and other borderlands also experience continuous shame of who we are, of our history and of our inability to fit fully someone else's imagination of that which is worthy, beautiful, acceptable, and "normal." We deal with the shame by bonding against others who are different from us and positioned even lower on the racial, political, and civilizational hierarchies created by European, Soviet, and American colonialists, scientists, and ideologues. But we can change that and the change begins by questioning, refusing, and unlearning "beliefs unstilled in us" by those possessing more wealth and power.[45] These beliefs include the racial categories that organize much of our knowledge.

For example, at the borderlands, where all is always in transition and on the move, terms such as "white" and "non-white" do not capture the complexity of life. As Anzaldúa put it, the term "white" cannot be applied to all white people because some "possess non-white consciousness" and the terms "non-white," "Black," or "of colour" do not enfold all non-whites because many of them "bear white consciousness."[46] These racial binaries depend on reductionism and exclusion that "diminish our humanness" and complexity, especially at the borderlands. These categories also inhibit politics seeking political togetherness, alliances, coalitions, and mutuality. Critical interrogations of "whiteness," "white," and "non-white" categories (applied to different social groups in Bulgaria, the Balkans, and the world at large) would be a major step towards bridging and opening a third space in between these racial types, where different identifications, complex consciousness, and hybridity capture our fluidity, humanity, and capacity for liberation, togetherness, and change. Transnational feminist anti-racism calls on us to engage in creating more and greater spaces of the "third kind" laying in between worlds and types, where mixing and ambiguity is accepted, loved, and purposefully articulated in public education, the arts, political discourse, and at the family dinner table. Creating more such third spaces in postsocialist Bulgaria does not need institutional structures and foreign sponsorship; rather, it is in the hands of local artists, educators, teachers, activists, creative people, and all other people who, like the Roma performing artist Azis, cross worlds and have built bridges, or are willing to learn how to construct them.

We should embrace the multiple genealogical and epistemological lineages that cross East and West and find in such hybridity not shame but strength. Racial, cultural, political, and linguistic hybridity is a bridge connecting our multiple selves, thus defying binaries and final truths about good and evil people; developed, civilized, and unworthy nations; and superior and inferior races. Peoples straddling the borderlands that stand in between the ends of these oppressive binaries are best positioned to invent new social forms by building upon and reinforcing the foundations of our hybrid identifications and extending them to embrace new influences and ideas. The knowledge that "we are in a symbolic relationship to all that exists and co-creators of ideology – attitudes, beliefs and cultural values"[47] is enough to motivate us to act. Doubt about the emancipatory capacities of socialism, capitalism, neo-liberalism, and other modern ideologies is also motivating and productive, propelling our search for other ways of being in the world. This book is my way of acting and seeking political togetherness with other women in Bulgaria and the world who reject binary identifications, modern masculine ideologies, and the reductive but fiercely guarded social and political categories that are among the root causes of the violence and divisions defining our histories. The socialist state imagined itself to be undoing these divisions, but in the process of building a just and moral society, it singled out and erased or murdered all those genres of people who would not come aboard because they had their own ideals and visions of what constitutes a good life and a better future.

Notes

Introduction

1. Holmstrom, *Socialist Feminist Project*.
2. Leonard and Fraser, "Capitalism's Crisis of Care."
3. Ghodsee, *Why Women Have Better Sex*.
4. Campbell, "Marx and Engels's Vision."
5. Johnson, "What Is Cultural Studies Anyway?" 38.
6. McClintock, *Imperial Leather*, 5.
7. Grabowska, "Bringing the Second World In."
8. Koobak and Marling, "Decolonial Challenge."
9. Suchland, "Is Postsocialism Transnational?"
10. Mohanty, *Feminism without Borders*.
11. Burawoy, "Marxism after Communism"; Khan, "End of State-Socialism."
12. Hopkins, "Gender Inequality in Postcapitalism."
13. Guettel, *Marxism & Feminism*, 1–3.
14. Marks, "Word 'Capitalism.'"
15. Marks, "Word 'Capitalism,'" 163.
16. See Mohanty, *Feminism without Borders*; Mojab, *Marxism and Feminism*; Banerji, *Thinking Through*.
17. Siegel, *Totalitarian Paradigm*; Shorten, *Modernism and Totalitarianism*.
18. Bauman, "Communism."
19. Grabowska, "Bringing the Second World In"; Slavova, "Looking at Western Feminisms."
20. Davies, *Left of Karl Marx*; Davis, *Autobiography*.
21. Lorde, "Notes."
22. Todorova, "I Don't Know."
23. See Turda and Weindling, *Blood and Homeland*; Law, *Red Racisms*; Goldberg, "Precipitating Evaporation"; Baker, *Race*; Pistotnik and Brown, "Race in the Balkans"; Imre, "Whiteness"; Bjelić, "Toward a Genealogy."
24. Todorova, "Race Travels."

174   Notes to pages 13–26

25 Institute for Political Research, *Historicizing "Whiteness"*; Balkan Society for Theory and Practice, *Race and Racism in the Balkans Workshop*.
26 Roediger, *Wages of Whiteness*.
27 Allen, *Invention*; Lipsitz, *Possessive Investment in Whiteness*; Roediger, *Working toward Whiteness* and *Wages of Whiteness*.
28 Hartigan, "Establishing."
29 Omi and Winant, *Racial Formation Theory*; Feagin and Elias, "Rethinking Racial Formation"; Bonilla-Silva, *Racism without Racists*; HoSang, LaBennett, and Pulido, *Racial Formation*.
30 Warren, *Racial Revolutions*; Bora, "Problem without a Name"; Pagliai, "Conversational Agreement."
31 Goldberg, *Threat of Race*.
32 Turda and Weindling, *Blood and Homeland*; Law, *Red Racisms*.
33 Goldberg, *Threat of Race*, 4.
34 Peterson, *Up from Bondage*.
35 Neuberger, *Orient Within*.
36 Stafford, "This Map."
37 Hill-Collins, "Social Construction"; Harding, *Feminist Standpoint Theory*.
38 Fawcett and Hearn, "Researching Others."
39 Enns, "Locational Feminisms."
40 Grewal and Kaplan, *Scattered Hegemonies*.
41 Kaplan, Alarcon, and Moallem, *Between a Woman*, 4.
42 Chari and Verdery, "Thinking between the Posts."
43 Barot and Bird, "Racialization."
44 Hochman, "Racialization."
45 See, for example, Chiara Bonfiglioli's use of the East-West divide in "Former East, Former West."
46 Mohanty, *Feminism without Borders*.
47 See Mohanty, Russo, and Torres, *Third World Women*.

1. Race, Women, and Nation-Building in the 1930s and 1940s

1 Darkovski, "Dimiter Mihalchev," 8–9. Kiril Darkovski was Mihalchev's colleague at the philosophy department at Sofia University. Darkovski writes that Prof. Dimiter Mihalchev usually delivered public lectures in Auditorium 15 at the university. Describing Mihalchev's oratorical skills and intellectual sharpness, Darkovski states: "[I] understood well what attracted as a magnet the colorful crowd regularly filling the famous Auditorium 15, then the largest at the university: this was the spectacle of a rare master of discourse and thinking, or maybe more correctly, the functioning of a living machine for though and speech" (p. 9). My translation.

2 Kavalski, "Balkan America?"
3 Statelova and Gruncharov, *Istoria na Nova Bulgaria*, 7–9, 13.
4 Statelova and Gruncharov, *Istoria na Nova Bulgaria*, 13–14.
5 Statelova and Gruncharov, *Istoria na Nova Bulgaria*, 15–16.
6 Statelova and Gruncharov, *Istoria na Nova Bulgaria*, 194.
7 Statelova and Gruncharov, *Istoria na Nova Bulgaria*, 198.
8 Brazitsov, "Edin Den Mejdu Sofiiskite Tsigani," 18. My translation.
9 Brazitsov, "Edin Den Mejdu Sofiiskite Tsigani," 19.
10 Brazitsov, "Edin Den Mejdu Sofiiskite Tsigani," 19.
11 "Gypsies," *lostbulgaria.com*. http://www.lostbulgaria.com/?cat=507.
12 MIRIS, "Etnicheski Sustav na Naselenieto v Bulgaria."
13 MIRIS, "Etnicheski Sustav na Naselenieto v Bulgaria."
14 Mihalchev, "Rasizmut kato Filosofsko-Istoricheska Teoria," 342.
15 Popov, *Bulgarskiat Narod Mejdu Evropeiskite Rasi I Narodi*, 13, 86.
16 Popov, *Bulgarskiat Narod Mejdu Evropeiskite Rasi I Narodi*, 34.
17 Popov, *Nasledsvenost, Rasa I Narod*, 48.
18 Popov, *Nasledsvenost, Rasa I Narod*, 57, 68.
19 Popov, *Bulgarskiat Narod mejdu Evropeiskite Rasi i Narodi*, 33–4.
20 Popov, *Bulgarskiat Narod mejdu Evropeiskite Rasi i Narodi*, 32.
21 Popov, *Bulgarskiat Narod mejdu Evropeiskite Rasi i Narodi*, 32.
22 Popov, *Nasledstvenost, Rasa i Narod*, 51.
23 Popov, *Nasledstvenost, Rasa i Narod*, 113–21.
24 Popov, *Nasledstvenost, Rasa i Narod*, 116.
25 Popov, *Nasledstvenost, Rasa i Narod*, 120, 122.
26 Popov, *Nasledstvenost, Rasa i Narod*, 148.
27 Mihalchev, "Rasizmut kato FIlosofsko-Istoricheska Teoria," 341.
28 Statelova and Gruncharov, *Istoria na Nova Bulgaria*, 495.
29 Mihalchev, "Rasizmuet kato Folosofsko-Istoricheska Teoria," 351–3.
30 Mihalchev, "Rasizmuet kato Folosofsko-Istoricheska Teoria," 381.
31 Mihalchev, "Rasizmuet kato Folosofsko-Istoricheska Teoria," 358.
32 Mihalchev, "Rasizmuet kato Folosofsko-Istoricheska Teoria," 362.
33 Mihalchev, "Rasizmuct kato Folosofsko-Istoricheska Teoria," 366.
34 Mihalchev, "Rasizmuet kato Folosofsko-Istoricheska Teoria," 386.
35 Mihalchev, "Rasizmuet kato Folosofsko-Istoricheska Teoria," 386.
36 Mihalchev, "Rasizmuet kato Folosofsko-Istoricheska Teoria," 386–7.
37 Mihalchev, "Rasizmut pod Zakrilata na Biologiata," 423.
38 Mihalchev, "Rasizmut pod Zakrilata na Biologiata," 420.
39 Mihalchev, "Rasizmut pod Zakrilata na Biologiata," 435.
40 Mihalchev, "Rasizmut pod Zakrilata na Biologiata," 435.
41 Mihalchev, "Rasizmut pod Zakrilata na Biologiata," 436.
42 Mihalchev, "Rasizmut pod Zakrilata na Biologiata," 424.

43 Mihalchev, "Rasizmut pod Zakrilata na Biologiata," 425.
44 Mihalchev, "Rasizmut pod Zakrilata na Biologiata," 435.
45 Mihalchev, "Rasizmut pod Zakrilata na Biologiata," 413.
46 Mihalchev, "Rasizmut pod Zakrilata na Biologiata," 413.
47 Mihalchev, "Rasizmut kato Filosofsko-Istoricheska Teoria," 372.
48 Mihalchev, "Rasizmut pod Zakrilata na Biologiata," 425.
49 Mihalchev, "Rasizmut pod Zakrilata na Biologiata," 426.
50 Konsulov, "Edin Filosof, Competenten po Vsichko," 1065.
51 Konsulov, "Shto e Natsia?" 645–9.
52 Konsulov, "Edin Filosof, Competenten po Vsichko," 1976; Konsulov, "Shto e Natsia?" 664.
53 Konsulov, "Shto e Natsia?" 664.
54 Konsulov, "Shto e Natsia?" 649.
55 Konsulov, "Shto e Natsia?" 658.
56 Konsulov, "Shto e Natsia?" 665.
57 Kinkel, "Priroda i Obshestvo," 162.
58 Kinkel, "Priroda i Obshestvo," 169.
59 Kinkel, "Priroda i Obshestvo," 191.
60 Kinkel, "Priroda i Obshestvo," 193.
61 Kinkel, "Priroda i Obshestvo," 194.
62 Kinkel, "Priroda i Obshestvo," 193, footnote.
63 McKee, *Sociology and the Race Problem*, 88.
64 Kinkel, "Priroda i Obshestvo," 196.
65 Quoted in Promitzer, "Taking Care of the National Body," 228.
66 Nazurska, *Universitetskoto Obrazovanie*, 79–80. My translation.
67 Nazurska, *Universitetskoto Obrazovanie*, 246.
68 Daskalova, *Ot Siankata na Istoriata*, 34.
69 Popova and Muratova, "Dimensions of the Women's Voices."
70 Daskalova, *Ot Siankata na Istoriata*, 136.
71 Popova, "Pozhelavam ti Evropa."
72 Popova, "Pozhelavam ti Evropa," 62.
73 Popova, "Pozhelavam ti Evropa," 62–3.
74 Popova-Mutafova, "Kakvo Zhenata."
75 Blagoeva, "Ikonomicheska ili Polticheska Nezavisimost na Zhenata Triabva?" 132.
76 Bulgarian Women's Union, "To the Union's Units, Regional Number 2," 4.
77 Pashova et al., *Iskam Blagorodna Profesia*.
78 Pashova and Muratova, *Romski Arhif*, 23–5.
79 Vassilev, "Rescue of Bulgaria's Jews."
80 Todorov, *Fragility of Goodness*.
81 Georgieff, "Sofia."
82 Bjelić, "Toward a Genealogy."

2. Socialist Racialism: Desired and Undesired Genres of Women, and the Paradoxes of Socialism

1 Todorova, "Race and Women of Color."
2 Genov, Marinov, and Tairov, *Tsiganskoto Naselenie v NR Bulgaria po Putia na Sotsialisma*, 5.
3 Araújo and Maeso, *Eurocentrism, Racism and Knowledge*.
4 Shohat and Stam, *Unthinking Eurocentrism*.
5 Hostettler, *Eurocentrism*.
6 Hostettler, *Eurocentrism*, 68.
7 Hall, "West and the Rest: Discourse and Power."
8 Hall, "West and the Rest," 221–2.
9 Marx, "On the Jewish Question."
10 Marx, "On the Jewish Question," 46.
11 Marx, "On the Jewish Question," 48.
12 Fine and Phillip, *Antisemitism and the Left*.
13 Lorde, "Notes from a Trip to Russia."
14 Lorde, "Notes from a Trip to Russia," 23–4.
15 Lorde, "Notes from a Trip to Russia," 24.
16 Lorde, "Notes from a Trip to Russia," 30.
17 See Anastasakis, "Europeanization of the Balkans"; Eriksen, "Europeanization of the Balkans."
18 Central Committee of the Bulgarian Communist Party, "Postanovlenie na Tsentralnia Komitet na Bulgarskata Komunisticheska Partia za Zasilvane na Borbata Protiv Alkoholizma," 47.
19 Central Committee of the Bulgarian Communist Party, "Postanovlenie na Tsentralnia Komitet na Bulgarskata Komunisticheska Partia za Zasilvane na Borbata Protiv Alkoholizma."
20 Zhivkov, "The New Party Program," excerpts from the report of the Central Committee of the Bulgarian Communist Party to the 10th Congress of BCP, 20 April 1971, in Zhivkov, *Selected Works*, 63.
21 Zhivkov, *Problems of the Construction of an Advanced Socialist Society*.
22 Zhivkov, *Problems of the Construction of an Advanced Socialist Society*.
23 Popov, *Antropologia na Bulgaskiat Narod*.
24 Popov, *Antropologia na Bulgaskiat Narod*, 265.
25 Bulgarian Council of Ministers. *Report*, 1, 4, 5.
26 Connor, *National Question*, 8–11.
27 Connor, *National Question*, xiv–xv.
28 Connor, *National Question*, xv.
29 Lemon, *Between Two Fires*.
30 Martin, *Affirmative Action Empire*.
31 Wheeler, *Racial Problems in Soviet Muslim Asia*.

32 Connor, *National Question*, 47.
33 Wheeler, *Racial Problems in Soviet Muslim Asia*, 22.
34 Wheeler, *Racial Problems in Soviet Muslim Asia*, 22.
35 Martin, *Affirmative Action Empire*.
36 Rainbow, *Ideologies of Race*.
37 Hirsch, *Empire of Nations*.
38 Gratzer, *Undergrowth of Science*.
39 Marushiakova and Popov, "Bulgarian Gypsies."
40 Genov, Marinov, and Tairov, *Tsiganskoto Naselenie v NR Bulgaria*.
41 Genov, Marinov, and Tairov, *Tsiganskoto Naselenie v NR Bulgaria*, 43.
42 Genov, Marinov, and Tairov, *Tsiganskoto Naselenie v NR Bulgaria*, 42.
43 Genov, Marinov, and Tairov, *Tsiganskoto Naselenie v NR Bulgaria*, 48.
44 Muratova, "Politki na Socialisticheskata Vlast v Bulgaria kum Zhenite Musulmanki," 74.
45 Pashova et al., *Iskam Blagorodna Profesia*.
46 McClintock, *Imperial Leather*.
47 Young, *White Mythologies*.
48 Prochner, May, and Kaur, "Blessings of Civilisation.'"
49 Bloch, *Red Ties and Residential Schools*.
50 Tlostanova, *Gender Epistemologies and Eurasian Borderlands*, 117.
51 Nunev, *Romskoto Dete I Negovata Semeina Sreda*, 18.
52 Genov, Marinov, and Tairov, *Tsiganskoto Naselenie v NR Bulgaria*, 32.
53 Popov and Marushiakova, *Etnicheskata Kartina v Bulgaria*.
54 Tomova, "Demografska Haracteristika na Tsiganskoto Naselenie v Bulgaria."
55 Ferguson, *Aberrations in Black*.
56 Ferguson, *Aberrations in Black*, 18.

3. Women's Work: Gendered and Racialized Socialist State Governmentality

1 Budd, *Thought of Work*, 2.
2 Eisenstein, "Constructing a Theory."
3 Einstein, "Constructing a Theory," 205.
4 Mohanty, *Feminism without Borders*, 139–68.
5 Mohanty, *Feminism without Borders*, 13.
6 Lange, "Communist Legacies."
7 Karin and Blagić, "Ambivalence of Socialist Working Women's Heritage."
8 Stoilova, "Post-socialist Gender Transformations."
9 Pollert, "Women, Work and Equal Opportunities."
10 Ghodsee, *Why Women Have Better Sex*.
11 Ghodsee, *Why Women Have Better Sex*, ix, 9, 16–17, 22.
12 Ghodsee and Mead, "What Has Socialism Ever Done?"
13 Ghodsee and Mead, "What Has Socialism Ever Done?" 105–9.

14 Lemke, "Foucault, Governmentality, and Critique."
15 Kanushev, "Nakazania I Infranakazania ili za Socialisticheskata Ikonomia na Represiata." My translation.
16 Birkett, "'White Woman's Burden.'"
17 Jacobs, "Give a Thought to Africa."
18 Rich, "'Saving' Muslims Women."
19 Nahodilova, "Communist Modernization and Gender," 42.
20 Nahodilova, "Communist Modernization and Gender," 42.
21 Delap, "'Woman Question' and the Origins of Feminism."
22 Eisenstein, "Constructing a Theory"; Ghodsee, "State Feminism and the Woman Question," in *Second World, Second Sex*, 31–52.
23 Bebel, *Woman and Socialism*.
24 Engels, *Origin of the Family*.
25 Lischke, *Lily Braun*.
26 Sudarkasa, "Status of Women.'"
27 McCallum, *Indigenous Women*, 231.
28 Muratova, "Muslim Women in Socialist Bulgaria," 132–3.
29 Muratova, "Muslim Women in Socialist Bulgaria," 137.
30 Nazarska, "Muslim Women and the Women's Movement in Bulgaria."
31 Muratova, "Muslim Women in Socialist Bulgaria," 134.
32 Muratova, "Muslim Women in Socialist Bulgaria," 133.
33 Muratova, "Muslim Women in Socialist Bulgaria," 140, 142.
34 Muratova, "Muslim Women in Socialist Bulgaria," 141.
35 Muratova, "Muslim Women in Socialist Bulgaria," 141.
36 Muratova, "Mulsim Women in Socialist Bulgaria," 137–8.
37 Marinova, "Kakvo e da si Uchitelka." My translation.
38 Pashova et al., *Iskam Blagorodna Profesia*, 120–55. My translation.
39 Pashova et al., *Iskam Blagorodna Profesia*, 120–55.
40 Nahodilova, "Communist Modernization and Gender," 47.
41 Nahodilova, "Communist Modernization and Gender," 51.
42 Garvanova, "Problemut za Prostituciata."
43 Garvanova, "Problemut za Prostituciata," 36.
44 Garvanova, "Sto e Prostitucia."
45 Markov, "Prostituciata." English translation by Dimiter Kenarov.
46 Personal interview, 9 October 2018.
47 Todorka Nikolova, *Zhivot Pod Muzhe*. My translation.
48 Nikolova, *Zhivot Pod Muzhe*, 25, 47.
49 Nikolova, *Zhivot Pod Muzhe*, 47.
50 Garvanova, "Sto e Prostitucia," 33.
51 Nikolova, *Zhivot Pod Muzhe*, 23–5.
52 Nikolova, *Zhivot Pod Muzhe*, 73–4.
53 Personal interview, 2018.

54 Bulgarian Women's Movement Sofia-region Archive, Transcript. My translation.
55 Bulgarian Women's Movement Sofia-region Archive, Transcript, 39.
56 Bulgarian Women's Movement Sofia-region Archive, Transcript, 43–4.
57 Bulgarian Women's Movement Sofia-region Archive, Transcript, 31–3.
58 Sofia Committee of the Fatherland Front, Transcript. My translation.
59 Sofia Committee of the Fatherland Front, Transcript, 33.
60 Ghodsee, "Pressuring the Politburo."
61 Ghodsee, "Pressuring the Politburo," 543.
62 Ghodsee, "Pressuring the Politburo," 549.
63 Ghodsee, "Pressuring the Politburo," 539.
64 Nikolova, *Zhivot Pod Muzhe*, 76.
65 Nazarska, "Muslim Women and the Women's Movement in Bulgaria," 125.

4. Second and Third World Women: Socialist State Feminisms and Internationalisms

1 For example, Ghodsee, "A Brief History of Women's Activism in Domestic Political Context: Case 1: Bulgaria," in *Second World, Second Sex*, 53–75; Ibrosheva and Stover, "Case Study"; Todorova, "Historical Tradition and Transformation."
2 Todorova, "Race and Women of Color."
3 I borrow the concept "between woman and nation" from transnational feminists; see Kaplan, Alarcon, and Moallem, *Between Woman and Nation*.
4 Dinkova, "Besedvame po Problemi."
5 Andreeva, "Zhenite Protiv Ravnopravieto."
6 "Tova Me Naraniava."
7 Georgieva, "Krasotata na Vseki Chovek."
8 "Gore Glavata Momiche!"
9 "Gore Glavata Momiche!"
10 Kiranova, "Pod Zvucite na Tam-tama."
11 Ghodsee, "Research Note," 255; see also Ghodsee, *Second World, Second Sex*.
12 Brayton, "Soviet Involvement in Africa."
13 Odinga, *Not Yet Uhuru*, 187.
14 Ghodsee, "Research Note," 258–9.
15 Todorova, "Pri Grandiozna Afera."
16 Boev, "Vechnite Priateli na Bulgaria."
17 Yergan, *African Students in Communist Countries*.
18 Yergan, *African Students in Communist Countries*, 5.
19 Yergan, *African Students in Communist Countries*, 5.
20 Butovski, "Chuzhdestrani Studenti i Socgastbaiteri Zalivat NRB."

21 Krasteva, *Imigraciata v Bulgaria*, 76–8.
22 Ferber, "Culture of Privilege," 70.
23 Todorova, "Historical Tradition and Transformation," 137.
24 Todorova, "Historical Tradition and Transformation," 137.
25 Todorova, *Imagining the Balkans*, 188.
26 Zhivkov, *Memoari*, 134–5.
27 Zhivkova, *Her Many Worlds*, 125–35.
28 Mathur, "Hindu Influence in Communist Bulgaria."
29 Zhivkova, *Her Many Worlds*, 127.
30 Zhivkova, *Her Many Worlds*, 128.
31 See Dragostinova, "'Natural Ally' of the 'Developing World.'"
32 Baleva, "'Slona Moia Priatel' za Kogoto Vsichki Plachehme."
33 Zhivkova, *Her Many Worlds*, 65, 148.
34 Cited in Dragostinova, "'Natural Ally' of the 'Developing World,'" 681.
35 Zhivkova, *Her Many Worlds*, 14–15.
36 Zhivkova, *Her Many Worlds*, 13–15.
37 "Our Children's Corner."
38 Gandhi, "Women's Role."
39 Panyotova, "Ninova Privetstva Reshenieto."
40 Atanasova, "Lyudmila Zhivkova"; Ivanova, "Occult Communism"; Blagov, *Zagadkata Ludmila Zhivkova*.
41 Zhivkova, *Her Many Worlds*, 146.
42 Zhivkova, *Her Many Worlds*, 81.
43 See, for example, the biographies and academic and language training of oft-quoted historians and gender studies experts Krasimira Daskalova (*Women, Gender, and Modernization in Bulgaria, 1878–1944*, 2012 (in Bulgarian), Maria Todorova (*Imagining the Balkans*), or Kornelia Slavova (editor of *Gender/Genre* [Sofia: Sofia University Press, 2010], and author of *Identities in Transition: Gender, Popular Culture and the Media in Bulgaria after 1989* [Polis, 2011]).
44 Hall, "Life and Times," 177.
45 Blagov, *Zagadkata Ludmila Zhivkova*, 76–7.
46 Nayyar, "India's Trade with the Socialist Countries."
47 Gandhi, "True Liberation of Women."
48 See Pande, "The History of Feminism"; Kumar, History of Doing; Daskalova, "Women's Movement in Bulgaria."

5. Challenging the Modern/Postmodern Duality: Race, Socialist Masculinity, and Global American Culture

1 Bauman, "Communism: A Postmortem."
2 Bauman, "Communism: A Postmortem," 167.

3 Bauman, "Communism: A Postmortem," 169.
4 Bauman, "Communism: A Postmortem," ix.
5 Jameson, "Postmodernism," 188.
6 Jameson, "Postmodernism," 200–1, 226–7.
7 Spivak, *Outside in the Teaching Machine*, 284.
8 Kaplan and Grewal, "Transnational Feminist Cultural Studies," 432.
9 Kaplan and Grewal, "Transnational Feminist Cultural Studies," 436.
10 Johnson, "What Is Cultural Studies Anyway?" 38–80.
11 Richard Rorty, *Contingency, Irony, and Solidarity*.
12 Krasteva and Bouroudjieva, "Mass Information," 376.
13 Zhivkov, "The New Party Program," in *Selected Works*, 49, 55.
14 Mantarova, "Cultural Activities and Practices," 419.
15 Zhivkova, *In Her Many Words*, 27–9.
16 Znepolsky, "V Tursene na Edna Satrudnichesta Publika."
17 Znepolsky, "V Tursene na Edna Satrudnichesta Publika," 32.
18 Znepolsky, "V Tursene na Edna Satrudnichesta Publika," 28–31.
19 Znepolsky, "V Tursene na Edna Satrudnichesta Publika," 31, 33, 36.
20 Znepolsky, "V Tursene na Edna Satrudnichesta Publika," 33, 38.
21 Ikonomov, "Prikluchensko-kriminalniat Zhanr v Bulgarskata Televizia."
22 Mihailov, "Video v Mnogo Posoki," 28; Chernev, "Videoto."
23 Stoianov, "Za po-visoko Kachestvo na Bulgarskite Filmi," 13.
24 Svilenov, 'Tvorcheskoto Edinomislie," 14.
25 Svilenov, 'Tvorcheskoto Edinomislie," 14.
26 *Missing in Action* (Joseph Zito, 1984), *Missing in Action II: The Beginning* (Lance Hool, 1985), *Braddock: Missing in Action III* (Aaron Norris, 1988), *Lone Wolfe McQuade* (Steve Carver, 1983).
27 *Above the Law* (Andrew Davis, 1988).
28 *Dirty Harry* (Don Siegel, 1971), *Magnum Force* (Ted Post, 1973), *The Enforcer* (James Fargo, 1976), *Sudden Impact* (Clint Eastwood, 1983), *The Dead Pool* (Buddy Van Horn, 1988).
29 *Death Wish* (Michael Winner, 1974), *Death Wish II* (Michael Winner, 1982), *Death Wish III* (Michael Winner, 1985), *Death Wish IV: The Crackdown* (J. Lee Thompson, 1987).
30 Connell and Messerschmidt, "Hegemonic Masculinity," 832.
31 Personal interview by author, 12 July 2003.
32 Personal interview by author, 7 January 2001.
33 Kotseva, "Women."
34 Kaneva, "Mediating Post-socialist Femininities."
35 State authorities did not collect or publish data on domestic or sexual violence against women in socialist Bulgaria. However, the issue was widespread and mostly unreported and unaddressed. See United Nations. "Domestic Violence against Women."

36 Novikova, "Soviet and Post-Soviet Masculinities."
37 Slapšak, "Hunting, Ruling, Sacrificing."
38 Tomova, *Ciganie v Prehodnia Period*, 79–88; Crowe, "Bulgaria," 27.
39 Personal interview by author, 12 June 2003.
40 Personal interview by author, 12 January 2001.
41 Personal interview by author, 19 December 2000.
42 Personal interview by author, 20 December 2000.
43 Personal interview by author, 8 January 2001.
44 Personal interview by author, 7 August 2003.
45 Personal interview by author, 24 July 2003.
46 Todorova, "I Don't Know My Color."
47 An estimated three hundred thousand Bulgarian immigrants settled in the United States; about 2.5 million Bulgarian live abroad in countries around the world. See "Bulgarian Diaspora," *Wikipedia, the Free Encyclopedia*, https://en.wikipedia.org/wiki/Bulgarian_diaspora.
48 Dimitrov, "Sylvester Stallone Kum Boyco Borisov."
49 Boiana-MG, "Don't Go To Bulgaria ..."; Sheneva, "Sylvester Stallone."
50 "Bewitching Bulgaria."
51 Hadjiev, "Devin Kato Indijski Grad."

Conclusion

1 Todorova and Gille, *Post-communist Nostalgia*.
2 See Mujanovic, *Hunger and Fury*.
3 Zeneli, "Economic Development in the Western Balkans."
4 See Dorian, "From 'Balkanization' to 'Europeanization'"; Džankić, Keil, and Kmezić, *Europeanization of the Western Balkans*.
5 See Rorke, "Bigger Than Football"; Rrustemi, *Far-Right Trends in South Eastern Europe*; Stojarová, *Far Right in the Balkans*.
6 Minca, Šantić, and Umek, "Managing the 'Refugee Crisis.'"
7 See Amalipe Center for Interethnic Dialogue and Tolerance, *Civil Society Monitoring Report*.
8 See Mancel, "Roma in Sweden"; Crumley, "France Deports Gypsies."
9 See Levine-Rasky, Beaudoin, and St. Clair, "Exclusion of Roma Claimants."
10 See Council of Europe, *Stratégie pour la promotion*.
11 Marushiakova and Popov, "European Policies for Social Inclusion of Roma."
12 Marushiakova and Popov, "European Policies for Social Inclusion of Roma," 29.
13 See World Bank Group, *Gender Dimensions of Roma Inclusion*.
14 European Commission, *EU Framework for National Roma Integration Strategies up to 2020*.

15 See World Bank Group, *Development Marketplace*; Ostry et al., "Economic Gains from Gender Inclusion."
16 See European Commission, *Development of European Identity/Identities*.
17 Hartocollis, "Why Migrants Don't Want to Stay in Hungary."
18 See Rodat, "Cultural Racism."
19 See Kim, "Eastern Europeans."
20 See Horn, "Is Eastern Europe More Xenophobic Than Western Europe?"
21 Rechel, "Ethnic Diversity in Bulgaria."
22 Tereshchenko, Bradbury, and Archer, "Eastern European Migrants' Experiences of Racism."
23 Dâmaso et al., "Acting European."
24 Mihailova, "More Damaging Bigotry"; see also Bulgarian Helsinki Committee, *Written Comments*, 12–13.
25 Panyotova, "Ninova Privetstva Reshenieto."
26 "Kornelia Ninova kum Zhenite: Budete Blagosloveni i Stastlivi s Muzhete do Vas," *24Chasa* (8 May 2020). https://www.24chasa.bg/novini/article/8274709 © www.24chasa.bg.
27 Bhabha, *Location of Culture*.
28 See V.S. Naipaul's novels *A House for Mr Biswas* (1961); *The Mimic Men* (1967), and *In A Free State* (1971).
29 Bhabha, *Location of Culture*, xii–xiv.
30 Bhabha, *Location of Culture*, 7.
31 See Darling-Wolfe, "Disturbingly Hybrid or Distressingly Patriarchal?"
32 Sokolova and Stavreva, "'The Readiness is All.'"
33 "Azis: Stremezhut kum skupoto i luksoznoto e chalga." DarikNews.com, 23 February 2020,.https://dariknews.bg/novini/liubopitno/azis-stremezhyt-kym-skypoto-i-luksoznoto-e-chalga-video-2213270.
34 "AZIS in Love with the USA – АЗИС Влюбен в Америка!"
35 "Nichija zemja: Lice nazaem?"
36 "Nichija zemja: Lice nazaem?"
37 "AZIS – Pozna li me? / Азис - Позна ли ме?"
38 "AZIS – MOTEL / Азис – Мотел."
39 Gilroy, *Black Atlantic*.
40 "AZIS – Ciganche / АЗИС – Циганче."
41 "Nichija zemja: Lice nazaem?"
42 For a brief statement of dominant notions of multiculturalism in Canada, see Kymlicka, "Liberal Multiculturalism." For analysis of "multiculturalism" debates and politics in Germany, Britain and France, see the *International Journal on Multicultural Societies (IJMS)* 5, no. 1 (2003), edited by Paul de Guchteneire, Matthias Koenig, Gurharpal Singh, and John Rex.
43 Anzaldúa, "Border Arte," in *Gloria Anzaldúa Reader*, 176–86.

44 Moraga and Anzaldúa, *This Bridge Called My Back*, 204–5.
45 Anzaldúa, "La Prieta," in *Gloria Anzaldúa Reader*, 42–3.
46 Anzaldúa, "(Un)natural Bridges, (Un)safe Spaces," in *Gloria Anzaldúa Reader*, 244.
47 Anzaldúa, "(Un)natural Bridges, (Un)safe Spaces," in *Gloria Anzaldúa Reader*, 244.

Bibliography

Allen, Theodore. *The Invention of the White Race, Volume 1*. New York: Verso, 1994.

Amalipe Center for Interethnic Dialogue and Tolerance, *Civil Society Monitoring Report on Implementation of the National Roma Integration Strategy in Bulgaria*. Luxembourg: Publications Office of the European Union, 2019.

Anastasakis, Othon. "The Europeanization of the Balkans." *Brown Journal of World Affairs* 12, no. 1 (2005): 77–88.

Andreeva, Liliana. "Zhenite Protiv Ravnopravieto." *Zhenata Dnes* no. 6 (1975): 10–11.

Anzaldúa, Gloria. "Border Arte" and "(Un)natural Bridges, (Un)safe Spaces." In *The Gloria Anzaldúa Reader*. Edited by AnaLouise Keating. Durham, NC: Duke University Press, 2009.

Araújo, Marta, and Silvia Maeso. *Eurocentrism, Racism and Knowledge: Debates on History and Power in Europe and the Americas*. London: Palgrave Macmillan, 2015.

Atanasova, Ivanka N. "Lyudmila Zhivkova and the Paradox of Ideology and Identity in Communist Bulgaria." *East European Politics and Societies* 18, no. 2 (2004): 278–315.

Baker, Catherine. *Race and the Yugoslav Region: Postsocialist, Post-conflict, Postcolonial?* Manchester: Manchester University Press, 2018.

Baleva, Mariela. "'Slona Moia Priatel' za Kogoto Vsichki Plachehme." *Trud*, 19 May 2019. https://trud.bg/slonut-mojat prijatel-za-kogoto-vsich/.

Balkan Society for Theory and Practice. *Race and Racism in the Balkans Workshop*. Balkan Society for Theory and Practice, Pristina, Kosovo, 1 July 2020. https://www.balkansocietytp.com/copy-of-2019-workshop.

Banerji, Himani. *Thinking Through: Essays on Feminism, Marxism and Anti-racism*. Toronto: Women's Press, 1995.

Barot, Rohit, and John Bird. "Racialization: The Genealogy and Critique of a Concept." *Ethnic and Racial Studies* 24, no. 4 (2010): 601–18.

Bauman, Zygmunt. "Communism: A Postmortem." In *Intimations of Postmodernity*, 156–74. London: Routledge, 1992.

Bebel, August. *Woman and Socialism*. Translated by Meta L. Stern. New York: Socialist Literature, 2010.
"Bewitching Bulgaria." *BoxOffice India*, 8 December 2018. https://boxofficeindia.co.in/bewitching-bulgaria.
Bhabha, Homi. *The Location of Culture*. London: Psychology Press, 1994.
Birkett, Dea. "The 'White Woman's Burden' in the 'White Mans Grave': The Introduction of British Nurses in Colonial West Africa." In *Western Women and Imperialism: Complicity and Resistance*, edited by Nupur Chaudhiri and Margaret Strobel, 177–206. Bloomington: Indiana University Press, 1992.
Bjelić, Dušan. "Toward a Genealogy of the Balkan Discourses on Race." *Interventions* 20, no. 6 (2018): 906–29.
Blagoeva, Vella. "Ikonomicheska ili Politicheska Nezavisimost na Zhenata Triabva?" In *Ot Siankata na Istoriiata: Zhenite v Bulgarskoto Obstestvo I Kultura (1840–1940)*, edited by Krasimra Daskalova. Sofia: Dom na naukite za choveka i obshtestvoto, 1998.
Blagov, Krum. *Zagadkata Ludmila Zhivkova*. Sofia: Izdatelstvo Reporter, 2012.
Bloch, Alexia. *Red Ties and Residential Schools: Indigenous Siberians in a Post-Soviet State*. Philadelphia: University of Pennsylvania Press, 2004.
Boev, Boyko. "Vechnite Priateli na Bulgaria." *Dnevnik*, 12 June 2016. https://www.dnevnik.bg/istorii_na_denia/2016/06/12/2773349_vechnite_priiateli_na_bulgariia/.
Boiana-MG. "Don't Go to Bulgaria ... Unless You Want to Have a Great Time!" *Boiana – MG Travel*, 14 August 2015. http://blog.boiana-mg.com/bulgaria/slay-dont-go-to-bulgaria-unless-you-want-to-have-a-great-time/.
Bonfiglioli, Chiara. "Former East, Former West: Post-socialist Nostalgia and Feminist Genealogies in Today's Europe." *Environmental Science & Policy* 59 (2011): 115–26.
Bonilla-Silva, Eduardo. *Racism without Racists: Color-Blind Racism and the Persistence of Racial Inequality in America*. 5th edition. London: Rowman & Littlefield, 2017.
Bora, Papori. "The Problem without a Name: Comments on Cultural Difference (Racism) in India, South Asia." *Journal of South Asian Studies* 42, no. 5 (2019): 845–60.
Brayton, Abbott. "Soviet Involvement in Africa." *Journal of Modern African Studies* 17, no. 2 (June 1979): 253–69.
Brazitsov, Hristo. "Edin Den Mejdu Sofiiskite Tsigani" [A day among Sofia's Gypsies]. *Az Znam Vsichko* [I know everything] 1 (1931): 18–19.
Budd, John. *The Thought of Work*. Ithaca, NY: Cornell University Press, 2011.
Bulgarian Council of Ministers. *Report of the Commission Appointed by the Bulgarian Council of Ministers Regarding the Complete Resolution of the Questions for the Gypsy Population in the People's Republic of Bulgaria*, September 1958, Council of Ministers entry number 1–41 from 27 June 1958.

Bulgarian Helsinki Committee. *Written Comments of the Bulgarian Helsinki Committee Concerning Bulgaria for Consideration by the United Nations Committee on the Elimination of Racial Discrimination at its 92nd Session.* Sofia: 2017. https://tbinternet.ohchr.org/Treaties/CERD/Shared%20Documents/BGR/INT_CERD_NGO_BGR_27032_E.pdf.

Bulgarian Women's Movement Sofia-region Archive. Transcript of seminar, 3 November 1982. Archival fond 2582, 1/54.

Bulgarian Women's Union. "To the Union's Units, Regional Number 2." Bulgarian Women's Union, Sofia, 5 February 1931. File number 132.

Burawoy, Michael. "Marxism after Communism." *Theory and Society* 29, no. 2 (2000): 151–74.

Butovski, Ivan. "Chuzhdestrani Studenti i Socgastbaiteri Zalivat NRB: Vietnam ni Vrusta Durzhaven Dulg s 35000 svoi Rabotnici." *168 Chasa*. 17 February 2019.

Campbell, Al. "Marx and Engels's Vision of Building a Good Society." In *Alternative Perspectives of a Good Society. Perspectives from Social Economics*, edited by John Marangos, 9–31. New York: Palgrave Macmillan, 2012.

Central Committee of the Bulgarian Communist Party. "Postanovlenie na Tsentralnia Komitet na Bulgarskata Komunisticheska Partia za Zasilvane na Borbata Protiv Alkoholizma" [Directive of the Central Committee of the Bulgarian Communist Party for increased fight against alcoholism]. *Rabotnichesko Delo*, br. 50, god. 31, 19 February 1958. Reprinted in *Zakon za Borba Sreshtu Protivoobshestvenite Proiavi na Maloletnite I Nepulnoletnite* [Law for fight against anti-social acts of juveniles and minors]. Sofia: Izdatelstvo Nauka i Kultura, 1961.

Chari, Sharad, and Katherine Verdery. "Thinking between the Posts: Postcolonialism, Postsocialism, and Ethnography after the Cold War." *Comparative Studies in Society and History* 51, no. 1 (2009): 16–34.

Chernev, Grigor. "Videoto: predi da Izkristalizirat Definiciite" [The video: Before crystallizing definitions]. *Kinoizkustvo*, 40, no. 11 (November 1985): 13.

Connell, R.W., and James Messerschmidt. "Hegemonic Masculinity: Rethinking the Concept." *Gender & Society* 19, no. 6 (2005): 829–59.

Connor, Walker. *The National Question in Marxist-Leninist Theory and Strategy*. Princeton, NJ: Princeton University Press, 1984.

Council of Europe. *Stratégie pour la promotion des femmes et des filles Roms en Europe (2014–2020)* ["Strategy on the advancement of Roma women and girls 2014–2020]. Strasbourg: Council of Europe, 2016. https://rm.coe.int/16806f32fd.

Crowe, David. "Bulgaria." In *A History of the Gypsies in Eastern Europe and Russia*, 1–30. New York: St. Martin's Press, 1995.

Crumley, Bruce. "France Deports Gypsies: Courting the Xenophobes?" *Time*, 19 August 2010. http://content.time.com/time/world/article/0,8599,2011848,00.html. Accessed 8 July 2020.

Dâmaso, Mafalda, Luke John Davies, Kuba Jablonowski, and Seamus Montgomery. "Acting European: Identity, Belonging and the EU of Tomorrow." Foundation for European Progressive Studies, 2019.

Darkovski, Kiril D. "Dimiter Mihalchev – Opit za Intelectualen Portret" [Dimiter Mihalchev – an attempt at an intellectual portrait]. In *Izbrani Suchinenia* [Selected works] by Dimiter Mihalchev, edited by Kiril Darkovski. Sofia: Izdatelstvo Nauka i Iskustvo, 1981.

Darling-Wolfe, Fabienne. "Disturbingly Hybrid or Distressingly Patriarchal? In *Gender Hybridity in a Global Environment*, edited by Keri E. Iyall Smith and Patricia Leavy, 63–79. Leiden, the Netherlands: Brill, 2008.

Daskalova, Krasimira. *Krasymyra Daskalova, Ot Syankata na Ystoryyata: Zhenyte v Bʺlharskoto Obshhestvo y Kultura (1840–1940)*. Sofia: Bulharska Hrupa za Yzsledvanyya po Ystoryya na Zhenyte y Pola, 1998.

– "The Women's Movement in Bulgaria in a Life Story." *Women's History Review* 13, no. 1 (2004): 91–103.

Davies, Carole Boyce. *Left of Karl Marx: The Political Life of Black Communist Claudia Jones* Durham, NC: Duke University Press, 2008.

Davis, Angela. *Angela Davis: An Autobiography*. New York: International, 1988.

Delap, Lucy. "The 'Woman Question' and the Origins of Feminism." In *The Cambridge History of Nineteenth-Century Political Thought*, edited by G. Stedman Jones and G. Claeys, 319–48. Cambridge: Cambridge University Press, 2011.

Dimitrov, Ivan. "Sylvester Stallone Kum Boyco Borisov: 'Produljavaj da Udriash.'" *Dnevnik* 2 November 2019. https://www.dnevnik.bg/razvlechenie/2019/11/02/3986140_silvestur_staloun_kum_boiko_borisov_produljavai_da/. Accessed 8 May 2020.

Dinkova, Maria. "Besedvame po Problemi na Suvremeniia Semeen Zhivot." *Zhenata Dnes* no. 4 (1975): 16–17.

Dorian, Jano. "From 'Balkanization' to 'Europeanization': The Stages of Western Balkans Complex Transformations." *L'Europe en Formation* 3 (2008): 55–69.

Dragostinova, Theodora. "The 'Natural Ally' of the "Developing World': Bulgarian Culture in India and Mexico." *Slavic Review* 77, no. 3 (2018): 661–84.

Džankić, Jelena, Soeren Keil, and Marko Kmezić, eds. *The Europeanization of the Western Balkans: A Failure of EU Conditionality?* London: Palgrave Macmillan, 2019.

Eisenstein, Zellah. "Constructing a Theory of Capitalist Patriarchy and Socialist Feminism." *Insurgent Sociologist* 7, no. 3 (1977): 3–17.

Engels, Friedrich. *The Origin of the Family, Private Property and the State*. New York: Penguin Classics 2010.

Enns, Carol Zerbe. "Locational Feminisms and Feminist Social Identity Analysis." *Professional Psychology Research and Practice* 41 (2010): 333–9.

Eriksen, Monika. "Europeanization of the Balkans within an Identity-based Framework." *Politeja* no. 37 (2015): 193–208.
European Commission. *The Development of European Identity/Identities: Unfinished Business (A Policy Review)*. European Commission, August 2012. https://ec.europa.eu/research/social-sciences/pdf/policy_reviews/development-of-european-identity-identities_en.pdf.
– *An EU Framework for National Roma Integration Strategies up to 2020*. European Commission, 5 April 2011. https://www.google.com/search?client=firefox-b-e&q=Framework+for+National+Roma+Integration+Strategies+up+to+2020.
Fawcett, Barbara, and Jeff Hearn "Researching Others: Epistemology, Experience, Standpoints and Participation." *International Journal of Social Research Methodology* 7, no. 3 (2004): 201–18.
Feagin, Joe, and Sean Elias. "Rethinking Racial Formation: A Systemic Racism Critique." *Ethnic and Racial Studies* 36, no. 6 (2013): 931–60.
Ferber, Abby. "The Culture of Privilege: Color-blindness, Postfeminism, and Christonormativity." *Journal of Social Issues* 68 (2012): 63–77.
Ferguson, Roderick A. *Aberrations in Black: Toward a Queer of Color Critique*. Minneapolis: University of Minnesota Press, 2004.
Fine, Robert, and Spenser Phillip. *Antisemitism and the Left*. Manchester: Manchester University Press, 2017.
Gandhi, Indira. "True Liberation of Women." Speech delivered at the Inauguration of the All-India Women's Conference Building Complex, New Delhi, 26 March 1980.
– "Women's Role in a Changing World." *Women on the March*, 10 October 1966, 23–5.
Garvanova, Magdalena. "Problemut za Prostituciata v Bulgaria sled Osvobozdenieto do Svetovnite Voini – mezhdu reglamentarizma I Abolicionizma." *Pogledi* 5–6 (2015): 27–53.
– "Sto e Prostitucia I Ima li Tia Pochva v Socialisticheska Bulgaria?" *Filosofski Alternativi* 1 (2016): 20–37.
Genov, Dimiter, Veselin Marinov, and Tihomir Tairov. *Tsiganskoto Naselenie v NR Bulgaria po Putia na Sotsialisma* [The Gypsy population in the People's Republic of Bulgaria on the road to socialism]. Sofia: Izdatelstvo na Natsionalnia Suvet na Otechestvenia Front, 1968.
Georgieff, Anthony. "Sofia: Double-faced Bulgaria." In *Civil Society and the Holocaust: International Perspectives on Resistance and Rescue*, edited by Cecilie Felicia, Stokholm Banke, Anders Jerichow, Judith Goldstein, and Paul Larkin, 56–74. Amsterdam: Humanity in Action Press, 2013. https://www.humanityinaction.org/knowledge_detail/sofia-double-faced-bulgaria/.
Georgieva, Dimitrinka. "Krasotata na Vseki Chovek" [Every person's beauty]. *Zhenata Dnes* no. 9 (1974): 22.

Ghodsee, Kristen. "Pressuring the Politburo: The Committee of the Bulgarian Women's Movement and State Socialist Feminism." *Slavic Review* 73, no. 3 (Fall 2014): 538–62.
– "Research Note: The Historiographical Challenges of Exploring Second World–Third World Alliances in the International Women's Movement." *Global Social Policy* 14, no. 2 (2014): 244–64.
– *Second World, Second Sex: Socialist Women's Activism and Global Solidarity during the Cold War*. Durham, NC: Duke University Press, 2019.
– *Why Women Have Better Sex under Socialism: And Other Arguments for Economic Independence*. Durham, NC: Duke University Press, 2018.
Ghodsee, Kristen, and Julia Mead. "What Has Socialism Ever Done for Women?" *Catalyst* 2, no. 2 (2018): 101–33.
Gilroy, Paul. *The Black Atlantic: Modernity and Double Consciousness*. Cambridge, MA: Harvard University Press, 1995.
Goldberg, David Theo. "Precipitating Evaporation: On Racial Europeanization" In *The Threat of Race: Reflections on Racial Neoliberalism*, 151–98. Malden, MA: Wiley-Blackwell, 2009.
"Gore Glavata Momiche!" *Zhenata Dnes* no. 1 (1975): 23.
Grabowska, Magdalena. "Bringing the Second World In: Conservative Revolution(s), Socialist Legacies, and Transnational Silences in the Trajectories of Polish Feminism." *Signs* 37, no. 2 (January 2012): 385–411.
Gratzer, Walter. *The Undergrowth of Science: Delusion, Self-deception and Human Frailty*. London: Oxford University Press, 2000.
Grewal, Inderpal, and Caren Kaplan, eds. *Scattered Hegemonies: Postmodernity and Transnational Feminist Practices*. Minneapolis: University of Minnesota Press, 1994.
Guettel, Charnie. *Marxism & Feminism*. Toronto: Women's Press, 1974.
Hadjiev, Valentin. "Devin Kato Indijski Grad, Bolivud Hanulni 7 Hotela, Zatvori Putista." 24Чaca.bg. https://www.24chasa.bg/novini/article/6962381. Accessed 8 July 2020.
Hall, Stuart. "Life and Times of the First New Left." *New Left Review* 61 (January–February 2010): 177–96.
– "The West and the Rest: Discourse and Power. In *The Formations of Modernity*, edited by Bram Gieben and Stuart Hall, 275–331. London: Polity, 1993.
Harding, Sandra. *The Feminist Standpoint Theory: Intellectual and Political Controversies*. New York: Routledge, 2003.
Hartigan, John. "Establishing the Fact of Whiteness." *American Anthropologist*, n.s., 99, no. 3 (1997): 495–505.
Hartocollis, Anemona. "Why Migrants Don't Want to Stay in Hungary." *New York Times*, 5 September 2015. https://www.nytimes.com/interactive/projects/cp/reporters-notebook/migrants/hungary-treatment-refugees.

Hill-Collins, Patricia. "The Social Construction of Black Feminist Thought." *Signs* 14, no. 4 (1989): 745–73.

Hirsch, Francine. *Empire of Nations: Ethnographic Knowledge and the Making of the Soviet Union*. Ithaca, NY: Cornell University Press, 2014.

Hochman, Adam. "Racialization: A Defense of the Concept," *Ethnic and Racial Studies* 42, no. 8 (2019): 1245–62.

Holmstrom, Nancy. *The Socialist Feminist Project: A Contemporary Reader in Theory and Politics*. New York: Monthly Review, 2002.

Hopkins, Barbara. "Gender Inequality in Postcapitalism: Theorizing Institutions for a Democratic Socialism." *Review of Radical Political Economics* 50, no. 4 (2018): 668–74.

Horn, Heather. "Is Eastern Europe More Xenophobic than Western Europe?" *Atlantic*, 16 October 2015. https://www.theatlantic.com/international/archive/2015/10/xenophobia-eastern-europe-refugees/410800/.

HoSang, Daniel Martinez, Oneka LaBennett, and Laura Pulido, eds. *Racial Formation in the Twenty-First Century*. Berkeley: University of California Press, 2012.

Hostettler, Nick. *Eurocentrism*. New York: Routledge, 2012.

Ibrosheva, Elza, and Maria Stover. "Case Study: The Bulgarian Woman as 'Free and Happy Individual' (A Cultural Analysis of a Bulgarian Magazine's Covers over Seven Decades)." In *The Handbook of Magazine Studies*, edited by Miglena Sternadori and Tim Holmes, 462–71. Hoboken, NJ: Wiley, 2020.

Ikonomov, Vladislav. "Prikluchensko-kriminalniat Zhanr v Bulgarskata Televizia; Niakoi Suobrazhenia v praktikata i Vazmozhnostite" [The crime-adventure genre in Bulgarian television: Some ideas for practice and possibilities]. *Kinoizkustvo* 32, no. 6 (June 1977): 39–47.

Imre, Anikó. "Whiteness in Post-Socialist Eastern Europe: The Time of the Gypsies, the End of Race." In *Postcolonial Whiteness: A Critical Reader on Race and Empire*, edited by Alfred Lopez, 79–102. New York: SUNY Press, 2005.

Institute for Political Research. *Historicizing "Whiteness" in Eastern Europe and Russia*. Conference proceedings, 25–6 June 2019, Bucharest, Romania. Bucharest: Institute for Political Research, 2019.

Ivanova, Veneta. "Occult Communism: Culture, Science and Spirituality in Late Socialist Bulgaria." PhD diss., University of Illinois at Urbana-Champaign, 2017.

Jacobs, Sylvia. "Give a Thought to Africa: Black Women Missionaries in Southern Africa." In *Western Women and Imperialism: Complicity and Resistance*, edited by Nupur Chaudhiri and Margaret Strobel, 207–30. Bloomington: Indiana University Press, 1992.

Jameson, Fredric. "Postmodernism, or the Cultural Logic of Late Capitalism." In *The Jameson Reader*, edited by Michael Hardt and Kathi Weeks, 188–232. Oxford: Blackwell Publishing, 2000.

Janakiev, Alexander. "Nesocialisticheskite Kinematografii i Miastoto im v Nashia Repertoar" [Non-socialist cinematographies and their place in out repertoire]. *Kinoizkustvo* 33, no. 6 (June 1978): 50.

Johnson, Richard. "What Is Cultural Studies Anyway?" *Social Text* 16 (1987): 38–80.

Kaneva. Nadia. "Mediating Post-Socialist Femininities." *Feminist Media Studies* 15, no. 1 (2015): 1–17.

Kanushev, Martin. "Nakazania I Infranakazania ili za Socialisticheskata Ikonomia na Represiata." *Sociologicheski Problemi* 43, nos. 3–4 (2011): 165–93.

Kaplan, Caren, Norma Alarcon, and Minoo Moallem, eds., *Between a Woman and Nation: Nationalisms, Transnational Feminisms and the State.* Durham, NC: Duke University Press, 1999.

Kaplan, Caren, and Inderpal Grewal. "Transnational Feminist Cultural Studies: Beyond the Marxism/Poststructuralism/Feminism Divides." *positions* 2, no. 2 (1994): 349–63.

Karin, Renata, and Marina Blagić. "The Ambivalence of Socialist Working Women's Heritage: A Case Study of the Jugoplastika Factory." *Narodna Umjetnost* 50, no. 1 (2013): 40–73.

Kavalski, Emilian. "The Balkan America? The Myth of America in the Creation of Bulgarian National Identity." *New Zealand Slavonic Journal* 38 (2004): 131–57.

Khan, Nasir. "The End of State-Socialism and the Future of Marxism." *Socialist Viewpoint* 7, no. 3 (May–June 2007). http://www.socialistviewpoint.org/mayjun_07/0507001.html.

Kim, Albert. "Eastern Europeans More Inclined to See Their Culture as Superior (Survey)." *Globe Post*, 29 October 2018. https://theglobepost.com/2018/10/29/eastern-europe-culture-superior/.

Kinkel, Ivan. "Priroda i Obshestvo" [Nature and society]. *Arhiv za Stopanska i Socialna Politika* [Archive for economic and social policy] Year 15, book 3 (June 1940): 161–98.

Kiranova, Evgenia. "Pod Zvucite na Tam-tama." *Zhenata Dnes* no. 2 (1975): 8–9.

Konsulov, Stefan. "Edin Filosof, Competenten po Vsichko" [A philosopher competent in everything]. *Prosveta* [Education] Year 4, book 9 (May 1939): 1065–76.

– "Shto e Natsia?" [What is a nation?]. *Prosveta* [Education] Year 4, book 6 (February 1939): 647–65.

Koobak, Redi, and Raili Marling. "The Decolonial Challenge: Framing Post-socialist Central and Eastern Europe within Transnational Feminist Studies." *European Journal of Women Studies* 21 (July 2014): 330–43.

"Kornelia Ninova kum Zhenite: Budete Blagosloveni i Stastlivi s Muzhete do Vas." *24Chasa.* 8 March 2020. https://www.24chasa.bg/novini/article/8274709.

Kotseva, Tatyana. "Women." In *Recent Social Trends in Bulgaria 1960–1995*, edited by Nikolai Genov and Anna Krasteva, 107–18. Montreal: McGill-Queen's University Press, 2001.

Krasteva, Anna. *Imigraciata v Bulgaria*. Sofia: Mezhdunaroden Center za Isledvane na Malcinstvatata I kulturnite vzamimodejstvia, 2005.

Krasteva, Anna, and Tatyana Bouroudjieva. "Mass Information." In *Recent Social Trends in Bulgaria 1960–1995*, edited by Nikolai Genov and Anna Krasteva, 294–301. Montreal: McGill-Queen's University Press, 2001.

Kumar, Radha. *The History of Doing: An Illustrated Account of Movements for Women's Rights and Feminism in India 1800–1990*. New York: Verso, 1993.

Kymlicka, Will. "Liberal Multiculturalism as a Political Theory of State–Minority Relations." *Political Theory* 46 no.1 (2018): 81–9.

Lange, Thomas. "Communist Legacies, Gender and the Impact of Job Satisfaction in Central and Eastern Europe." *European Journal of Industrial Relations* 14, no. 3 (2008): 327–46.

Law, Ian. *Red Racisms: Racism in Communist and Post-Communist Contexts*. New York: Palgrave Macmillan, 2012.

Lemke, Thomas. "Foucault, Governmentality, and Critique." *Rethinking Marxism* 14, no. 3 (Fall 2002): 49–64.

Lemon, Alaina. *Between Two Fires: Gypsy Performance and Romani Memory from Pushkin to Post-Socialism*. Durham, NC: Duke University Press, 2000.

Levine-Rasky, Cynthia, Julianna Beaudoin, and Paul St. Clair. "The Exclusion of Roma Claimants in Canadian Refugee Policy." *Patterns of Prejudice* 48, no. 1 (2013): 67–93.

Leonard, Sarah, and Nancy Fraser. "Capitalism's Crisis of Care." *Dissent* (Fall 2006). https://www.dissentmagazine.org/article/nancy-fraser-interview-capitalism-crisis-of-care.

Lipsitz, George. *The Possessive Investment in Whiteness: How White People Profit from Identity Politics*. Philadelphia: Temple University Press, 1998.

Lischke, Ute. *Lily Braun 1865–1916: German Writer, Feminist, Socialist*. Rochester, NY: Camden House, 2000.

Lorde, Audre. "Notes From a Trip to Russia." In *Sister Outsider: Essays and Speeches*, by Audre Lorde, 13–35. Berkeley, CA: Crossing Press, 1984.

Mancel, Tim. "Roma in Sweden: A Nation Questions Itself." BBC News, 4 December 2013. https://www.bbc.com/news/magazine-25200449.

Mantarova, Anna. "Cultural Activities and Practices." In *Recent Social Trends in Bulgaria 1960–1995*, edited by Nikolai Genov and Anna Krasteva, 418–25. Montreal: McGill-Queen's University Press, 2001.

Marinova, Nadejda. "Kakvo e da si Uchitelka v Rodopite Celi 44 Godini" [What it is to be a teacher in the Rhodope region for 44 years]. *Nov Zhivot*, 24 November 2017. http://www.novjivot.info/2017/11/24/какво-е-да-си-учителка-в-родопите-цели-44/.

Markov, Georgi. "Prostituciata." *Zadochni Reportazhi za Bulgaria*. Sofia: Izdatelstvo Profizdat, 1990. "Prostitution." Translation by Dimiter Kenarov. *Ploughshares* 44, no. 3 (2018): 179+. Gale Academic Onefile.

Marks, Steven. "The Word 'Capitalism': The Soviet Union's Gift to America," *Soc* 49 (2012): 155–63.

Martin, Terry. *The Affirmative Action Empire: Nations and Nationalism in the Soviet Union, 1923–1939*. Ithaca, NY: Cornell University Press, 2001.

Marushiakova, Elena, and Vesselin Popov. "European Policies for Social Inlcusion of Roma: Catch 22?" *Social Inclusion* 3, no. 5 (2015): 19–31.

– "The Bulgarian Gypsies – Searching Their Place in the Society." *Balkanologie* 4, no. 2 (2000): 1–17.

Marx, Karl. "On the Jewish Question." In *The Marx-Engels Reader*, edited by Robert Tucker, 26–46. New York: Norton & Company, 1978.

Mathur, Rakesh. "Hindu Influence in Communist Bulgaria: President's Daughter Opens Eastern European Nation to Spiritual Interchange with India." *Hinduism Today*, September 1989. https://www.hinduismtoday.com/modules/smartsection/item.php?itemid=655.

McCallum, Mary J.L. *Indigenous Women, Work, and History 1940–1980*. Winnipeg, Manitoba: University of Manitoba Press, 2014.

McClintock, Anne. *Imperial Leather: Race, Gender and Sexuality in the Imperial Conquest*. New York: Routledge, 1995.

McKee, James. *Sociology and the Race Problem: The Failure of a Perspective*. Urbana: University of Illinois Press, 1993.

Mihailov, Vladimir. "Video v Mnogo Posoki" [The video in many directions]. *Kinoizkustvo*, 40, no. 6 (June 1985): 28.

Mihailova, Daniela. "More Damaging Bigotry and Intolerance from Bulgaria's Deputy Prime Minister Simeonov." European Roma Rights Centre, 24 October 2018. http://www.errc.org/news/more-damaging-bigotry-and-intolerance-from-bulgarias-deputy-prime-minister-simeonov.

Mihalchev, Dimiter. "Rasizmut kato Filosofsko-Istoricheska Teoria" [Racism as a philosophico-historical theory]. In *Izbrani Suchinenia* [Selected works], edited by Krasimir Darkovski, 341–400. Sofia: Izdatelstvo Nauka i Iskustvo, 1981. Originally published in *Filosofski Pregled* [Philosophical review] vol. 10, book 6 (1938): 293–332.

– "Rasizmut pod Zakrilata na Biologiata" [Racism under the protection of biology]. In *Izbrani Suchinenia* [Selected works], edited by Krasimir Darkovski, 401–41. Sofia; Izdatelstvo Nauka i Iskustvo, 1981. Originally published in *Filosofical Pregled* [Philosophical review] vol. 11, book 2 (1939).

Minca, Claudio, Danica Šantić, and Dragan Umek. "Managing the 'Refugee Crisis' along the Balkan Route: Field Notes from Serbia." In *The Oxford*

Handbook of Migration Crises, edited by Cecilia Menjívar, Marie Ruiz, and Immanuel Ness, 445–64. Oxford: Oxford University Press, 2019.
MIRIS. "Etnicheski Sustav na Naselenieto v Bulgaria" [Ethnic make-up of the population in Bulgaria]. MIRIS: Minority Rights Information System. http://miris.eurac.edu/mugs2/do/blob.html?type=html&serial =1039432230349. Accessed 4 April 2019.
Mohanty, Chandra Talpade. *Feminism Without Borders: Decolonizing Theory, Practicing Solidarity*. Durham, NC: Duke University Press, 2003.
Mohanty, Chandra Talpade, Ann Russo, and Lourdes Torres. *Third World Women and the Politics of Feminism*. Bloomington: Indiana University Press, 1999.
Mojab, Shahrzad, ed., *Marxism and Feminism*. London: Zed Books, 2015.
Moraga, Cherríe, and Gloria Anzaldúa. *This Bridge Called My Back: Writings by Radical Women of Color*. Latham, NY: Kitchen Table Press, 1984.
Mujanovic, Jasmin. *Hunger and Fury: The Crisis of Democracy in the Balkans*. Oxford: Oxford University Press, 2018.
Muratova, Nurie. "Muslim Women in Socialist Bulgaria." *Balkanistic Forum* 2 (2013): 128–49.
– "Politiki na Socialisticheskite Vlast v Bulgaria kum Zhenite Musulmanki v Bulgaria." *Arhivi na Zheni i Malcinstva* 3 (2011): 59–105.
Nahodilova, Lenka. "Communist Modernization and Gender: The Experience of Bulgarian Muslims, 1970–1990." *Contemporary European History* 19, no. 1 (2010): 37–53.
Nayyar, Deepak. "India's Trade with the Socialist Countries." In *Economic Relations between Socialist Countries and the Third World*. London: Palgrave Macmillan, 1977.
Nazarska, Zhorzheta. "Muslim Women and the Women's Movement in Bulgaria (1940s–1960s)." *Archive Documentation and Historical Problems* (2009): 123–32.
– *Universitetskoto Obrazovanie I Bulgarskite Zheni 1879–1944*. Sofia: IMIR, 2003.
Neuberger, Mary. *The Orient Within: Muslim Minorities and the Negotiation of Nationhood in Modern Bulgaria*. Ithaca, NY: Cornell University Press, 2004.
Nikolova, Todorka. *Zhivot Pod Muzhe: Otkroveniata na Edna Prostitutka*. Haskovo: EF "Sedmodiev," 1992.
Novikova, Irina. "Soviet and Post-Soviet Masculinities: After Men's Wars in Women's Memories." In *Male Roles, Masculinities and Violence: A Culture of Peace Perspective*, edited by Ingeborg Breines, Robert Connell, and Ingrid Eide, 117–29. Paris: UNESCO, 2000.
Nunev, Yosif. *Romskoto Dete I Negovata Semeina Sreda* [The Roma child and its family environment]. Sofia: Mezhdunroden Center po Problemite na Maltsinstvata I Kulturnite Vzaimodeistvia, 1998.
Odinga, Ogonga. *Not Yet Uhuru: An Autobiography*. Nairobi: East African Educational Publishers, 1976.

Omi, Michael, and Howard Winant, *Racial Formation Theory in the United States*. New York: Routledge, 2014.
Ostry, J.D., J. Alvarez, R. Espinoza, and C. Papageorgiou. "Economic Gains from Gender Inclusion: New Mechanisms, New Evidence." International Monetary Fund, 8 October 2018. https://www.imf.org/en/Publications/Staff-Discussion-Notes/Issues/2018/10/09/Economic-Gains-From-Gender-Inclusion-New-Mechanisms-New-Evidence-45543.
"Our Children's Corner." *Women on the March* (January 1966): 24.
Pagliai, Valentina. "Conversational Agreement and Racial Formation Processes." *Language in Society* 38, no. 5 (2009): 549–79.
Pande, Rekha. "The History of Feminism and Doing Gender in India." *Estudos Feministas* 26, no. 3 (2018): 1–17.
Panyotova, Diliana. "Ninova Privetstva Reshenieto na KS za Istanbulskata Konvencia." *NewsBg*. 27 July 2018. https://news.bg/politics/ninova-privetstva-reshenieto-na-ks-za-istanbulskata-konventsiya.html.
Pashova, Anastasia i Nurie Muratova. *Romski Arhif: Demokratichna Publichnost chrez Pravo na Istoria*. Blagoevgrad: Universitetsko Izdatrelsvo Neofit Rilski, 2017.
Pashova, Anastasia, Krisitna Popova, Milena Angelova, Nurie Muratova, Petur Vodenicharov, and Hristofor Popovski. *Iskam Blagorodna Profesia: Tradicii, Moda, Modernost v Zapadnite Rodopi* [I want a noble profession: Traditions, fashion, modernity in the West Rhodope region]. Blagoevgrad: Klub Otvoreno Obstestvo, 2000.
Peterson, Dale. *Up from Bondage: The Literatures of Russian and African American Soul*. Durham, NC: Duke University Press, 2000.
Pistotnik, Sara, and David Alexander Brown. "Race in the Balkans: The Case of Erased Residents of Slovenia." *Interventions* 20, no. 6 (2019): 832–85.
Pollert, Anna. "Women, Work and Equal Opportunities in post-Communist Transition." *Work, Employment and Society* 17, no. 2 (2003): 331–57.
Popov, Methody. *Antropologia na Bulgaskiat Narod: Fizicheski Oblik na Bulgarite* [Anthropology of the Bulgarian people: Physical portrait of Bulgarians]. Sofia: Bulgarian Academy of Sciences, 1959.
– *Bulgarskiat Narod Mejdu Evropeiskite Rasi I Narodi* [The Bulgarian people among the European races and peoples]. Lecture delivered at the founding meeting of the Union of Bulgarian Naturalists. Sofia: Izdatelsvo Nauka i Iskustvo, 12 January 1938.
– *Nasledsvenost, Rasa I Narod: Rasova Prinadlezhnost na Bulgarite* [Heredity, race and a people: Racial belonging of Bulgarians]. Sofia: Izdatelstvo Nauka i Iskustvo, 1938.
Popov, Veselin, and Elena Marushiakova. *Etnicheskata Kartina v Bulgaria: Prouchvania 1992* [The ethnic picture in Bulgaria: Research 1992]. Sofia: Klub' 90, 1993.

Popova, Kristina. "Pozhelavam ti Evropa Vmesto Seloto! Devicheskata Gimnazia: Obstuvane I Zhizneni Planove v Nachaloto na XX vek," *Balkanistichen Forum*, no. 1–3 (2004): 55–64.

Popova, Kristina, and Nurie Muratova. "Dimensions of the Women's Voices: Following on the Documentary Tracks of the First Women's Participation in Elections in Bulgaria (1937–1939)." *Women and Minority Archives: Ways of Atchiving* 1 (2009): 133–55. https://www.ceeol.com/search/article-detail?id=17687.

Popova-Mutafova, Fani. "Kakvo Zhenata e Spechelila I Kakvo Tia e Zagubila chrez Svoiata Emancipacia." In *Ot Siankata na Istoriiata: Zhenite v Bulgarskoto Obstestvo I Kultura (1840–1940)*, edited by Krasimra Daskalova, 371–87. Sofia: Dom na Naukite za Choveka I Obshtestvoto, 1998.

Prochner, Larry, Helen May, and Baljit Kaur. "'The Blessings of Civilisation': Nineteenth-Century Missionary Infant Schools for Young Native Children in Three Colonial Settings – India, Canada and New Zealand 1820s–1840s." *Paedagogica Historica: International Journal of the History of Education* 45, nos. 1–2 (2009): 83–102.

Promitzer, Christian. "Taking Care of the National Body: Eugenic Visions in Interwar Bulgaria, 1905–1940." In *Blood and Homeland: Eugenics and Racial Nationalism in Central and Southeast Europe*, edited by Marius Turda and Paul Weindling, 223–51. Budapest: Central European University Press, 2007.

Racheva, Maria. "V Nadprevara za Bestselari" [In a race for bestsellers]. *Kinoizkustvo* 32, no. 12 (December 1977): 46.

Rainbow, David. *Ideologies of Race: Imperial Russia and the Soviet Union in Global Context*. Montreal: McGill-Queen's University Press, 2019.

Rechel, Berndt. "Ethnic Diversity in Bulgaria: Institutional Arrangements and Domestic Discourse." *Nationalities Papers* 36, no. 2 (May 2008): 331–50.

Rich, Janine. "'Saving' Muslim Women, Feminism, US Foreign Policy and War on Terror." *International Affairs Review* (Fall 2014): https://www.usfca.edu/sites/default/files/arts_and_sciences/international_studies/saving_muslim_women-_feminism_u.s_policy_and_the_war_on_terror-_university_of_san_francisco_usf.pdf.

Rodat, Simona. "Cultural Racism: A Conceptual Framework." *RSP* 54 (2017): 129–40.

Roediger, David. *The Wages of Whiteness: Race and the Making of the American Working Class*. New York: Verso, 2007.

– *Whiteness: Race and the Making of the American Working Class*. New York: Verso, 2007.

– *Working toward Whiteness: How America's Immigrants Became White*. New York: Basic Books, 2006.

Rorke, Bernard. "Bigger Than Football: Bulgaria Has a Problem with Neo-fascism." European Roma Rights Center, 18 October 2019. http://www

.errc.org/news/bigger-than-football-bulgaria-has-a-problem-with-neo-fascism. Accessed 8 July 2020.

Rorty, Richard. *Contingency, Irony, and Solidarity*. Cambridge: Cambridge University Press, 1989.

Rrustemi, Arlinda. *Far-Right Trends in South Eastern Europe: The Influences of Russia, Croatia, Serbia and Albania*. The Hague, Netherlands: The Hague Center for Strategic Studies, 2019. https://hcss.nl/report/far-right-trends-south-eastern-europe-influences-russia-croatia-serbia-and-albania. Accessed 8 July 2020.

Sandoval, Chela. "Fredric Jameson: Postmodernism is a Neocolonizing Global Force." In *Methodology of the Oppressed*. Minneapolis: University of Minnesota Press, 2000.

Sheneva, Tsvetelina. "Sylvester Stallone: Stavam po Silen Kogato Sum v Bulgaria." 12 August 2013. https://www.24chasa.bg/Article/2232159.

Shohat, Ella, and Robert Stam. *Unthinking Eurocentrism*. New York: Routledge, 2014.

Shorten, Richard. *Modernism and Totalitarianism: Rethinking the Intellectual Sources of Nazism and Stalinism*. New York: Palgrave Macmillan, 2012.

Siegel, Achim. *The Totalitarian Paradigm after the End of Communism: Towards a Theoretical Reassessment*. Amsterdam: Brill Rodopi Publishers, 1998.

Silova, Iveta, Nelly Piattoeva, and Zsuzsa Milley, eds. *Childhood and Schooling in (Post)socialist Societies: Memories of Everyday Life*. New York: Palgrave Macmillan, 2016.

Slapšak, Svetlana. "Hunting, Ruling, Sacrificing: Traditional Male Practices in Contemporary Balkan Cultures." In *Male Roles, Masculinities and Violence: A Culture of Peace Perspective*, edited by Ingeborg Breines, Robert Connell, and Ingrid Eide, 131–42. Paris: UNESCO, 2000.

Slavova, Kornelia. "Looking at Western Feminisms through the Double Lens of Eastern Europe and the Third World." In *Women and Citizenship in Central and Eastern Europe*, edited by Jasmina Lukić, Joanna Regulska, and Darja Zaviršek, 245–63. Farnham, UK: Ashgate, 2006.

Sofia Committee of the Fatherland Front. Transcript of seminar on issues related to the family and juveniles, Sofia, 10 May 1984. Archival Fond 2582, 1/40.

Sokolova, Boika, and Kirilka Stavreva. "'The Readiness is All,' or the Politics of Art in Post-Communist Bulgaria." n.p., n.d. http://sites.utoronto.ca/tsq/60/SokolovaStavreva1_60.pdf.

Spivak, Gayatri. *Outside in the Teaching Machine*. London: Psychology Press, 1993.

Stafford, Tom. "This Map Shows What White Europeans Associate with Race – and It Makes for Uncomfortable Reading." *Conversation*, 18 July 2017.

https://theconversation.com/this-map-shows-what-white-europeans-associate-with-race-and-it-makes-for-uncomfortable-reading-76661.
Statelova, Elena, and Stoicho Gruncharov. *Istoria na Nova Bulgaria 1878–1944* [History of New Bulgaria 1878–1944]. Sofia: Anubus, 1999.
Stoianov, Georgi. "Za po-visoko Kachestvo na Bulgarskite Filmi" [For a higher quality of Bulgarian films]. *Kinoizkustvo* 39, no. 7 (July 1984): 3–15.
Stoilova, Mariya. "Post-socialist Gender Transformations and Women's Experiences of Employment: Movements Between Continuity and Change in Bulgaria." *Journal of Organizational Change Management* 23, no. 6 (2010): 731–54.
Stojarová, Věra. *The Far Right in the Balkans*. Manchester: Manchester University Press, 2013.
Suchland, Jennifer. "Is Postsocialism Transnational?" *Signs* 36, no. 4 (2011): 837–62.
Sudarkasa, Niara. "'The Status of Women' in Indigenous African Societies." *Feminist Studies* 12, no. 1 (1986): 91–103.
Svilenov, Atanas. "Tvorcheskoto Edinomislie- Osnovi za Uspeh" [Creative consensus – a basis for success]. *Kinoizkustvo* 37, no. 6 (June 1982): 3–15.
Tereshchenko, Antonina, Alice Bradbury, and Louise Archer, "Eastern European Migrants' Experiences of Racism in English Schools: Positions of Marginal Whiteness and Linguistic Otherness." *Whiteness and Education* 4, no.1 (2019): 53–71.
Tlostanova, Madina. *Gender Epistemologies and Eurasian Borderlands*. New York: Palgrave Macmillan, 2010.
Todorov, Tzvetan. *The Fragility of Goodness: Why Bulgaria's Jews Survived the Holocaust*. Princeton, NJ: Princeton University Press, 2003.
Todorova, Maria. "Historical Tradition and Transformation in Bulgaria: Women's Issues or Feminist Issues?" *Journal of Women's History* 5, no. 3 (Winter 1994): 129–43.
– *Imagining the Balkans*. Oxford: Oxford University Press, 1997.
Todorova, Maria, and Zsuzsa Gille, eds. *Post-communist Nostalgia*. New York: Berghahn Books, 2010.
Todorova, Miglena S. "I Don't Know My Color, but I Do Know My Politics." In *Feminist Waves, Feminist Generations: Life Stories from the Academy*, edited by Hoku Aikau, Karla Erickson, and Jennifer Pierce, 197–210. Minneapolis: University of Minnesota Press, 2007.
– "Race Travels: Whiteness and Modernity across National Borders." PhD diss., University of Minnesota, 2006.
– "Race and Women of Color in Socialist/Postsocialist Transnational Feminisms in Central and Southeastern Europe." *Meridians: Feminism, Race, Transnationalism* 16, no. 1 (2018): 114–41.
Todorova, Petia. "Pri Grandiozna Afera po Vreme na Komunizma v Afrika Potuvat $840 miliona." *168 Chasa*, 17 January 2019. https://www.168chasa.bg/article/7247714.

Tomova, Ilona. *Ciganite v Prehodnia Period* [Gypsies in the transition period]. Sofia: International Center for Problems with Minorites and Intercultural Relations, 1995.

— "Demografska Haracteristika na Tsiganskoto Naselenie v Bulgaria" [Demographic characteristics of the Gypsy population in Bulgaria]. *Romani Ilo* (March–April 1995): 14.

"Tova Me Naraniava." *Zhenata Dnes* no. 5 (1975): 23.

Turda, Marius, and Paul J. Weindling. *Blood and Homeland: Eugenics and Racial Nationalism in Central and Southeast Europe.* Budapest: Central European University Press, 2007.

United Nations. "Domestic Violence against Women a Serious Problem in Bulgaria, Women's Antidiscrimination Committee Told." United Nations Press Release WOM1017, 28 January 1998. https://www.un.org/press/en/1998/19980128.WOM1017.html.

Vassilev, Rossen. "The Rescue of Bulgaria's Jews in World War II." *New Politics* 12:4, no. 48 (2010): 114–21.

Warren, Jonathan. *Racial Revolutions: Antiracism and Indian Resurgence in Brazil.* Durham, NC: Duke University Press, 2001.

Wheeler, Geoffrey. *Racial Problems in Soviet Muslim Asia.* 2nd edition. London: Oxford University Press, 1962.

World Bank Group. *Development Marketplace: Innovations to Address Gender-based Violence.* World Bank, 8 August 2020. https://www.worldbank.org/en/programs/development-marketplace-innovations-to-address-gender-based-violence.

— *Gender Dimensions of Roma Inclusion: Perspectives from Four Roma Communities in Bulgaria.* Europe and Central Asia Social Development Unit, World Bank Group, January 2014. https://issuu.com/world.bank.europe.central.asia/docs/gender-dimensions-of-roma-inclusion. Accessed 8 July 2020.

Yergan, Max. *African Students in Communist Countries.* New York: American, Afro-Asian Educational Exchange, 1961. http://worldcat.org/identities/lccn-n80079855/.

Young, Robert. *White Mythologies: Writing History and the West.* London: Psychology Press, 2004.

Zeneli, Valbona. "Economic Development in the Western Balkans: On the Road to Competitive Market Economies?" *Connections* 13, no. 4 (2014): 53–64.

Zhivkov, Todor. *Memoari.* Sofia: IK Trud I Pravo, 2006.

— *Problems of the Construction of an Advanced Socialist Society in Bulgaria: Reports and Speeches.* Sofia: Sofia Press, 1969.

— *Selected Works.* New Delhi: People's Publishing House, 1982.

Zhivkova, Lyudmila. *Her Many Worlds, New Culture & Beauty, Concepts & Action.* Oxford: Pergamon Press, 1986.

Znepolsky, Ivaylo. "V Tursene na Edna Satrudnichesta Publika" [In search of one cooperating public]. *Kinoizkustvo* 32, no. 7 (July 1977): 29–38.

Music Videos

"AZIS in Love with the USA – АЗИС Влюбен в Америка!" 17 March 2013. https://www.youtube.com/watch?v=jI5hCHakF2I.

"Nichija zemja: Lice nazaem?" s Elena Chopakova, *Nova TV*. 6 July 2019. https://nova.bg/news/view/2019/07/06/256179/ничия-земя-лице-назаем.

"Azis: Bog me e suzdal, za da peja i da obedinjavam – Subudi se." 24 December 2017. https://www.youtube.com/watch?v=_-GG082L52g.

"AZIS – Pozna li me? / Азис – Позна ли ме?" Official video. 7 September 2018. https://www.youtube.com/watch?v=Smdc5GcCM-A.

"AZIS – MOTEL / Азис – Мотел." Official video. 26 July 2017. https://www.youtube.com/watch?v=v_ici9SWJ-Y.

"AZIS – Ciganche / АЗИС – Циганче." Official video. 7 July 2019. https://www.youtube.com/watch?v=i_mPzU2_72E.

Index

Africa, 12, 19, 41–2, 56, 57, 62–3, 79–83, 101, 104, 105, 108–10, 112, 126, 155. *See also* women: in African countries
African Americans, 40–1, 57, 74, 80, 131, 143–6
anti-racism, 56, 60–1, 161–72
anti-colonialism, 56–7
Anzaldúa, Gloria, 12, 21, 170–2, 184n43, 185nn44–7
Asia, 57, 59, 63, 83
Azis, 164–70

Baker, Catherine, 173n23
Balkans, 12–17, 22, 60–1, 149, 153–74
Bauman, Zygmunt, 129–30, 173n18, 181nn1–2, 182nn3–4
Bebel, August, 82, 179n23
Bhabha, Homi, 12, 162–3
Black women, 11, 12, 83, 100, 105, 108, 152; feminists, 11, 83. *See also* African Americans; women: in African countries
boarding schools/residential schools, 64, 71–2
Bollywood films, 147–8
Braun, Lily, 82–3

Bulgarian Communist Party, 61–2, 85–6
Bulgarian Socialist Party, 158–60
Bulgarian Women's Union, 48–51

Canada, 6, 12, 84, 150, 152
capitalism, 3–10, 129–30
Christian women, 6, 68–72, 80–90, 98–104, 112, 120. *See also* ethnic Bulgarian women
Cold War, 4, 74, 89–90, 93, 108–9, 116
colonialism, 23; Soviet, 56–7, 65–6, 71–2; European, 13, 70–1; Ottoman, 68, 72. *See also* boarding schools/residential schools
Committee of the Bulgarian Women's Movement, 99, 102–4
culture, 40–3, 130; socialist, 58, 60, 116–18, 124–5, 131–46; postmodern, 131; postsocialist, 146–8, 161–71. *See also* postsocialist cultural "third space"; transnational feminist cultural studies; United States: popular culture

Davis, Angela, 11, 12, 57, 103
democratic socialism, 6–9, 77, 122–4
demographics, 36, 73

East, 23, 114–24, 129–30, 138–48, 156–7, 164, 167–71
Eastern Europe, 8–9, 61, 122–3, 128
economy: capitalist, 76, 81, 84; global 79; socialist, 75–101
education, 29, 48, 49, 71; of women, 68–9, 70
Engels, Fredric, 46, 64, 65, 82, 83, 90, 179n24
epistemology of doubt, 4–5, 164, 172
ethnic Bulgarian women, 3, 32, 47, 49–51, 78–9, 84–5, 87, 89, 98, 99, 152, 158–9
ethnicity, 7, 17, 36, 56, 64, 76, 155, 168
eugenics: American, 66; in Bulgaria, 45–6; Soviet, 46
Eurocentricity, 37, 47–58, 60–1, 78–164
Europe, 27–62, 113–18, 150–70
European Union, 4, 8, 21, 24, 60–1, 101; policies and identities, 149–57
europic complex, 58

feminisms: white and middle-class, 8, 83. See also postsocialist race-based feminism; socialist feminism; state feminism; transnational feminisms
feminist bridges, 4, 5, 6. See also solidarity; women's relations
Ferguson, Roderick, 12, 56, 74n55
film audiences (in socialist Bulgaria), 131–5
films, socialist Bulgarian, 132–5, 140–1. See also Bollywood films; Hollywood films
First World women, 23

Gandhi, Indira, 20, 102, 114–22, 125–6
Ghodsee, Kristen, 6, 12, 77, 173n3, 178nn10–13, 180nn60–3 (ch. 3), 180n14 (ch. 4)

Gilroy, Paul, 12, 13, 168, 184n39
global North, 5, 6, 8, 11, 20, 23, 83, 105, 126
global South, 5, 8, 11, 83, 105, 126
Goldberg, David Theo, 12, 174nn31, 33
good society, 130–1
governmentality, 19; socialist state, 78–84, 89–90
Gypsies, 30–74, 166–7. See also Roma

Hall, Stuart, 58, 177nn7–8, 181n44
Hill-Collins, Patricia, 12, 174n37
Hollywood films, 136, 138, 141; action movies, 20, 136–8, 142–3, 145; stars, 135, 143, 147
hybridity, 161–72

India, 115–19, 162
Indigenous peoples, 71, 83–4
international students from Africa, 94, 109–10
internationalism, 12, 19–20, 43, 103–6, 114–27

Jameson, Fredric, 128–30, 136, 182nn5–6
Jews, 43–4, 45, 53–4, 58–9, 63

Kaplan, Caren, 12, 129, 174nn40–1, 180n3, 182nn8–9
Kinkel, Ivan, 45–7, 176nn57–62, 64
Konsulov, Stefan, 43–5, 176nn50–6

Law, Ian, 15, 173n23, 174n32
Lenin, Vladimir I., 42, 64–6, 131
liberal bourgeoise, 29–30, 51
liberalism, 4, 5, 7, 10, 25, 28–37, 58, 77, 127, 161, 164, 170, 172
Lorde, Audre, 59–60, 173n21, 177nn13–16

Marx, Karl, 6, 9, 46, 58, 59, 65, 73, 82, 83, 90, 123, 124, 177nn9–11
Marxism, 3–10, 18, 19–24, 39–72, 86, 102, 116–25, 163, 164; theory and practice, 24–5
Marxist ideology, 48–9, 58; paradox, 59
masculinity, 128, 131–48, 154, 167
migrant workers from Vietnam, 19, 110–11
Mihalchev, Dimiter, 39–43, 174n1, 175nn27, 29–42, 176nn43–9
Mohanty, Chandra Talpade, 12, 21, 75, 76, 173nn10, 16, 174n46, 178nn4–5
Muratova, Nurie, 12, 176nn69, 78, 178n44, 179nn28–9, 31–6
Muslims, 67, 146, 155–6; women, 15, 18, 19, 24, 47, 51–2, 67–74, 78, 80–1, 84–90, 98–100, 103, 120, 146, 151–9; Roma, 60, 68

nation, 39, 43–6
nation-building, 4, 28–9
nationalism, 65, 66, 163
nationalities, 64–7, 74
New Left, 122–6
North America, 19, 41, 42, 56, 101, 105

Ottoman empire, 27–8, 36, 43, 53, 72, 166

patriarchy: capitalist, 75, 94; postsocialist, 157–61; socialist, 88–9, 91, 92, 94–5
political Left, 103, 157–63; global New Left, 122–6. *See also* New Left
political Right, 157–63
Popov, Methody, 37–9, 175nn15–26
postmodernity, 128, 130
postsocialism, 22, 147–71
postsocialist cultural "third space," 161–71

postsocialist feminist analytic, 3–4
postsocialist race-based feminism, 7
postsocialist women, 8, 24, 157–63; feminists, 11
prostitution, 90–2. *See also* sex work

queer, 149, 158–9, 161, 164–8

race, 7–18, 26–55, 56–63, 66–7, 74–5, 88, 93, 103–14, 124, 129–48, 153–62, 168–72. *See also* racial sciences; racialization
racial formation, 12–16, 54
racial hygiene, 43–5
racial sciences, 27, 37–47
racial whiteness, 8, 13, 14, 30, 42, 47, 59, 61, 74, 79, 171; United States–based, 135–8, 142–6
racialization, 3, 6, 12–17, 26–56, 127, 135–48, 153–67
racism, 5, 8, 9, 13–16, 20–1, 39–44, 56, 60, 66, 74, 110–13, 121, 149–51, 153, 161, 164, 167; "cultural racism," 155–6
refugees, 155, 158
resistance, 20, 122; male, 131, 141, 146; women's, 21, 92, 105, 120–4, 129
Roma, 41–6, 60, 64, 72–4; women, 18, 21, 24, 29–36, 51–3, 57, 67–9, 71, 79, 98, 100–7, 120, 149–59. *See also* Gypsies

Second World, 7, 24, 125, 142; women, 7–8, 23, 24
sex work, 78, 90–5, 145. *See also* prostitution
social difference, 4, 6–7, 37, 129
socialist feminism, 95–101, 104–14, 152. *See also* state feminism
socialist humanism, 103, 116, 122–3
socialist modernity, 60, 67, 71–3, 78, 88–9, 99, 105, 129–30

socialist personality, 61–2
socialist racialism, 16, 18, 56–74, 80, 131, 143–6
Socialist Women's Union, 50–1
socially useful labour, 19, 60–2, 68, 91
solidarity, 108–9, 111–31, 161, 168
South America, 12, 83, 102, 105, 126
Soviet Empire, 11, 27, 64–7, 71
Soviet Union, 5, 6, 8, 10–12, 19, 22, 24, 37, 59–60, 65, 75, 91, 101, 108, 109, 114, 124, 145
spirituality and socialist culture, 116–19
Spivak, Gayatri, 129, 182n7
standpoint, 30, 125; analytic, 16–18
state feminism, 102, 126–7; feminists, 100, 103–4, 120–1

Third World, 8, 24, 123, 162, 170; women, 7–8, 11, 23, 102–25
Todorova, Maria, 180n1, 181nn23–5, 43, 183n1
transgender, 159–60, 164–70. *See also* Azis
transnational feminisms, 3–4, 7, 19, 149, 170–2; feminists, 8, 10–12, 21, 169
transnational feminist cultural studies: of borderlands, 162–72; theorizing, 129
transnationalism, 21–2, 163

United States, 8, 25–7, 57, 60, 84, 167; popular culture, 131–43
useful knowledge, 6

Vietnam War, 135–8. *See also* migrant workers from Vietnam
violence against women, 71, 88, 92–5, 98–105, 112, 121, 141, 149, 151–3, 159–60

West, 4, 8–9, 57–8, 77, 84, 114–21
Western academia, 7, 9–10, 25, 83
"woman question," 48, 78, 82–3
women: in African countries, 83, 108–9, 112, 126; in India, 119; rural, 18, 51, 100; working class, 18, 51, 75, 76, 78, 82, 98, 100, 103, 112, 120. *See also* Black women; Christian women; ethnic Bulgarian women; Muslims: women; Roma: women; sex work
Women on the March, 118–19
women teachers, 48–50
women's emancipation under socialism, 48–50, 60, 77, 79–81, 84, 88, 92, 95, 98–101, 119, 152–3
women's relations, 4, 7–8, 10, 12, 19–20, 22–3, 76, 78, 102–4, 108–9, 113–16, 119–27, 152; political solidarity, 167–8. *See also* solidarity
women's studies, 3, 7, 8
women's vote, 27, 48
women's work, 19, 75–88, 90–8, 100

Zhenata Dnes, 19, 99, 102, 104–5, 109, 111–13, 119, 126
Zhivkov, Todor, 62, 69, 177nn20–2, 181n26, 182n13
Zhivkova, Ludmila, 20, 102–3, 113–26, 181nn27, 29–30, 33, 35–6, 41–2

www.ingramcontent.com/pod-product-compliance
Lightning Source LLC
Chambersburg PA
CBHW020408080526
44584CB00014B/1232